Calunga

and the Legacy of an
African Language in Brazil

Calunga
and the Legacy of an
African Language in Brazil

STEVEN BYRD

University of New Mexico Press
Albuquerque

© 2012 by the University of New Mexico Press
All rights reserved. Published 2012
Printed in the United States of America

First paperback edition, 2020
Paperback ISBN: 978-0-8263-5087-9

LIBRARY OF CONGRESS CATALOGING-IN-PUBLICATION DATA

Byrd, Steven, 1973—
Calunga and the legacy of an African language in Brazil / Steven Byrd.
p. cm.
Includes bibliographical references and index.
ISBN 978-0-8263-5086-2 (cloth : alk. paper)
— ISBN 978-0-8263-5088-6 (electronic)
1. Portuguese language—Dialects—Brazil—Minas Gerais. 2. Portuguese language—Dialects—Brazil—Foreign elements—African. 3. Portuguese language—Brazil—African influences. 4. African languages—Influence on Portuguese. 5. Brazil—Civilization—African influences. I. Title.
PC5447.M56B97 2010
469.7'98151—dc23
2012022589

DESIGN AND LAYOUT: CATHERINE LEONARDO
Composed in 9.5/14 Charis SIL
Display type is Goudy Old Style

Contents

Illustrations | vii

Acknowledgments | ix

PART ONE: Overview

CHAPTER ONE:
Introduction | 3

CHAPTER TWO:
Historical Overview | 15

CHAPTER THREE:
Linguistic Overview | 52

PART TWO: Linguistic Description

CHAPTER FOUR:
Sociolinguistic and Sociohistorical
Considerations of Calunga | 103

CHAPTER FIVE:
The Calunga Lexicon | 123

CHAPTER SIX:
Calunga Grammar | 166

Appendix | 199

Abbreviations | 239

Notes | 241

References | 249

Index | 265

Illustrations

FIGURES

Figure 2.1.	Depiction in stone of a Portuguese caravel	18
Figure 2.2.	Torre de Belém	23
Figure 2.3.	Brazilwood tree	31
Figure 2.4.	Slave dungeon	36
Figure 2.5.	Shackles, handcuffs, and branding iron	39
Figure 3.1.	Afro-Brazilian village of Quartel de Indaiá	68
Figure 4.1.	Galera's Bar in Patrocínio	107
Figure 4.2.	Stone wall built by slaves	113
Figure 4.3.	Cattle fazenda	114
Figure 4.4.	Area of former Ambrósio *quilombo*	117

MAPS

Map 1.	Brazil, with locations of selected Afro-Brazilian speech communities	5
Map 2.	Lusophone countries and territories in Europe, the Atlantic islands, Africa, and South America	16

TABLES

Table 3.1.	African languages and language families	53
Table 3.2.	Niger-Congo languages	54
Table 3.3.	Comparison of Afro-Hispanic dialects and Afro-Portuguese creoles	97

Table 5.1.	Comparison of lexical items documented in Afro-Brazilian speech communities of Minas Gerais, São Paulo, and Bahia	149
Table 6.1.	Calunga vowels	167
Table 6.2.	Calunga consonants	167
Table 6.3.	Calunga subject and object pronouns	179
Table 6.4.	Calunga present tense	180
Table 6.5.	Calunga present tense, progressive aspect	180
Table 6.6.	Calunga past tense, perfect aspect	181
Table 6.7.	Calunga past tense, imperfect aspect	181
Table 6.8.	Calunga past tense, progressive aspect	181
Table 6.9.	Calunga future tense	181
Table 6.10.	Noun phrase comparison, Calunga and BPV	185
Table 6.11.	Noun phrase comparison with adjectives, Calunga and BPV	186
Table 6.12.	Subject pronoun comparison, Calunga and BPV	186
Table 6.13.	Calunga and BPV present indicative	188
Table 6.14.	BPV and SBP present indicative	188
Table 6.15.	Calunga and BPV indicative, perfect aspect (quinhamá(r)/andar)	188
Table 6.16.	Calunga and BPV indicative, perfect aspect (curiá(r)/comê(r))	189
Table 6.17.	Calunga and BPV indicative, imperfect aspect	189
Table 6.18.	Conjugation of the verb 'to do' in the present indicative in Kimbundu, Calunga, BPV, and SBP	194
Table 6.19.	Verbal paradigms of Língua do Negro da Costa	196

Acknowledgments

The word *companion* originates from Latin, *cum panis*, meaning 'with bread'. This Latin expression is a reference to the person or persons with whom we share our bread. My time living and studying in Brazil and the United States has brought me some memorable and loving companions who have inspired me and often made me look at life with a smile—what the celebrated Portuguese poet Fernando Pessoa once called "o espectáculo do mundo." With that in mind, I would like to highlight some outstanding companions who have been present before and during this project.

First and foremost, "meu amorzinho" Daniela has been an amazing and brilliant companion who has, quite literally, been there every step of the way. After spending uncountable hours traveling, thinking, writing, revising, revising, and more revising, she has stood by me. Words are not enough to thank her for her love and compassion.

My mom and dad, my first companions in life, have been incredibly loving and supportive no matter what crazy ideas come into my head, which have been many for sure. But somehow, through it all, they have always managed to be behind me, offer me guidance, and make me smile on life. From my dad I inherited a love for language, books, music, Socratic questioning, and especially my students. From my mom I inherited persistence, a fascination with travel, and a sense of how to love and laugh. When I told her that I was thinking about dedicating this book to the fictional character Irwin R. Fletcher (from *Fletch*, one of my favorite movies), she said, "That's a great idea!"

Two very special companions who have been around a long time now are "mis hermanos" Salvador Servín and Alfonso Abad. Our conversations about where we are going in life, our favorite music, and soccer are always the best.

My academic companions have been the Socratics in my life. At the University of Texas–Austin, Chiyo Nishida, Orlando Kelm, Fritz Hensey, and Carlos Solé—all wonderful teachers, advisors, inspirations, and most importantly, "gente fina," as Brazilians say. At the University of New England, I thank Paul Burlin, Sam McReynolds, Matthew Anderson, and Elaine Brouillette for their wisdom, support, encouragement, and especially their friendship. I also extend a special thanks to Armin Schwegler at University of California–Irvine and John Lipski at Penn State University for their recommendations and brilliant insight into the African contribution to Spanish and Portuguese.

My abstract companions, late persons whom I never had a chance to meet but who have been strongly present in my life with their music and words and, in some mysterious way, helped me write this book: Antônio Carlos Jobim with his sublime Brazilian soundscapes; Miles Davis with his timeless album *Kind of Blue*, which has always reminded me that I need to improve; and the magnificent Portuguese writer José Saramago, who, in a personal letter, offered me two unforgettable pieces of advice for writing and living: "você já sabe" and "ler, ler, ler."

Lastly, I must thank one of the best and funniest persons I ever met in Brazil: Tadeu de Barros. After my wife, Daniela, and I had been frustrated for weeks with finding Calunga speakers in Patrocínio, one day, literally out of the blue, Tadeu walked into our hotel lobby and said, "Hi, I speak that language." From that day on he found us as many speakers as he possibly could within Patrocínio and thereabouts. From him, besides the nature of the Calunga speech community, we learned how anteater is actually a delicacy, how ants mixed with coffee is not bad to drink and good for you, and how to successfully drive a 1970s Volkswagen Bug through rampant brush fires with a shot clutch and a leaky gas tank. In short, without Tadeu's gracious, unconditional, and memorable collaboration on this project, the book before you would not exist. He is the hero of this story . . .

Part One

OVERVIEW

CHAPTER ONE

Introduction

Os estudos sôbre o negro brasileiro têm se ressentido da falta de um conhecimento mais exato da língua que falavam os pretos importados pelo tráfico, talvez porque hoje, quando o interêsse por êsses assuntos cresceu à altura da sua importância, já quasi não existem mais africanos ou descendentes próximos de africanos que conheçam a língua dos seus maiores.

E o conhecimento dêsse ramo do assunto é fundamental a uma análise perfeita, porque a língua, nas suas características, no seu gênio, nas suas formas diversas, é a chave de muitos problemas de folclore, sociologia, etnografia e outros prismas da questão.

(Studies about the black Brazilian have suffered from the lack of an exact understanding of the language that the imported blacks of the [slave] traffic spoke, perhaps because today, when interest in these subjects has increased according to their importance, there are almost no more Africans or near descendants of Africans who know the language of their ancestors.

And the understanding of this subject is fundamental for a complete analysis [of Afro-Brazilian culture], because language—in its characteristics, by its nature, in its diverse forms—is the key to many problems of folklore, sociology, ethnography and other prisms related to the subject.)

—João Dornas Filho (1943:71),
twentieth-century Brazilian historian/sociologist

From the mid-sixteenth century to the end of the nineteenth century millions of Africans were forcibly transported to Brazil. Although exact numbers are not known, estimates of 4 to 4.5 million slaves have been suggested by scholars (Bueno 2003:120; Klein 2002:93; Olsen

2003:57). But, given that many African slaves were smuggled to Brazil, the numbers could be higher, possibly in the range of 5 to 8 million (Castro 2001:62). At any rate, researchers agree that Brazil received more African slaves than any other country, accounting for approximately 40 percent of the entire Atlantic slave trade (Dodson 2001:119). Such a large influx of people typically will influence the culture. In fact, Brazilian music, dance, religion, folklore, art, and cuisine have African roots or notable African influence. But our understanding of the Africa-Brazil connection in regard to language is rudimentary at best.

Studies on Afro-Brazilian language, which span more than a century, have mostly attempted to establish the African contribution to Brazilian Portuguese. Bonvini and Petter (1998:79) note that these studies tend to focus on two features: the lexical component of Brazilian Portuguese and the phonological and morphosyntactic characteristics of Brazilian Portuguese vernacular through possible creolization, semi-creolization, or decreolization. But African languages and subsequent varieties that have persisted in Brazil have not been the focus of much research. As Bonvini and Petter (74) rightly question, what do we really know about the languages spoken by slaves in Brazil? According to Castro (2001:71), the answer is close to nothing. And as Bonvini (2008a:21) asserts, the lack of data regarding African languages on Brazilian soil is surprising given that varieties of these languages have survived in various forms, such as liturgical languages (e.g., Candomblé) and cryptolects (e.g., Cupópia of the Cafundó community), into the twenty-first century. With this in mind, the present book is a modest attempt to provide description and analysis of the contemporary Afro-Brazilian speech community of Calunga and of how this particular speech community fits into the larger picture of the African legacy in Brazil.

Calunga is an Afro-Brazilian speech spoken primarily in and around Patrocínio, Minas Gerais—a rural town of 81,589 inhabitants located near the Serra da Canastra in the Triângulo Mineiro (see map 1).[1] Although the speech has been reported elsewhere in the region and in the nearby state of Goiás, the speakers—known as *calungadores*—are generally older Afro-Brazilian men numbering perhaps in the hundreds. In the first decade of the twenty-first century this Afro-Brazilian speech exists in a moribund state.

Map 1. Brazil, with locations of selected Afro-Brazilian speech communities.

The history and origins of Calunga are largely unknown, but some scholarly attempts have been made to document and learn about this speech community. In the 1990s, for example, there were two studies that offered some lexical and anthropological observations: Batinga's (1994) book, *Aspectos de presença do negro no triângulo mineiro/alto paranaíba: Kalunga*, provides a sketchy anthropological and lexical overview of Calunga; and Vogt and Fry (1996) dedicate part of their book, *Cafundó: A África no Brasil*, to comparing Calunga to the Afro-Brazilian Cupópia speech spoken in the state of São Paulo. Most recently, Byrd (2006, 2007, 2010a, 2010b) and Byrd and Bassani Moraes (2007) have published a series of linguistic and sociolinguistic studies on Calunga.

Using the terminology of Castro (2001), Calunga may be best categorized in Portuguese as a *falar africano*, which is perhaps best translated and characterized in English as an *Afro-Brazilian speech*. As will be argued, this Afro-Brazilian speech is primarily a lexical phenomenon with some peculiar grammatical aspects. Clearly, while some of Calunga's lexicon has terms of African origin—mostly from Kimbundu, Umbundu, and Kikongo (the latter probably to a lesser extent)—its phonetics/phonology and morphosyntax are on par with the rural, regional Brazilian Portuguese vernacular, known within Brazil as *português caipira* (Caipira Portuguese). The field research for this study revealed that the primary language of all Calunga speakers is the regional Caipira Portuguese; Calunga is reserved for contexts in which they wish to communicate "in secrecy" or in solidarity.

The contemporary secrecy of Calunga reflects Brazil's history of slavery and its aftermath. That is, the speech was utilized by slaves and Afro-descendants so that they would not be understood by people with authority over them—a common theme articulated by older Calunga speakers. In this respect Calunga represents an ethnolinguistic speech community that has maintained its Afro-Brazilian speech as a form of intragroup cryptolect. However, today Calunga is no longer a race-specific or ethnic language, as European descendants have also acquired it, though the latter speakers constitute a small minority of documented calungadores. Also, there is an intriguing mystery as to why there are not more female speakers of Calunga, a question that was not completely uncovered in the field research.

The following excerpted dialogue with a linear English translation was recorded June 27, 2004, in Patrocínio, Minas Gerais. It offers some insight into the context within which Calunga has traditionally been spoken.[2]

Participants:
JL: Joaquim Luís, Calunga speaker, born 1928
DB: Daniela Bassani Moraes, researcher

Calunga	*English*
JL: Os camanu maioral, os maioral, punha os imbundu pá curimá, né? Intão aqueis ibuninhu qui os camanu pegava e levava pá omenha pá aprumá saravo na custela dus imbuninhu. Os camanu mucafo ficava de cá aprumanu a calunga de jambi (oi!) aprumanu aquela calunga de ambi pá aquela omenha estraviá . . . pá . . . aquei saravu de omenha do embunim, pegá só a omenha. Tá, há, o saravo num pegava nu imbunim. Aí, eis calungava de cá, ficava caluganu, aí os camanu maioral vinha com os camanu, tirava, pucurava, os camanu macafu oiava os camanim e sarava pá, pá, pá uranu, sá? Cê sá que é uranu?	JL: The powerful men, the powerful men ['owners, bosses'] used to make the black men work, right? So the little black kids that the powerful men used to grab and take to the water to beat the backs of the little kids. The black men stayed on one side praying (oi!) praying so that the water would go another way . . . so that water would whip only the water [not the kids]. So the whip would not beat the kids. There, they [the blacks, who] were on one side, would pray, there the powerful men would come with the black men, would take down [the black kids], would look for [the wounds on the black kids], the blacks would look at the boys and would thank *urano* ['God'], you know? Do you know what *urano* is?
DB: Não.	DB: No.
JL: Vai, uranu é pá, pu céu, pra Deus, pra ajudá a num acontecê nada, sá? É p'que quem ia apanhá era os camanim, né? Ia pu injó da água, a água tocava, pegava na correia e pegava nu imbunim, vap, vap, vap, vap.	JL: Well, *urano* is for, for heaven, for God, to help that nothing happens, you know? It is because the kids were going to be whipped, right? They were going to the water house ['mill'], the water would run, it would impulse the whip, and it would beat the black kids, vap, vap, vap, vap.
DB: Batia nu coru.	DB: It would beat their skin.
JL: É. Aí, os camanu, os imbundu-cá, ficava nu jambi, rezanu, sabe? Rezanu pa aquilu pegá nus, nus camanim.	JL: Yes. Then, the men, we black men, would stay with a saint, praying, you know? Praying that that would not beat the black kids.

Calunga	*English*
DB: Nus imbunim.	DB: [Beat] the black kids.
JL: É. Aí dava, vencia o horário lá assim, os camanu ia tirava o camanim saia mesma coisa.	JL: Yes. Then the time would come, the men would take down the kids, the black kids would come out the same way [would come out all right].

The history of this Afro-Brazilian speech begins with the Portuguese slave trade on the western central African coast, in what is today the region of Congo and Angola. Millions of Bantu-speaking slaves were sent to the Brazilian colony from this region for agricultural and mining work. From the etymologies of Calunga's Bantu words it is evident that these slaves were speakers of Kimbundu, Umbundu, and Kikongo—Bantu languages commonly spoken today in Congo and Angola. During Brazil's colonial period African slaves were the majority of the Brazilian population, especially in Minas Gerais, as well as in some other regions. Because of the millions of African and Afro-Brazilian slaves, varieties of African languages, pidginized/creolized Portuguese, and/or intertwined languages were spoken throughout colonial plantations and mining communities, within urban areas, and in maroon villages known as *quilombos*. Thus Calunga is likely the remnant of the linguistic complexity among Brazil's former slave population of the Triângulo Mineiro.

It must be underscored, however, that the history of Calunga's evolution into its current form is essentially unknown. It is this author's position that Calunga evolved as a type of Bantu-Portuguese hybrid language from the linguistic complexity found in the colonial estates of Minas Gerais, which could have been some type of pidgin, creole, or intertwined variety. Moreover, this author concurs with the research of Yeda Pessoa de Castro, whose studies on falares africanos and the African influence on Brazilian Portuguese indicate that there was as an "africanização do português" (Africanization of Portuguese) and an "aportuguesamento dos africanismos" (Portuguesement of Africanisms) (Castro 1997:57, 2001:125), which need to be taken into account for Calunga as well as for the Caipira Portuguese that influenced Calunga.

Afro-Brazilian speech communities such as Calunga are valuable in presenting a more comprehensive picture of what might be referred to as a "Brazilian linguistic puzzle." It is a puzzle in the sense that the picture is incomplete with respect to the African-language contribution to Brazil, unlike other areas of culture where the African contribution is better understood. That is, research on Afro-Brazilian speech communities like Calunga can provide a more comprehensive picture of the Brazilian linguistic landscape, including a better understanding of the African contribution to Brazilian Portuguese. Hence this book is a modest attempt to add a small piece to the puzzle. In this sense Calunga should be viewed as a type of "microdialect" (Lipski 2004)—that is, a puzzle piece—that may aid scholars in better comprehending and evaluating the African-language contribution to Brazilian Portuguese.

The proceeding chapters explore the following questions:

- What is the history and historical context of Calunga?
- What is the linguistic context of Calunga? And what types of scholarly literature have been written on African languages spoken in Brazil and the African contribution to Brazilian Portuguese?
- What is the sociolinguistic profile of the Calunga speech community?
- What are the lexical and grammatical aspects of Calunga?

Part one of the book addresses questions one and two by providing a historical and linguistic overview. Part two addresses all four questions to some extent but focuses particularly on questions three and four.

In order to answer to the above questions, empirical data from in situ interviews and bibliographical resources have been employed. Regarding the latter, an array of literature has been consulted, in linguistics, history, anthropology, archaeology, sociology, economics, journalism, and fiction. Regarding the former, empirical data were collected by means of impromptu recording of informants from 2003 to 2005 in Patrocínio, Minas Gerais, and thereabouts. All recordings were conducted with the verbal consent of the informants. Other informants declined being recorded but agreed instead to pencil-and-paper interviews. Some interviewed informants elected anonymity, which has been respected. The subjects were selected on the basis of their fluency in Calunga; all had little formal education. Women were particularly difficult to interview, usually denying any knowledge of Calunga and often declining even pencil-and-paper interviews. No research was conducted in contemporary quilombo communities or any other area that requires authorization from the Brazilian government.

The primary objective of this book is to provide a comprehensive linguistic description of Calunga and of the Calunga speech community. A secondary aim is to provide an understanding of Calunga within the larger context of Portuguese language, history, and culture, particularly within the context of Afro-Brazilian language studies.

There are, of course, limitations to this study. Most importantly, the history and linguistic evolution of Calunga are largely unknown, which creates difficulties for analyses and conclusions in regard to this speech. Any conclusions reached herein should be regarded as tentative. Finally, it is an open question whether or not Calunga will continue to be spoken and thus be available for future study.

PRELIMINARIES

Since Calunga is not an official written language, spelling is based on the 1971 standard for Brazilian Portuguese orthography, though some strategies have been employed to better render the informants' speaking patterns: for example, *aprumar* > *aprumá(r)*, *camano* > *camanu*. The phonetic transcriptions of Calunga are based on a slightly modified version of the International Phonetic Alphabet in which syllables are divided with periods for ease of reading (e.g., *fala* ['fa.la]). All translations in this book were done by this author, unless noted otherwise. Lastly, there are some technical and foreign terms that appear in the book, defined below.

anti-creole. A creole variant, which is different from traditional creoles in that it employs grammatical elements from the superstrate language and lexical elements from the substrate language (Couto 1992a, 1997, 2002). *See also* creole.

bandeirantes. Inland Portuguese explorers and hunters of indigenous South Americans to enslave (ca. 1550–1775). They were responsible for the discovery of several regions of Brazil and South America.

Bantu. A term first coined in 1862 by German philologist Wilhelm Bleek, from the reconstructed word *ba-ntò* 'people,' which is the plural of *mo-ntò* 'person' (Reader 1999:182; Wald 1990:992). The term refers to the language(s) of migrant groups in Africa, making it one of a linguistic (and archaeological) nature, not a demographic designation (Falola 2002:49). Greenberg (1966) has categorized Bantu with Mande languages of West Africa, which together form the Niger-Congo language family (or "phylum"). But, as Lipski (2005:200n2) correctly points out, "A complete genealogy of Bantu languages is an ongoing enterprise." Recent estimates put the number of Bantu languages at 400 to 670 (Batibo 2005:5–9; Falola 2002:49; Isichei 1997:52; Lipski 2005:200). However, Wald (1990:992) writes that "Bantu speakers themselves tend to recognise the essential unity of their own and neighbouring Bantu languages with which they are familiar," in spite of the large number of these languages. On that point Isichei (1997:52) notes that the Bantu languages "are so closely related that it has often been assumed that they spread relatively recently" within Africa. To illustrate, Kikongo and Kimbundu were described in the late sixteenth century as being as similar as Spanish and Portuguese, with Umbundu being less similar but with "strong convergences" in vocabulary and grammar to Kikongo and Kimbundu (Thornton 2006:95). The linguistic characteristic that sets the Bantu languages apart is a series of similar morphological class prefixes, such as *ki-* (e.g., *ki-kongo*) and *ba-* (e.g., *ba-ntu*), and corresponding grammatical patterns. Bantu prefixes, for example, can distinguish a group of people (e.g., Mbundu) from their language (e.g., Kimbundu) (Isichei 1997:53). See especially Dimmendaal (2011) for a detailed explanation of the classification of Bantu and Bantoid languages.

Brazilian Portuguese vernacular (BPV). Adapted from Holm's (2004) term "Brazilian Vernacular Portuguese," BPV refers to the colloquial Portuguese of Brazilians. This dialect employs certain grammatical features that are considered incorrect or uneducated within certain sociolects.

caipira. A person from the rural regions of Brazil, particularly the southeastern region (i.e., São Paulo state, Minas Gerais, Goiás, and surrounding states), who is often caricatured as a country bumpkin.

Caipira Portuguese. The variety of Brazilian Portuguese vernacular (BPV) spoken in southern and western Minas Gerais, São Paulo state, and Goiás. Its major defining characteristics are a lack of subject-verb agreement (e.g., *nóis é*), bare plurals (e.g., *as casa*), and a strong retroflex /r/ ([ɻ]) in syllable- and word-final position (e.g., *carta* ['kaɻ.ta], although deletion can occur in verbal infinitives: *falar* [fa.'la]).

calungador(a). A speaker of Calunga.

casa grande. A slave owner's estate during Brazil's colonial era (Freyre 1956).

congado. An Afro-Brazilian religious ceremony of song and dance that represents the coronation of the king of Congo (Cunha 2001:206).

creole. A controversial term among speakers whose language is thus designated, and a problematic term among linguists. In regard to the latter point, Schwegler writes,

> [M]any creolists continue operating under a deeply felt conviction that creoles or subsets of creoles (e.g. the Portuguese-based creoles of the Atlantic world) (1) indeed share many grammatical properties, (2) have arisen under similar sociohistorical circumstances (slave trade, colonialization), and (3) are languages whose paradigmatic complexity was significantly and abruptly reduced during the initial phase of their existence. As such, these *can* be said to share a "special relationship," and therefore merit scholarly inquiry as a "special class." It is thus the *combination* of internal linguistic features and shared external history that gives creoles "exceptional status." (Schwegler 2010:438, italics his)

> Controversy and theoretical problems aside, this book recognizes Holm's (2004:xiii) definition as a "fully restructured language" resulting from language contact.

cryptolect ("secret language"). A type of cryptic speech or language utilized by a close-knit or ethnic group that desires not to be understood in certain social situations.

decreolization. A linguistic shift from a creolized language to a standard or dominant language.

falar africano. An Africanized Brazilian speech. It is not an African language per se but contains grammatical and lexical elements from African languages and/or pidginized or creolized Portuguese (Castro 2001).

fazenda. A Brazilian estate. *See also* casa grande.

feitoria. A Portuguese commercial fort established on the African coasts, often for the purpose of slave trafficking.

grumetes. African middlemen who dealt with African peoples and the Portuguese. They were often speakers and disseminators of creole languages (Kihm 1994:4).

lançados. Early Portuguese settlers—usually criminals or societal outcasts—who were often responsible for establishing commercial contacts with African peoples and often began Luso-African families.

Língua Geral. The koine variety of Tupi (an indigenous language family of South America) that was widely spoken during the first two centuries of the Portuguese colonization of Brazil (Holm 2004:48; Reinecke 1975:110).

lumbalú. An Afro-Colombian funeral ritual practiced in the village of El Palenque de San Basilio. It is somewhat similar to Haitian Voodoo and Brazilian Candomblé (Schwegler 1996).

Mina-Jeje. The Portuguese term for the Ewe-Fon or Akan languages of the Kwa subfamily. Mina-Jeje was spoken in Ouro Preto, Minas Gerais, in the eighteenth century (Castro 2002).

mixed (intertwined) language. The mixing of grammars and lexical items from unrelated languages that produces a peculiar sharing of each of the languages involved (Bakker and Muysken 1995; Thomason 1995).

Nagô. Yoruba-speaking Africans, especially those from Nigeria and Benin, who were sent as slaves primarily to Salvador, Bahia (Castro 2002:44).

Negros Congos. Afro-Panamanian communities that speak a ritualistic speech known as "Congo" during the Carnival season (Lipski 1989).

Palenquero. A creole spoken in the Colombian village of El Palenque de San Basilio.

pidgin. An improvised contact language used by speakers of different languages, often for reasons of commerce. By definition it is not a native language of any speaker.

quilombola. An inhabitant of a quilombo.

quilombos. Maroon slave villages in Brazil. These villages were inhabited mostly by African-born slaves, though Brazilian-born and indigenous slaves were also present. Some former villages have survived in rural areas of Brazil into the twenty-first century (Rohter 2001).

reisado. An Afro-Brazilian dance commonly performed in celebration of the Day of Kings (Cunha 2001:672).

semi-creole. A "partially restructured language" (Holm 2004:xiii), as opposed to a creole. Schwegler (2010) has also used the term "in-between variety" for semi-creoles. *See also* creole.

sertão. A non-specific reference to the Brazilian backlands, characterized as a poor and dry region. The Sertão Mineiro (i.e., northern and western regions of Minas Gerais) has been popularized by the fiction of João Guimarães Rosa (2001).

Triângulo Mineiro. The westernmost region of Minas Gerais, which borders the states of São Paulo to the south, Mato Grosso do Sul to the west, and Goiás to the north (see map 1). The name is derived from its peculiar triangle shape.

tropeiro. A Brazilian cowboy, typically from the southeastern region (i.e., the states of Minas Gerais, São Paulo, Goiás, etc.).

vissungo. A choral Afro-Brazilian religious song of the Catopé group from the central region of Minas Gerais. It is characteristically sung with percussion and in a call-and-response fashion between the leader and the choir (Cadernos do arquivo 1988:68).

CHAPTER TWO

Historical Overview

In your voice—
> the voice of the sugarfields, the ricefields,
> the coffeefields, the rubberlands
> the cottonlands . . .
> the plantations of Virginia
> the fields of the Carolinas
> of Alabama
> > Cuba
> > > Brazil
>
> rising from the mills that grind the sugarcane
> the voice of Harlem District South . . .
> wailing the blues, breasting the Mississippi
> chanting the groan of wagon wheels . . .
> the voice of all America, of all Africa
> the voice of every voice united

—Viriato da Cruz, twentieth-century Angolan poet and revolutionary, from "Black Mother: A Song of Hope" (quoted in Davidson 1973:151)

The origins of Calunga can be attributed to a series of historical factors. Of particular importance are the fifteenth-century Portuguese explorations and the subsequent establishment of the Portuguese Empire. Another key factor is the Atlantic slave trade, which "transformed the economic, political, and cultural character of the peoples, nations, and continents involved in the largest, albeit involuntary, migration in the history of humankind" (Dodson 2001:118). But it must be underscored that little is actually known regarding the specific history of Calunga. This problem is a consequence of a general lack of knowledge regarding Africa and the African diaspora, which have been themes of objective scholarship only since the latter half of the twentieth century (Azevedo 1998:25).

This chapter draws on the writings of scholars—particularly historians of Africa and the African diaspora, Portugal, and Brazil—to provide a general sociohistorical overview of the context in which Calunga evolved. A more specific historical overview of Minas Gerais and Calunga is in chapter 4.

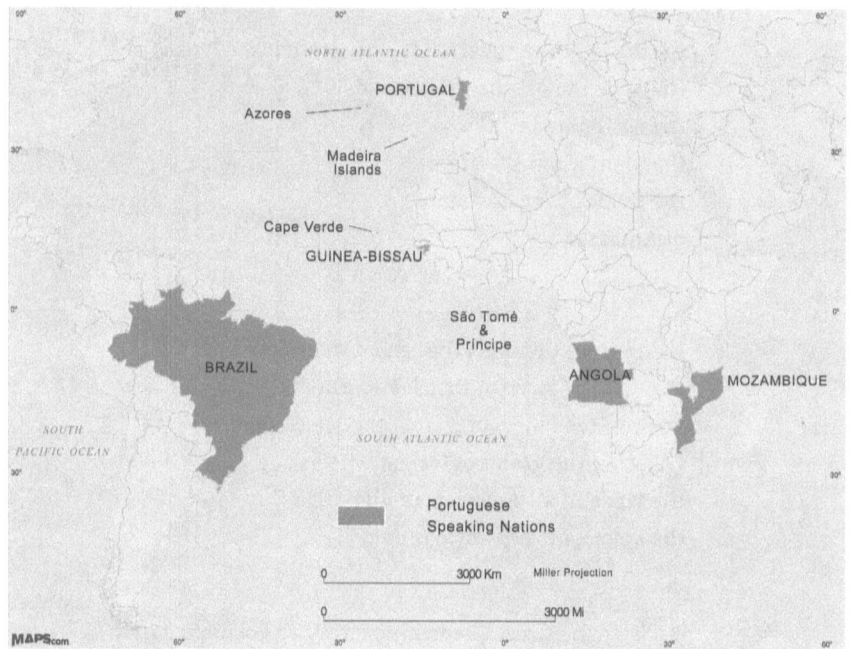

Map 2. Lusophone countries and territories in Europe, the Atlantic islands, Africa, and South America.

THE IBERIA-AFRICA CONNECTION

The Iberian Peninsula has an extensive history with Africa. One standard historical period to highlight is the Moorish conquest and occupation of the peninsula from AD 711 to 1492. Arriving from contemporary Morocco via the Straits of Gibraltar, the Moors subsequently conquered most of the peninsula, establishing themselves in the region they named al-Andalus. By 718 the Iberian Peninsula was divided: Islamic al-Andalus in the central and southern regions and the Christian dominions of Portugal, Galicia, León, Castilla, Navarro, Aragón, and Catalonia in the north (Azevedo 2005:9).

During the Muslim occupation of Iberia, Christian Iberians learned of great cities, schools, trading systems, and armies in sub-Saharan West Africa (Landers 2006:2). Much of the knowledge of northern and sub-Saharan African cultures came from Moorish scholars and traders. One example is Abu Ubayd al-Bakri, a scholar from Córdoba, who wrote an important book in Arabic, *The Book of the Routes and Realms*. Completed in 1068, this book detailed some of the peoples and cultures of sub-Saharan Africa. Interestingly, al-Bakri did not travel much out of al-Andalus but rather used travelers and traders as sources for his book (Davidson 1998:25). Note, for example, al-Bakri's description of King Tunka Manin of ancient Ghana:

> When the king gives audience to his people, to listen to their complaints and to set them to rights, he sits in a pavilion around which stand ten pages holding shields and gold-mounted swords. On his right hand are the sons of the princes of his empire, splendidly clad and with gold plaited in their hair.
>
> The governor of the city is seated on the ground in front of the king, and all around him are his counselors in the same position. The gate of the chamber is guarded by dogs of an excellent breed. These dogs never leave their place of duty. They wear collars of gold and silver, ornamented with metals.
>
> The beginning of a royal meeting is announced by the beating of a kind of drum they call *deba*. This drum is made of a long piece of hollowed wood. The people gather when they hear its sound. (Quoted in Davidson 1998:28–29, italics his)

In the medieval era ancient Ghana was a key supplier of gold and diamonds to northern Africa, western Europe, and the Near East. "Even kings in distant England," writes Africa historian Basil Davidson (1998:31), "had to buy West African gold before they could order their craftsman to make coins." Muslim traders also provided spices, from as far away as India and China, to medieval Iberians by means of a system of trading routes spanning from West and North Africa into the Middle East and beyond (Davidson 1998:177). In 1375 the Cresques Atlas, elaborated for the king of Portugal by a Majorcan geographer, presented caravan traders meeting with the ruler of the Mali kingdom (Davidson 1998:35–36).

Ultimately, a direct pursuit of such commodities, among other objectives, inspired the Portuguese to explore the Atlantic Ocean in the fifteenth century.

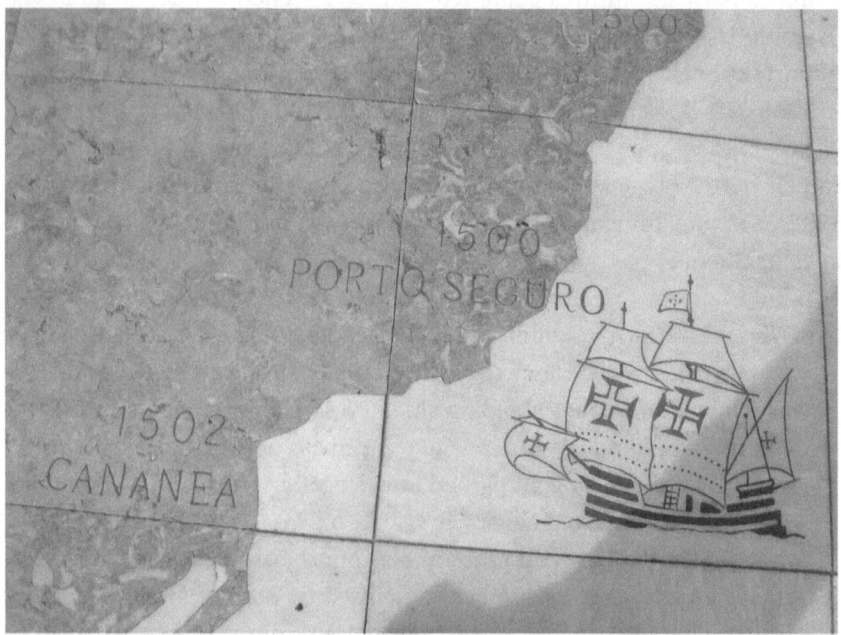

Figure 2.1. Depiction in stone of a Portuguese caravel off the coast of Brazil, near the Torre de Belém in Lisbon, Portugal. Photograph courtesy of Daniela Bassani Moraes Byrd, 2010.

PORTUGUESE EXPLORATIONS AND EXPANSION

In *The Wealth of Nations*, economist Adam Smith explains European motives for establishing new colonies around the world. In regard to Portugal's motives, which were inspired especially by Venetians' profitable trade in East Indian goods, Smith writes,

> The Venetians, during the fourteenth and fifteenth centuries, carried on a very advantageous commerce in spiceries, and other East India goods, which they distributed among the other nations of Europe. They purchased them chiefly in Egypt, at that time under the dominion of the Mammeluks, the enemies of the Turks,

of whom the Venetians were the enemies; and this union of interest, assisted by the money of Venice, formed such a connection as gave the Venetians almost a monopoly of the trade.

The great profits of the Venetians tempted the avidity of the Portuguese. They had been endeavouring, during the course of the fifteenth century, to find out by sea a way to the countries from which the Moors brought them ivory and gold dust across the Desart [sic]. They discovered the Madeiras, the Canaries, the Azores, the Cape de Verd islands, the coast of Guinea, that of Loango, Congo, Angola, and Benguela, and finally, the Cape of Good Hope. They had long wished to share in the profitable traffic of the Venetians, and this discovery opened to them a probable prospect of doing so. (Smith 1776/1976: vol. 2, pp. 68–69)

Historian A. J. R. Russell-Wood (1998:1) writes that the history of Portugal is an "unceasing ebb and flow of people, commodities, flora and fauna, ideas, and influences, with the globe as their stage." The Portuguese Empire, dated from 1415 to 1808 by Russell-Wood (1998, 2009), extended by sea and land to Africa, South America, India, Indonesia, Persia, and Asia—even to Tibet and Nepal (Russell-Wood 1998:14–15). During this period "Portuguese became the most widely spoken European language in the Atlantic sphere" (Russell-Wood 2009:81). To this day Portuguese holds the status of official language in some seven countries around the globe.

Unlike their Spanish neighbors, whose "hard power" empire engaged in military and religious conquests, the Portuguese Empire was one of "soft power": trade, commerce, and political and religious diplomacy. In fact, the Portuguese rarely engaged in any wars of conquest (Angola being one exception). Instead, the Portuguese were strategic in establishing "key points" to their interests and identifying what kind of presence was necessary to achieve them and the best way to establish that presence: colonization, building diplomatic ties, establishing trading forts, and so on (Russell-Wood 1998:21–22). Examining specifically the Atlantic sphere, Russell-Wood (2009:82) views the Portuguese presence there as one of "commerce, movement of peoples, creation of pan-Atlantic families, settlements, economic production, and boundary crossings—despite the [Portuguese] Crown."

There are a few explanations for the Portuguese explorations. Most importantly, the Portuguese sought an alternative passage to Asia that bypassed the Islamic monopoly of the North African and Middle Eastern land routes. Moreover, the Portuguese desired to gain direct access to the gold trade of western, southern, and eastern Africa (Alpha Bah 1998:70). Besides stirring commercial interests, the reconquest of the Moorish-occupied Iberian Peninsula sparked a Christian crusade to the Muslim lands in Africa (Ryder 1969:217–18). Lastly, medieval scientific interest in the Atlantic Ocean and Africa ignited a sense of adventurism in Europe. For instance, Ptolemy's *Geographia*, which had been known by Arab scholars previously, was translated into Latin for the first time in 1406 (Chaplin 2009:37). Plus, romanticized notions of Africa, also popular during the medieval era, were offered by the Roman poet Pliny in his *Summary of the Antiquities and Wonders of the World* (Reader 1999:325).

Given Portugal's geography, the Atlantic Ocean was the best prospect for Portuguese explorations and expansion. Prior to their explorations the Portuguese had known of Genoese sailors who had ventured past the Straits of Gibraltar in the late thirteenth and early fourteenth centuries. Lanzarote Malocello, for example, landed on the Canary Islands in 1336, one of which, Lanzarote, today bears his name (Reader 1999:331). Shortly thereafter, in 1341, King Afonso IV of Portugal declared the Canaries within the Portuguese domain (Portugal later ceded these islands to Castile under the 1479 Treaty of Alcáçovas-Toledo). Such Atlantic islands marked the beginnings of the Portuguese presence outside of Europe. Portuguese people, plants, manufactured products, language, and culture moved from Europe to Africa to the Americas and beyond via such islands.

While Portuguese commercial, religious, adventurist, and scientific aspirations were factors for expansion, so too was local poverty. "It can be argued," writes historian David Birmingham (2000:2), "that the price of bread in the city of Lisbon was the single most important factor in launching the age of empire." That is, instead of relying on wheat imports from England and Flanders, which were not always dependable, the Portuguese sought to grow their own wheat. As such, the Portuguese Crown sought fertile lands in order to provide a steady supply of bread flour for its citizens. Hence, in this analysis the Portuguese Empire initially was established on uninhabited Atlantic islands for the purposes of agricultural independence.

In 1419 the Portuguese began to colonize the Madeira Islands, which were uninhabited but densely wooded (i.e., *madeira* 'wood'). Portuguese colonial farmers there were expected to grow wheat for export to Portugal and Morocco. Around 1427 the Portuguese landed on the Azores, where the cooler, wetter climate and volcanic soils proved to be excellent for wheat cultivation. By the sixteenth century some four hundred thousand bushels of wheat were shipped to Portugal each year from the Azores (Birmingham 2000:8). With the advent of the Azores' successful wheat exports, the Madeira Islands began to cultivate a different cash crop: sugarcane. Birmingham (2000:8) notes that "the quasi-revolutionary change from cereal farming to sugar milling created an economic model that was later to be adopted throughout the Atlantic world." A subsequent aspect of this "quasi-revolutionary change" was the establishment of the plantation model that required a large workforce of slaves.

The Portuguese expansion into Africa began in 1415 when Prince Henry led a force to capture the Moroccan city of Ceuta, a strategic port where the Mediterranean intersected the Atlantic. The Portuguese established a series of coastal forts there to serve the interests of artisans, merchants, and traders (Russell-Wood 1998:86–87). Upon his return to Portugal in the 1430s, Prince Henry settled into a new residence near Cabo São Vicente where he established the Sagres navigation school—the first modern naval academy—thus earning him the title of the Navigator. Inspired by rumors of a great African gold trade and in search of the legendary Prester John, Henry began to dispatch ships along the West African coast (Reader 1999:329–30). In the 1430s, however, the Portuguese had not yet ventured beyond the coasts of southern Morocco. Portuguese boats and technology were not sufficiently sophisticated to sail back to Europe against the strong currents. The Chinese provided the missing pieces for long-range ships: the triangular lateen sail, the central rudder, and the compass—introduced to the Portuguese via Arab traders (Russell-Wood 1998:17). Further advances in cartography, mathematics, and maritime science enabled the Portuguese to sail farther out and safely return.

Portuguese explorations of Africa intensified in 1433 when Prince Henry's brother, Duarte, became king of Portugal. In 1435 Henry sent Portuguese captain Gil Eanes to sail beyond Cape Bojador (in contemporary Morocco)—a notorious landmark where the currents became dangerous and ships could be blown off course. Although terrified of this reconnaissance mission, Eanes managed to sail 250 kilometers beyond Cape Bojador, where he found traces of men and camels (Reader 1999:333). A year later Henry sent Captain Affonso Gonçalves Baldaia beyond Eanes's marker, where he discovered a river inlet he named Rio d'Ouro (River of Gold, which in reality had no gold). Shortly thereafter, while searching for villages near the Rio d'Ouro, Captains Antão Gonçalves and Nuno Tristão raided two African encampments, killing four inhabitants and taking ten captives. These captives were delivered to Henry, and Gonçalves was subsequently knighted. By the early 1440s the slave trade in Africa had effectively begun.

The Portuguese established a fort (*feitoria* in Portuguese) on Arguim Island in 1444, which provided an entrance to African trade routes. From the Arguim fort Henry had hoped to initiate gold trading with Wadan, an important access point to Guinea and Mauritania. Some shipments of African gold, ivory, pepper, and slaves began to flow to Portugal. But gold was scarce throughout this region, which forced the Portuguese farther down the African coast. In 1455 papal legislation granted Portugal monopoly powers over all African trade (Reader 1999:381). At the time of Henry the Navigator's death in 1460, the Portuguese had reached the shores of contemporary Sierra Leone and Liberia. And the explorations continued with unabated fervor.

Circa 1460 the Portuguese began to form their first colonies in sub-Saharan Africa. Portuguese settlers known as *lançados* (outcasts) began to colonize the uninhabited archipelago of the Cape Verde Islands. Along with the lançados, the Portuguese used West African slaves from the mainland of Guinea-Bissau. The Portuguese settlers replicated the sugarcane plantations from Madeira, also cultivating orchil (for dye) and later cotton. A Luso-African population and subsequent creole language were born there (see chapter 3). A similar colonization was repeated on the São Tomé and Príncipe Islands in the following decades. Eventually this colonization model would be repeated in Brazil as well.

From 1460 to 1500 Portuguese fleets made major headway in exploration and expansion. For example, in 1462 Pedro da Sintra explored Sierra Leone, and from 1469 to 1473 Fernão Gomes mapped the African gold trade routes between the upper Guinea coast and Sierra Leone. In contemporary Ghana Gomes finally found the foremost source of gold in West Africa. Throughout the 1470s the Portuguese established a number of commercial and diplomatic ties in the "gold coast" region and in the Bight of Benin and the Niger Delta—the so-called slave coast. In the latter region the Portuguese often bought or captured slaves, particularly Benin and Igbo peoples, and exchanged them for gold (Reader 1999:342). Horses were also highly valued among West African nobles in exchange for slaves, though horses were difficult to ship and had significant trouble adapting to the tropical climate (Reader 1999:393). Meanwhile, the Portuguese continued southward along the African coast, building feitorias on the coast or nearby islands. In 1482–1483 Diogo Cão sailed into the Zaire River, and by 1487 Bartolomeu Dias had reached the southern tip of the African continent, the Cape of Good Hope. During a 1497–1499 voyage Vasco da Gama reached the East African coast for the first time, and his ships eventually reached India with help from local traders.[1] In 1500, en route to India on a commercial voyage, Pedro Álvares Cabral landed on the northeastern shores of South America.

In a span of eighty-five years, from 1415 to 1500, the Portuguese had colonized four Atlantic islands, reconnoitered the coasts of western and

Figure 2.2. Torre de Belém, symbol of Portuguese exploration and expansion, sits along the Rio Tejo in Lisbon, Portugal. Photograph by Steven Byrd, 2010.

eastern Africa and established various trading forts there, established diplomatic relations with African kingdoms, reached India, and landed on the northeastern beaches of South America. Combined with the Spanish conquest of the Americas, the Portuguese voyages to Africa, India, and South America ultimately altered the course of human history. Adam Smith declared the changes brought about by these two empires as "the most important events recorded in the history of mankind" (quoted in Chomsky 1993:4).

After 1492 other European powers entered the Atlantic sphere. The Spanish, of course, expanded into the Americas, and so too did the French, English, Dutch, and Danish as well as pirates.

Portuguese Expansion in Congo and Angola

The Portuguese expanded into the region of Congo and Angola following their arrival in the late fifteenth century. The native peoples of this land spoke Bantu languages and would influence many cultures throughout the Americas, as expressed eloquently by the Angolan poet and revolutionary Viriato da Cruz. Indeed, according to the Africa historian/anthropologist Jan Vansina, the Bantu peoples of Congo and Angola "provided the common glue, the cultural background common to African American communities everywhere" (quoted in Morgan 2009:231).

In 1482–1483 Portuguese captain Diogo Cão sailed into the Nzadi (Great River), known today as the Congo or Zaire River, an action that "opened a new phase in Portuguese history" (Russell-Wood 2009:87). The Portuguese discovered a kingdom of villages that worked iron and copper, wove clothing and mats, and raised pigs, sheep, chickens, and cattle (Segal 1962:11).

Bantu groups had colonized the areas of contemporary Congo and Angola circa AD 500. Warrior leaders and kingdoms evolved in these regions, particularly around the Congo River valley, in the late fourteenth century (Warner-Lewis 2003:1–2). Davidson notes,

> By about 1450, the strongest kingdom in the western area ... was that of the Kongo people; and the Kongo have conserved their history with some care. Their traditions sketch a picture of migration, new settlement, and adjustment to local conditions that is

> markedly similar in its essence to the consequences of the Norman invasion of Anglo-Saxon England three centuries earlier. Around 1350 a leader and his warriors crossed southward over the Congo River from the region west of Stanley Pool, their homeland, and obtained supremacy south of the river. . . . They grafted their rule upon a people, the Ambundu, who had already developed an embryonic kingship of their own. (Davidson 1973:56)

With the exception of the hunter-gatherer Khoi of southern Angola, "nearly all Angola's people . . . share ultimately common origins and cultures, and speak related languages that are often little more than variants of a few of the western Bantu tongues" (Davidson 1973:38). However, even in the modern era, "there are zones of Angola about which little is known, about which one can really write nothing," noted Portuguese ethnographer Mesquelita de Lima in 1964 (quoted in Davidson 1973:36).

In the Congo Diogo Cão left behind four men with gifts and, before he sailed out, erected a stone cross known as a *padrão*. On the padrão were etched the arms of Portugal and the following message: "In the year 6681 of the world, and in that of 1482 since the birth of our Lord Jesus Christ, the most serene, most excellent and potent prince, King John II of Portugal did order this land to be discovered and these [padrãoes] to be set up by Diogo Cão, an esquire of his household" (quoted in Reader 1999:344). Farther south Cão erected a second padrão on the shores of an arid region near contemporary Luanda, Angola. Upon his return from this reconnaissance mission, Cão met King Nzinga Nkuwu of the Congo, the *manicongo*. After reporting this encounter to Portuguese king João II, Cão was sent on a second mission in 1484–1485. He arrived in the Congo bearing gifts and with a request that the manicongo convert to Christianity.

The Portuguese policy in the Congo was one of economic and cultural exchange, perhaps benign at the outset. Diplomatic relations were established, and from 1490 to 1492 King João II sent missionaries, artisans, traders, and two German printers. Both the manicongo and his son Mbemba Nzinga (baptized under the name Dom Affonso I) converted to Christianity. A capital city was established at São Salvador, or Mbanza. As part of the diplomatic exchange Congolese nobles traveled to Lisbon for education in European laws, religion, and culture. Portuguese customs, such as European courts and clothing, were subsequently adopted in the Congo. From 1506 to 1543 Dom Affonso I disseminated Christianity and other European traditions in his kingdom.

However, relations between Portugal and the Congo deteriorated throughout the sixteenth century. The Portuguese had learned that within the Congo Kingdom there were "disposable persons" who could be bought and sold, in addition to ivory, which was highly valued. These persons, typically men, had lost their freedom and civic rights either by judicial decree or by being captured in warfare. But they were not slaves in the European sense. Davidson (1973:60) writes, "The economies of these kingdoms had no use for plantation labor and thus for large quantities of slaves." However, the Portuguese were successful in corrupting leaders of the Congo Kingdom to ensure a steady flow of these "disposable persons." Davidson (60) further explains that "[t]he sale or gift [to the Portuguese] of the Kongo's 'disposable persons' was the key that opened the gate to a slave trade that afterward engulfed the whole . . . country." Such practices led the Portuguese and other Europeans to believe that parts of Africa were basically a basin of slaves to be bought and sold (Davidson 1973:60)—a distorted view of the Congolese that began to dominate Portuguese commercial efforts. This distortion was fueled particularly by Portuguese colonizers on the nearby islands of São Tomé and Príncipe, who demanded labor for their sugarcane plantations. Even Jesuit priests became involved in the slave trade, which created a bitter antagonism with the Congolese.

The insatiable appetite for slaves did not go unnoticed by the Congolese nobles. Dom Affonso I pled passionately to Portuguese king João II to stop slave trading in his kingdom. As Affonso wrote the king of Portugal in a letter dated July 6, 1526:

> Sir, Your Highness should know how our Kingdom is being lost in so many ways that it is convenient to provide for the necessary remedy, since this is caused by the excessive freedom given by your factors and officials to the men and merchants who are allowed to come to this Kingdom to set up shops with goods and many things which have been prohibited by us, and which they spread throughout our Kingdoms and Domains in such an abundance that many of our vassals, whom we had in obedience, do not comply because they have the things in greater abundance

than we ourselves; and it was with these things that we had them content and subjected under our vassalage and jurisdiction, so it is doing a great harm not only to the service of God, but the security and peace of our Kingdoms and State as well.

And we cannot reckon how great the damage is, since the mentioned merchants are taking every day our natives, sons of the land and the sons of our noblemen and vassals and our relatives, because the thieves and men of bad conscience grab them wishing to have the things and wares of this Kingdom which they are ambitious of; they grab them and get them to be sold; and so great, Sir, is the corruption and licentiousness that our country is being completely depopulated, and Your Highness should not agree with this nor accept it as in your service.... That is why we beg of Your Highness to help assist us in this matter, commanding your factors that they should not send here either merchants or wares, because it is *our will that in these Kingdoms there should not be any trade of slaves nor outlet for them.* (Quoted in Davidson 1993:223–24, italics in original)

Affonso's pleas went unanswered.

After Affonso's death in the 1540s Portugal's influence in the Congo took a turn for the worse. A violent war involving the Jagas and Anzicos left the Congo Kingdom in ruin. Amid such violence, the Portuguese eventually left the Congo after 1570.

During his Africa reporting trips of the 1870s, journalist Henry Morton Stanley found no remaining traces of the Portuguese presence in the Congo basin (Duffy 1962:45). Historian James Duffy (1962:46) concludes about the Portuguese presence, "The degradations and frictions arising from the slave-trade and the demands of the empire in the East, which distracted Lisbon's interest from the Congo in the crucial years of the Portuguese-African alliance, were responsible for the failure of the project. Without encouragement and moral authority, it succumbed to the purely material exploitations which have so often characterized the presence of Europe in Africa."

Of course, the Portuguese did not altogether abandon the region, and the territory that is known today as Angola emerged as a new attempt at a Portuguese colony in Africa. There the Portuguese encountered the

Ndongo Kingdom of the Kimbundu people. Their dynastic king held the title of *ngola,* which later gave the country its name.

The Portuguese initially sent a cohort of diplomats to the ngola in 1520 to request permission to search for silver mines. The ngola denied their request. So, in 1560, Paulo Dias de Novais (the grandson of Bartolomeu Dias) introduced the ngola to Jesuits priests in an attempt to court the African ruler. But again the ngola was not forthcoming. Interestingly, it turns out that the manicongo had advised the ngola not to have any type of political or religious affiliation with the Portuguese (Davidson 1973:80). Jesuit priest Father Gouveia, who served in the Ndongo Kingdom at the time, told the king of Portugal that the only way to convert the Kimbundu people was through military conquest (Davidson 1973:71). Birmingham (1966:44–45) notes that "Gouveia stressed that the Portuguese king must . . . show once and for all that he was the real master of all Africa."

In 1575 Paulo Dias de Novais landed with seven hundred troops at the newly founded city of São Paulo de Loanda, today Luanda. Shortly thereafter the Portuguese were at war with the Ndongo Kingdom. Dias de Novais's initial incursion failed, but "the hundred years' war" with Ndongo had begun. War lasted until the 1680s, ending with the African kingdom destroyed and the Portuguese rule of central and northern Angola in place (Davidson 1973:79–86).

Three principles dictated Portuguese colonial policy in Angola: generate revenue for the Crown, establish colonial white rule for the benefit of Portugal, and organize Africans as a labor pool to serve Portuguese interests locally and abroad. These objectives were achieved almost exclusively by providing a steady stream of slaves for Portuguese colonies, often working through the Catholic Church, as in the Congo. Furthermore, in addition to slave traders and mostly corrupt clergymen, the colonists that the Portuguese sent to Angola were often *degredados.* These 'banished ones' were usually poor, uneducated criminals in Portugal who held utter contempt for African cultures (Davidson 1973:89). Such degredados were sent to Angola well into the twentieth century.

Davidson (1973) concludes that, in general, the Portuguese treated Angola as a colony of slaves for export, particularly to Brazil, and as a godless wasteland to which they could send undesirable citizens. Thornton (2006:84), however, offers a different view: that there was indeed a "deep engagement" by the Portuguese. He writes that "by the mid-seventeenth century Angola resembled Latin American countries in ways that no other part of Africa did." As in Latin America, for example, there was an adoption of European culture, particularly religion and language.

However one evaluates the rule of the Portuguese in Angola, over time relations became bitter and eventually violent. Angolan journalist José de Fontes Pereira made the following observation in April 1882 in the newspaper *O Futuro d'Angola*: "How has Angola benefited under Portuguese rule? The darkest slavery, scorn, and the most complete ignorance. [E]ven the government have done their utmost to the extent of humiliating and vilifying the sons of this land who possess the necessary qualifications for advancement" (quoted in Davidson 1973:138–39). In the twentieth century a violent struggle against the Portuguese took place.[2] Angola's struggle against the Portuguese later evolved into a civil war that lasted until the 1990s.

By 1975 Portugal had effectively lost control of all its African colonies following violent revolutionary struggles.

Brazil

Karl Friedrich Philipp, a nineteenth-century German scientist who traveled through Brazil from 1817 to 1820 with his colleague Johann Baptist von Spix, wrote that "the history of Brazil will always be primarily a branch of Portuguese history. However, if Brazilian history is to be complete and to deserve the name history, it can never exclude the roles played by the Ethiopian [African] and Indian [indigenous] races" (quoted in Schwartz 1997:xviii).

The Americas were in dispute between Spain and Portugal in the 1490s. As Columbus returned to Europe from his historic 1492 voyage, a storm forced him to land in Lisbon. There Portuguese king João II interrogated him to learn whether he had sailed into Portuguese territory as adjudicated by the 1479 Treaty of Alcáçovas-Toledo (Phillips 2009:251). Later the pope was asked to rule on the matter, which resulted in the 1494 Treaty of Tordesillas. The Spanish nevertheless actively explored the waters around South America following the 1494 treaty. For instance, Vicente Yáñez Pinzón, the captain of the *Niña* on Columbus's first journey to the Americas, is credited with being the first to sail to the northeastern coast of Brazil and the Amazon River in January 1500. However, for political reasons related to the Treaty of Tordesillas, the Portuguese are traditionally credited with Brazil's discovery (Catz 1995–1996; *História do Brasil* 1997:26).

The official Portuguese "discovery" of Brazil came on April 22, 1500, when Captain Pedro Álvares Cabral and his fleet of thirteen ships landed on the northeastern Brazilian coast during a journey to India. The reason for this landing has never been conclusively determined, but historians theorize that it was made either by accident, in order to avoid the Atlantic doldrums, or by royal orders (Catz 1995–1996). Whatever the reason, Cabral erected a padrão on the Brazilian shore on May 1, 1500. The next day he sent one supply ship back to Portugal with news of the discovery; the rest of the fleet set sail on their original mission to India. Besides the padrão, Cabral also left behind two "tearful criminals" who were to learn about the land, the people, and the native language (Abreu 1907/1997:25).

In South America the Portuguese encountered indigenous peoples known today as the Tupi-Guaranis. These native peoples, both on the coast and in the interior regions, lived in small, communalist societies. They grew manioc, corn, and various fruits, hunted and fished, wove and made pottery, domesticated parrots and other tropical birds as pets, danced and sang, wore elaborate body decorations and piercings, and practiced ritualistic cannibalism on enemies, friends, and relatives. João Capistrano de Abreu, one of the "fathers of modern Brazilian historiography" according to Schwartz (1997:xix) and an accomplished linguist, describes some of the peoples that the Portuguese encountered:

> Based on linguistic evidence, modern ethnographers have succeeded in grouping certain more or less intimately related [Brazilian] tribes. The first group consists of those who spoke the coastal language, known as the *língua geral* (general language) because of its distribution. This was the largest native group living along the coast. They came from the backlands in three distinct migrations. The Carijós or Guaranis were located in Cananéia and Paranapanema and to the south and west of that area. The Tupiniquins settled along the Tietê River, the Jequitinhonha River, the Ibiapaba mountain range, and on the coast and backlands of Bahia. The Tupinambás settled around the area of present-day Rio de Janeiro. They also settled along the lower

banks of the São Francisco River, in Rio Grande do Norte, as well as in Maranhão and Pará. The point of origin for these three groups is the area between the Paraguay and Paraná Rivers. . . .

If we leave out the Amazon region, where there were many Maipures and not a few Caraíbas, we are left with only the Tupis and the Cariris as tribes that were incorporated into Brazil's present-day population. (Abreu 1907/1997:12–13, italics his)[3]

Portugal initially had little interest in Brazil. There was nothing sufficiently striking about the land or the inhabitants to begin a widespread colonization of the Terra dos Papagaios (land of parrots), as they called it (Catz 1995–1996:82). Adam Smith (1776/1976: vol. 2, p. 80) notes in *The Wealth of Nations*, "After the settlements of the Spaniards, that of the Portugueze in Brazil is the oldest of any European nation in America. But as for a long time after the first discovery, neither gold nor silver mines were found in it, and as it afforded, upon that account, little or no revenue to the crown, it was for a long time in a great measure neglected."

That said, during a 1501 expedition Italian explorer Amérigo Vespucci noticed something of interest: *pau-brasil* (brazilwood). The pulp of brazilwood was useful for crimson or purple dye—the color of kings and noblemen—which later provided the name Terra Brasilis. By 1505 the Portuguese had renamed the new colony Terra do Brasil, reducing the title in 1527 to simply Brasil (also written as *Brazil*) (*História do Brasil* 1997:22–23).

However, another European country was now also vying for a foothold in South America: France.

Figure 2.3. Brazilwood tree in Arceburgo, Minas Gerais. The sign reads in Portuguese, "Brazilwood: I learned in the first years of school that the origin of our country's name comes from this tree." Photograph by Steven Byrd, 2003.

The French claimed the territory of northeastern Brazil as La France Antartique, allying themselves with indigenous peoples who opposed the Portuguese presence (Phillips 2009:253). There they established a trading fort, La Pèlerine, on the shores of contemporary Pernambuco (Abreu 1907/1997:35). French sailors and merchants also were attracted to brazilwood for its properties as a crimson dye, which were "much prized in Europe's textile industries" (Phillips 2009:253).

Due to increasing French interests in the South American colony, in 1532 the Portuguese king sent Martim Affonso de Sousa (who appears in Luís de Camões's *Os Lusíadas*) to fortify the Portuguese presence there. The king announced the creation of captaincies (i.e., provinces): parallel sections of land that stretched from contemporary Pernambuco in the north to the River Plate in the south. Martim Affonso de Sousa himself was to receive some one hundred miles of coastline (Abreu 1907/1997:35). Around 1535 the Portuguese Crown divided up twelve captaincies from the contemporary states of Maranhão to Santa Catarina and donated them to twelve individual dignitaries, laying the path for the geographical form of contemporary Brazil (see Hufferd 2005:61 for a map and further explanation). São Vicente (near what is today São Paulo city) was the first declared Brazilian city in 1532 (Keen 1996:123).

Phillips (2009:263) calculates that some two thousand Portuguese colonizers migrated to Brazil during the 1530s, along with some four thousand African slaves. The initial objective of the Portuguese colonization of Brazil was "to feature high-volume, low-priced goods, especially brazilwood and various aromatic woods and construction timber" (265). However, after brazilwood rendered only small profits and coastline deforestation and no gold or majestic cities were found, the Portuguese instituted sugarcane production in the struggling colony. One of the most authoritative accounts of the early Brazilian colony, *Diálogos das Grandezas do Brasil*, written in 1618 and attributed to Ambrósio Fernandes Brandão, explains how the Portuguese organized Brazil economically: "[A]s riquezas do Brasil consistem em seis coisas, com as quais seus povoadores se fazem ricos, que são estas: a primeira a lavoura do açúcar, a segunda a mercancia, a terceira o pau a que chamam do Brasil, a quarta os algodões e madeiras, a quinta a lavoura de mantimentos, a sexta e última a criação de gados. De tôdas estas coisas o principal nervo e substância da riqueza da terra é a lavoura dos açúcares." (Quoted in Bosi 1980:28; The riches of Brazil consist of six things, with which its inhabitants enrich themselves, which are these: the first sugar farming, the second commerce, the third wood that they call from Brazil, the fourth cotton and wood, the fifth sustenance farming, the sixth and final cattle ranching. Of all these things the principal strength and substance of wealth from the land is sugar farming.)

Martim Affonso de Sousa initiated the Brazilian sugar industry in 1532 as part of the colonization efforts. Like the Spanish in the New World colonies, the Portuguese first attempted to use indigenous slaves, but with little success: such slaves were unproductive or were decimated by European-borne diseases. In order to fill the labor shortage, African slaves were requested by Jesuit priests (Duffy 1962:54; *História do Brasil* 1997:75). Using their feitorias on the African coasts, the Portuguese began sending Africans to the Brazilian colony as well as to other regions of Latin America at the request of the Spanish. During the sixteenth and seventeenth centuries the Portuguese were in the position of both supplying African slaves to the Americas and profiting from the labor of their slaves in Brazil (Phillips 2009:265).

In the seventeenth century the Dutch began to aggressively challenge the Portuguese colonies in Africa and South America. That is, the Dutch sought to undermine and take over Portugal's spice- and slave-trading ventures with the founding of the East Indies Company (considered one of the first business corporations) in 1602 and then the establishment of the West Indies Company in 1621 (Klein 1986:46). One strategy was to attack and capture Portuguese feitorias. For example, the Dutch captured Portuguese positions in the Brazilian northeast from 1624 to 1654, including the cities of Pernambuco and Salvador, the West African feitoria of Elmina in 1637, and the Angolan coastal ports of Luanda and Benguela in 1641. Interestingly, the Portuguese recovered their Angolan ports in 1648 by using a squadron of fifteen ships from Brazil (Birmingham 1993:48; Davidson 1973:75). Moreover, the Dutch incursions into South America laid the path for eventual establishment of British and French sugar plantations in the Caribbean, including the use of African slaves and contemporary milling technology of the mid-seventeenth century (Klein 1986:49).

Conflicts with the Dutch aside, the general process of Portuguese colonization of Brazil was diverse and largely dependent on the climate and terrain of the region in question. While the northeastern areas contained a concentration of sugarcane plantations, in the southeastern regions sugarcane did not grow as well, which left them largely unexplored and uncolonized.

From the late sixteenth to the late eighteenth centuries Portuguese teams of explorers known as *bandeirantes* (for the type of *bandeira* 'flag' that they traveled with) wandered into the interior of the Brazilian colony in search of gold and indigenous slaves. Such explorations covered tens of thousands of kilometers of the South American continent, stretching as far as the Amazon River in the north, the contemporary nation of Ecuador in the northwest, and contemporary Uruguay in the southeast. The demarcation line of the Treaty of Tordesillas was violated by these explorations, but Spanish protest was futile given that the two crowns had been united in 1580. Following Portugal's independence from Spain in 1640, the bandeirantes had initiated a massive territorial expansion of Brazil for Portugal.

In the region that was later known as Minas Gerais, the bandeirantes discovered gold, diamonds, and other precious stones in the 1690s. From these discoveries, Portugal diversified its colonial activities to both sugar and mining. This phase of colonization initiated an economic shift from the northeastern states of Bahia and Pernambuco to Rio de Janeiro and Minas Gerais. Besides Minas Gerais, settlements in the contemporary states of Goiás and Mato Grosso were also established specifically for mining purposes.

The mines of Minas Gerais made Brazil the leading producer of gold in the world during the eighteenth century. In 1703, for instance, the Portuguese extracted more gold from Brazil than all the gold obtained in West Africa. During the peak years of 1741–1760 an average of 14,600 kilos of Brazilian gold arrived in Europe each year. In particular the English, Spanish, and Dutch were important buyers of Brazilian gold during this period (Phillips 2009:269). Moreover, shipments of gold and diamonds from Minas Gerais contributed to a growth of global trade and a large economic expansion (i.e., mining, agriculture, and manufacturing) in Europe in the eighteenth century. By 1750 Ouro Preto, the major city of Minas Gerais, grew to a population of over eighty thousand (*História do Brasil* 1997:65–68).

Portugal moved the colonial capital from Salvador to Rio de Janeiro in 1763 in order to concentrate its political and economic activities in

Brazil's southeastern region (i.e., Rio de Janeiro, São Paulo, Minas Gerais). This political and economic transition enlarged the colonial bureaucracy, created internal transportation and commercial networks, produced competition with the northeastern sugar business, and increased the African slave trade (Burkholder and Johnson 2001:258, 261). An unprecedented increase in African slaves sent to Brazil was accompanied by a large increase in Portuguese migration. During the eighteenth century perhaps as many as five hundred thousand Portuguese migrated to Brazil (Phillips 2009:268). In order to better capitalize and control the Brazilian economy, the Marquês de Pombal enacted reforms. These reforms expelled the Jesuits—who were responsible for religious and secular instruction—diminished the use of indigenous labor, and advocated for large increases in the number of African slaves (Keen 1996:125).

After 1760, however, the Brazilian mines began to dry up, which forced the Portuguese to return to agriculture. Minas Gerais, in particular, sought to diversify its economy: farming, sugarcane plantations, *cachaça* (white rum) distilleries, cattle ranches, and pig farms began to flourish. Many mine owners began to invest their capital in local agriculture and local entrepreneurs, such as manufacturers of farming tools (Birmingham 1993:101). In short, Minas Gerais sought to become economically independent from Portugal. But the question of labor was still a problem. Hence, as was done previously, large numbers of African slaves were sent to Brazil to work on the sugarcane, tobacco, cotton, rice, and coffee farms (Burkholder and Johnson 2001:258).

In the latter half of the eighteenth century the white elites of Minas Gerais, many of whom were educated emigrants from northern Portugal, began the first independence movement in Brazil. Inspired in part by the American Revolution, the Inconfidência Mineira of 1789 aimed to break free from the Portuguese Crown and embraced a number of ambitious plans. Among the revolutionaries' ideas were economic, political, and educational freedom, the establishment of a local university, protectionism for local industries, an autonomous military of local citizens, and a whitening of the population (Birmingham 1993:102). To such demands the Portuguese Crown responded with force. A key revolutionary figure of the Inconfidência Mineira, Tiradentes, was captured and publicly executed.

Another independence movement occurred in Bahia in 1798. Poor *mestiços* (i.e., "semi-whites") who were teachers, craftsmen, soldiers, and various other types of workers, fought against the oppressive social order maintained by the Portuguese Crown. Inspired by the ideals of the French Revolution, they demanded democratic rule and an abolition of slavery—radical propositions at the time. Needless to say, the Bahian revolution was crushed violently, even more so than the Inconfidência Mineira (Birmingham 1993:103). Yet Brazilian independence was near.

Napoleon invaded Portugal in 1807. Aided by the British, the Portuguese ruler Queen Maria I escaped to Rio de Janeiro in 1807–1808. Portuguese and British forces battled the French to hold major cities such as Lisbon and Porto. As the Napoleonic wars came to a close, Queen Maria I died in Brazil in 1816, leaving her son João VI in control of Portugal. As calm returned to Europe, João VI returned to Lisbon. But João's son, Pedro IV, remained in Rio de Janeiro. On September 7, 1822, Pedro IV declared Brazil independent from Portugal, with no ensuing violence. Pedro IV was renamed Dom Pedro I, the emperor of Brazil.

Figure 2.4. Slave dungeon at Elmina feitoria in Ghana. Photograph by Steven Byrd, 2009.

THE ATLANTIC SLAVE TRADE

Reporter A. T. Steele of the *New York Herald Tribune* wrote on February 15, 1948, "When an Angolan plantation owner requires labor, he notifies the government of his needs. The demand is passed down to the village chiefs, who are ordered to supply fixed quotas of laborers from the communities. If the required number is not forthcoming, police are sent to round them up" (quoted in Davidson 1973:128). Steele's report highlights a twentieth-century version of an ancient practice.

Slavery and slave plantations had been established by Europeans long before their arrival in the Americas.[4] In fact, slavery and slave trading extend back to the rise of complex societies and are practices that have been known in virtually all world cultures (Klein 1986:1). For example, slavery in the European tradition has its origins in ancient Greece and Rome. The ancient Roman population of contemporary Italy had an estimated two to three million slaves, making up some 35 to 40 percent of the total population (Klein 1986:4). The elite Romans of Lusitania (modern-day Portugal) used slaves for farming olives, grapes, wheat, rye, figs, and cherries; for quarrying and mining; and for construction (Birmingham 1993:13). "In terms of the production of goods and services for the market, the Romans can be said to have created a modern slave system which would be similar to those established in the Western Hemisphere from the 16th to the end of the 19th century," writes historian Herbert S. Klein (1986:5). From the Latin word for slave—*servus*—are derived words such as *serve, servant, service,* and *serf.*

In the medieval era the Moors introduced slavery into the agriculture and industry of the Iberian Peninsula, including the enslavement of Christians (Klein 1986:7). During the Crusades European Christians became involved in slave trading after Genoese and Venetian merchants and traders witnessed Muslim sugar plantation systems in regions such as Palestine and Syria. The word *sugar* is, in fact, derived from Arabic: *as-sukkar.*

Europeans began to establish their own sugar plantations in the contemporary region of Lebanon in 1123, with such plantations moving westward into Mediterranean territories (Reader 1999:331). During the Black Death (1347–1351), about one-third of the agricultural workforce of Europe perished—particularly in the southern regions, where there were sugar plantations—which resulted in an intensive search for labor (Reader 1999:340). Enslavement at the time was deemed acceptable for virtually anyone but less acceptable for Christians. The word *slave* (and Romance-language equivalents: Portuguese *escravo*, Spanish *esclavo*, French *esclave*, Italian *schiavo*) originates from the word *slav*, which referred to mostly Russian (i.e., "Slavic") peasants from the Black Sea region who worked on sugar plantations in Syria, Cyprus, Sicily, and elsewhere (Reader 1999:331). Of course, not all these forced laborers were actually Slavs; in fact, on the Mediterranean plantations there were Muslims from North Africa and Asia Minor, Christians from Greece and the Balkans, and even Europeans from the north (Klein 1986:8). By the early fifteenth century such sugar plantations had expanded into the southern Portuguese province of the Algarve (Klein 1986:9).

In Africa, before the arrival of Europeans, slavery was employed, but in a different form than European serfdom. African societies had rights to slaves rather than rights to land. Plus, slaves in African societies were considered "aliens" in terms of their ethnicity, religion, or language (Morgan 2009:228). In fact, many slaves in African cultures were captured through warfare or lost their freedom by committing serious crimes (Alpha Bah 1998:73). However, in African societies slaves could work their way up to become outstanding and exemplary members of their respective societies. African societies also had distinctions between ethical and unethical forms of slavery. For instance, Muslims typically objected to the sale of Muslim slaves to Christians (Lovejoy 2006:10). Nevertheless, Arabs and Europeans alike did encounter a social system in sub-Saharan Africa that they regarded as slavery, which was "as old as its counterparts in Asia and Europe" (Alpha Bah 1998:73). To cite one example, the Berber traveler Muhammed ibn Battuta of Tangier provides a vivid description of slavery as employed in the Mali Empire circa 1352, calling it a "deplorable custom": "Women servants, slave women and young girls go about quite naked, not even concealing their sexual parts. I saw many like this during Ramadhan; because it is the custom with the Negroes that commanding officers should break their fast in the sultan's palace; and they are served with food which is brought by women slaves, twenty or more of them who are completely naked" (quoted in Davidson 1993:101). Similar types of slavery were present in non-Muslim African societies as well, something the Portuguese learned about during their own travels.

At any rate, it is clear that an enterprise such as the Atlantic slave trade could not have taken place without the consent of Africans. As Morgan (2009:240) concludes, "Even though Europeans initiated Atlantic trade, organized it for their benefit, and underpinned it with their shipping technology and financial institutions, Africans participated willingly and powerfully in the new commerce."

The first reports of Portuguese slaving activities in Africa appear in 1441, from a trip to Guinea by Portuguese captains Antão Gonçalves and Nuno Tristão. But the starting point of the Atlantic slave trade is argued to have begun on the island of Arguim, located just off the coast of modern-day Mauritania, where the Portuguese established a feitoria in 1448 (Reader 1999:339; Ryder 1969:220). From the Arguim feitoria the Portuguese established commercial relations with Arab traders and nomadic African groups (Reader 1999:339). In exchange for items such as wool, cotton, carpets, and silver, the Portuguese received hides, fish, goats, and especially gold and slaves. By the 1460s approximately one thousand slaves per year were being shipped from Arguim to Portugal (Reader 1999:341).

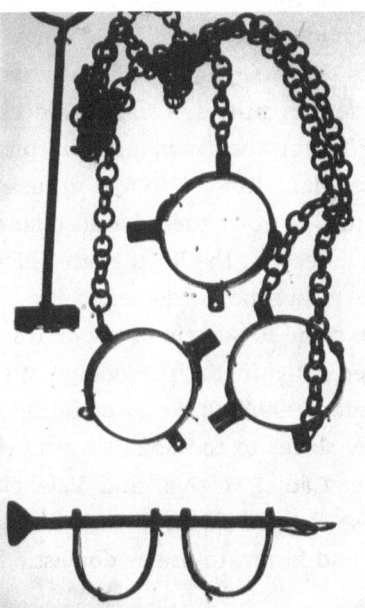

Figure 2.5. Shackles, handcuffs, and branding iron used at Elmina feitoria in Ghana. Photograph by Steven Byrd, 2009.

Morgan (2009:229) notes seven major regions that Europeans targeted on the African coast during the Atlantic slave trade: Senegambia (Senegal River to Rio Nunez), Sierra Leone (Rio Nunez to Cape Mount), the Windward Coast (Cape Mount to Assini River), Gold Coast (Assini River to Volta River), Bight of Benin (Rio Volta to Rio Nun), Bight of Biafra (Rio Nun to Cape Lopez), and West Central Africa (Cape Lopez to Kunene River). Overall, the region of Upper Guinea contributed much less to the Atlantic slave trade than West Central Africa (Morgan 2009:231). Much of this is explained by the strong and prolonged Portuguese presence in the region, a shorter Atlantic passage to South America, and a common Bantu culture among the Bakongo, Mbundu, and Ovimbundu. That said, it is evident that Europeans had at best a minimal understanding of Africans and African cultures. Names applied to Africans frequently came from their port of sale (e.g., Mina), a broad region (e.g., Angola), or a linguistic and/or cultural identity (e.g., Igbo). For their part, Africans identified themselves according to their village or kinship, not as ethnic or national groups, much less according to makeshift categories applied to them by Europeans (Morgan 2009:236–38).

In the early years of the slave trade the Portuguese managed their African subjects in a number of ways. First, some captured slaves were shipped to Portugal to learn Portuguese. These *grumetes* (apprentice sailors) were vital because they provided translation in various African languages, explained African customs, and aided in commercial negotiations. For instance, linguist Alain Kihm (1994:4) argues that grumetes were important disseminators of Portuguese-based creole languages, particularly in Guinea-Bissau. Second, the Portuguese shipped significant numbers of African slaves to Europe for domestic and agricultural labor. For example, by the 1570s some 10 percent of Lisbon was composed of African slaves, which provided a significant percentage of the country's agricultural labor force (Reader 1999:380; Weber de Kurlat 1963:383). Third, the Portuguese sold many slaves to the Spanish, who then shipped them to cities such as Seville, Cádiz, Huelva, and Valencia (Lipski 1994b:94). Fourth, the Portuguese shipped slaves to various Atlantic islands to work on sugar plantations and farms, to use as domestic servants, or to sell to other slave traders.

Following the arrival of the Spaniards in the Americas in 1492, a medieval labor system known as the encomienda was employed. Such a system granted the Spanish encomenderos possession of both land and the people living on the land. For instance, following their "discoveries" of the Caribbean islands, Columbus and his men enslaved the native Caribs (whom they called "Indians"). Like the African grumetes for the Portuguese, some enslaved Caribs were shipped to Spain to be trained as interpreters. As historian Hugh Thomas (2004:175) argues, "The Atlantic slave trade thus began in a west-east direction, not from Africa, but from the Caribbean to Europe."

Sometime before 1502 the first African slaves began to arrive in the Caribbean, shipped by the Spanish via Spain and Portugal (Reader 1999:382–83). There is some speculation that Columbus himself may have been involved in the shipping of the first Africans to the Americas. The Portuguese, for their part, sent the first African slaves to the shores of South America sometime in the early to mid-sixteenth century.

In particular, the Congo/Angola region was a primary area for slaves shipped to Latin America by the Portuguese (and other European) slave traders. Slaves from this region typically were shipped from the port cities of Cabinda, Luanda, and Benguela. Slave traffic to the Americas from Congo and Angola began to especially intensify during the Spanish-Portuguese unification of 1580–1640 (Landers 2006:4). Moreover, Lovejoy (2006:11) estimates that, during the seventeenth and eighteenth centuries, perhaps 85 percent of the total number of slaves sent to the Americas came from the region of the Congo and Angola. Duffy (1962:59–60) estimates that a total of some four million slaves from Congo/Angola were shipped to the Americas, with over 50 percent sent to Brazil and 30 percent to the Caribbean.

In Angola, for example, the slave trade was organized in the following manner. First there were *aviados* (executives), or trading colonists—merchants and traders who negotiated with the African kings for slaves. Second in line were the *negros calçados* (shod blacks), who served the aviados as middlemen. And third were the *pombeiros* (bare foots), who did the work of gathering and finding slaves to sell to the negros calçados (Davidson 1973:91–92). According to Morgan (2009:224), this slave-trading infrastructure comprised tens of thousands of people, particularly African middlemen who served as "the indispensable lubricants of the slaving system." Such an infrastructure was maintained by the constant influx of commodities—such as foodstuffs, clothing, metal, liquor, tobacco, and firearms—from Portuguese colonies, especially from Brazil, in exchange for the Angolan people. "[B]y the 1780s slaves comprised over 90 percent of the value of all African exports," notes Morgan (227).

Interestingly, the Angolans themselves lived in sparsely populated villages and were extremely mobile. Militant Angolans, including mercenary groups such as the Imbangala, were responsible for the enslavement of many fellow Angolans, including the capture and training of child soldiers. Thornton (2006:95) notes that in West Central Africa "it was through military service that people were most often enslaved; most Africans brought as slaves to Latin America were likely to have had military experience and organization as their last African experience."

It is worth noting that the Atlantic slave trade was a relatively minor affair in terms of slave shipments for the first 250 years. In the early years, from 1450 to 1600, the Atlantic slave trade was fairly small and dominated by the Portuguese. From 1600 to 1700 there was a rise in slaving activity, although it still mostly consisted of "scattered shipments of Africans," according to Chaplin (2009:41). The peak years of the slave trade, however, were from 1700 to 1800, due to the high demand for slaves in all the European colonies in the Americas and the colonies' subsequent entry into the slaving business. For example, Phillips (2009:269) notes that some 90 percent of the French Caribbean population consisted of African slaves and their descendants by the end of the eighteenth century.

Another important detail regarding the Atlantic slave trade was the disproportionate number of male versus female slaves. In fact, until the 1820s, when slave trafficking became illegal, African men greatly outnumbered African women among the slave populations. According to British statistics, in the eighteenth century only twenty-two women were sent to the Americas for every seventy-eight men (Fraginals 1984:10–11). After 1820 more women were shipped, as reproductive mates, particularly to Brazil and Cuba, as the British blockade of slave trafficking made it ever costlier to ship slaves.

By the end of the eighteenth century public opinion began to turn against slavery and slave trading in Europe and in the Americas. Changing religious norms and ideas born of the Enlightenment strongly challenged the status quo of the rights of kings, the power of the Church, and the ownership of people. The French Revolution's ideals of *Liberté, Egalité,*

Fraternité resonated throughout Europe and the American colonies. The 1789 memoirs of Olaudah Equiano, an enslaved Igbo from contemporary Nigeria who purchased his freedom, made an appeal for the colonizers to look at African civilizations with tolerance, understanding, and interest. There were also incidents that caused Europeans and colonists in the Americas to become critical of the Atlantic slave trade. One infamous example was the "Zong affair" of 1781: Captain Zong of Liverpool tossed a shipment of sick and starving slaves in the Atlantic, later collecting an insurance payment for their deaths (Chaplin 2009:48). And the Haitian slave rebellion of 1791 was a watershed event that eventually led to the independence of that country in 1804.

Even though slavery continued throughout the nineteenth century, the British Parliament introduced legislation banning the overseas traffic of slaves in 1807, with President Thomas Jefferson signing similar legislation in the United States in the same year. Interestingly, the modern African states of Sierra Leone and Liberia were a result of Britain's and the United States' abolition of the slave trade (Alpha Bah 1998:82–83). But even with such political efforts in full force in countries like Britain and the United States, more slaves were exported to the Americas in the nineteenth century than during the seventeenth century, when slavery was socially and politically acceptable (Reader 1999:380). A full end to slave trafficking and slavery itself in many of the American colonies—such as the United States, Cuba, and Brazil—would not come until the latter half of the nineteenth century.

Precise figures on the number of slaves sent to the Americas do not exist, but scholars' estimates range from ten to fifty million people (Alpha Bah 1998:83). Africa diaspora scholar Howard Dodson offers a strong view about our limited understanding of the slave trade:

> [M]ore than five out of every six people who came to the Americas in the first three centuries after their "discovery" were African. . . . As late as 1820, three times as many Africans as Europeans had come to the Americas. As a result, one of the major consequences of the slave trade was the peopling of the continents and islands of the Western Hemisphere with predominantly African peoples who constituted the demographic foundation on which the societies and cultures of the Americas were built.

> We have not studied these facts in history books, and this knowledge has not been a part of our understanding of the development of the Americas. To the contrary, the histories of the Americas have been written from colonial perspectives that have neglected to take into account the economic, political, and sociocultural consequences of the undeniable fact that the overwhelming majority of the people involved in the development of the Americas were African.
>
> ... If more than five-sixths of the peoples who developed the new societies of the Western Hemisphere have not been included in the telling of its history, then we do not know much about this history. (Dodson 2001:119–20)

The Atlantic Slave Trade and Brazil

Scholars' estimates of the number of Africans shipped to and living in Brazil are as problematic as the estimates of slaves sent to the Americas overall. In his census of the Atlantic slave trade Curtain (1969:89) estimates that some 3.6 million slaves were shipped to Brazil. More recent estimates are that some 4 to 4.5 million arrived in Brazil between the sixteenth and nineteenth centuries (Bueno 2003:120; Klein 2002:93; Olsen 2003:57). However, Castro (2001:62) believes the estimates should be higher: some 5 to 8 million. And Mendonça (1933:176) argues that there may have been an additional 2 million contraband slaves who entered Brazil. Estimates compiled by Klein (1986:295–97) show that there were on average 1 million slaves in Brazil in the late eighteenth century; in 1872 there were 1.5 million slaves and 4.2 million free coloreds. Burkholder and Johnson (2001:262) estimate that in the early nineteenth century African slaves or descendants of Africans made up approximately 66 percent of Brazil's population, whites constituted 28 percent, and indigenous people, 6 percent. Lastly, Leite and Callou (2002:13) note that the 1822 Brazilian census recorded some 1,347,000 whites (25 percent of the population) and 3,993,000 blacks (75 percent).[5] In the first decade of the twenty-first century it is estimated that Brazil's population comprises at least 80 million Afro-descendants (Boadi-Siaw 2007:164).[6]

Even though accurate figures cannot be calculated, it is agreed that Brazil was the largest single recipient of African slaves, accounting for approximately 40 percent of the entire Atlantic slave trade (Dodson 2001:119). Russell-Wood (2009:95–96) explains why: "What distinguished the slave trade to Brazil was its intensity, volume, and duration. Over a span of three centuries, chartered companies, merchant consortia, individuals, Portuguese and Brazilians, and illegal traders engaged in a trade carrying slaves variously from Upper Guinea to Pará and Maranhão, from Lower Guinea to ports between Belém and Rio de Janeiro, from Luanda and Benguela to Recife, Salvador, and Rio de Janeiro, and from Mozambique to Rio de Janeiro."

Portuguese king Dom João III declared the official beginning of Brazilian slave traffic on March 29, 1549 (Queiroz 1998:24). But some historians suggest an earlier arrival, circa 1531, coinciding with the beginning of sugarcane cultivation in Brazil (Megenney 1978:62). Like the early Spanish colonizers of the Caribbean, the Portuguese initially attempted enslaving the indigenous population. But this practice was unsuccessful for the Portuguese. Furthermore, as in some areas of Spanish America, Portuguese Jesuit priests in Brazil became advocates for indigenous Brazilians and requested an African workforce instead (Duffy 1962:53).

At the time it colonized Brazil, Portugal had a population of fewer than one million, with many of the Crown's resources dedicated to its trading empire of gold, spices, ivory, and slave trafficking in Asia and Africa. Hence, when the Crown decided to fully colonize Brazil, it looked to Portuguese sugarcane plantations established on Atlantic islands and the African slaves used there as the best colonial model. In fact, some of the first sugar plantations in Brazil were established by plantation owners from the islands of São Tomé and Príncipe, who brought their slaves with them (Holm 2004:51). African slaves also arrived in Brazil via Lisbon, accompanying Portuguese landowners who traveled there to establish plantations (Mellafe 1975:21). As the Brazilian colony developed, more and more Africans arrived directly from the Portuguese feitorias on the African coasts (Boadi-Siaw 2007:165).

The Africa-Brazil slave trade initially began from Guinea and the island of São Tomé. The trade then spread down the West African coast and eventually into Congo and Angola. A nineteenth-century British blockade of the West African coast resulted in Mozambique serving as the final region of slave trafficking destined for Brazil. Because there were many slave routes, however, the origins of the Africans in Brazil are not well known. Arthur Ramos (1979:183) explains, "Desde os tempos coloniais até os nossos dias, houve designações populares de Nagô, Mina, Angola, Moçambique . . . o que indicava vagamente os pontos do continente africano de onde provieram os negros. Mais comuns eram as designações gerais: 'peça da Índia,' 'preto da Guiné,' 'negro da Costa.' Para o senhor branco, não havia povos negros diversos, mas apenas o negro escravo." (From colonial times until our days, there were popular designations of Nagô, Mina, Angola, Mozambique . . . that indicated vaguely the points of the African continent where the blacks came from. More common were general designations: "goods from India," "black from Guinea," "black from the Coast." For the white master, there were not diverse black peoples, but only the black slave.)

That said, specific types of slaves were sought by slave traffickers for certain skills. For example, the Nagô (Yoruba speakers) and Mina-Jeje (Ewe-Fon, Gbe, or Akan speakers from the regions of contemporary Ghana, Togo, and Benin) were popular during the period of exploration for gold and diamonds in the eighteenth century due to their mining skills, acquired in Africa (Castro 2002; Queiroz 1998:28). But, as reviewed above, Angola became the major source for slaves sent to Brazil. As early as 1620 there was a heavy demand for *peças de Angola* (goods from Angola), as the Angolan slaves were referred to, arriving especially at the port of Rio de Janeiro (Carneiro 2005:107).

As the Brazilian colony grew, the importation of slaves from Angola increased. Davidson (1973:93) notes that by the nineteenth century "Angola . . . had become far more a colony of Brazil than of Portugal." For example, from 1823 to 1825, 92 percent of all exports from Angola (which were primarily slaves) went to Brazil. And from 1830 to 1832 the port of Luanda received nine ships from Portugal but ninety from Brazil (mostly from Rio de Janeiro and Salvador). Interestingly, after gaining its independence in 1822, Brazil unsuccessfully attempted to form a "Confederação Brazílica" with the Angolan port of Benguela due to their mutual commercial ties (Davidson 1973:93).

African slavery in Minas Gerais, as in most of Brazil, was substantial during the colonial period. In the first half of the eighteenth century slaves predominantly arrived in Minas Gerais from the feitoria of Elmina (in modern-day Ghana); by the latter half of the century, however, the region of Congo/Angola became the primary source for slaves (Barbosa 1970:309).

By 1776, 78 percent of the population of Minas Gerais was either African-born or mulatto; by 1821, 75 percent was African-born or mulatto; and at the time of the abolition of slavery in 1888, 53 percent was African-born or mulatto (Barbosa 1970:315). It wasn't until the end of the nineteenth century that the white population of Minas Gerais surpassed 50 percent, due largely to a substantial migration of Italians to the region.

Slavery in Colonial Brazil

During the colonial period the *fazenda* (estate) was the heart of rural Brazilian society. The fazenda revolved around the *casa grande*: a patriarchal community including the owner and his family, overseers, sharecroppers, retainers, and the slaves (Keen 1996:133). The *senhor de engenho*, or plantation owner, was at the top of the colonial hierarchy. His *engenhos* (lit. 'mills'), which were typically situated close to the shore, consisted of sugarcane fields, oxen, firewood, grinders, copper kettles and molds, boats, and slaves. From the engenhos sugarcane was exported to Portugal, and Portuguese products were imported: wheat, wine, and artisanal items. Wealthier engenhos were "autonomous economic systems," often including a church and a chaplain/teacher who was responsible for the secular and religious teaching of the owner's children (Abreu 1907/1997:65). Abreu (1907/1997:195–96) provides the following description of slavery on the engenho in nineteenth-century Brazil: "Slaves did all the household work. There were always too many of them. . . . Some of the slaves were employed in tasks of transportation on land and water. Some learned trades. Others, by paying their owners a fixed amount, sought occupations that appealed to them. They sometimes spoke African languages. They formed secret guilds. And they practiced sorcery. With their native joy, their persistent optimism, . . . they withstood the burden of slavery."

Also noteworthy in the colonial casa grande was the presence of the *mãe preta* (black mammy) (Castro 1995:32–33)—a domestic slave who took care of the master, his house, and his family. She cooked in an African style, sang nursery rhymes and told African myths and legends to the children, and likely spoke Portuguese influenced by her native African language.

Under the colonial regime Africans created (or re-created) their native culture in Brazil and in the Americas generally (Thornton 1998). Even though subservient to their masters, Africans in the Americas played music and danced, prayed to their gods, cultivated and cooked their foods, and spoke their languages, with the various aspects of European culture serving as "linking materials" (Thornton 1998:184). For instance, one needs only to note the many contemporary Afro-Brazilian congregations of Bahia, known as *terreiros*, which are estimated to number some two thousand (Castro 1995:31). These terreiros are divided into *nações* (nations), the names of which refer to particular ethno-religious cultures: for example, *congo, angola* (Bantu-derived ceremonies); *jeje* (Ewe-Fon-derived ceremonies); and *nagô, queto, ijexá* (Yoruba-derived ceremonies) (Castro 1995:28).

In Minas Gerais the cultural elements of Bantu slaves from Congo/Angola were of considerable importance. African celebrations and religious ceremonies such as *congados* and *reisados* are found in many rural areas throughout the state to this day. During congados the figure of the manicongo (king of Congo) is invoked in the celebratory songs. Furthermore, popular folklore, nursery rhymes, and work songs from Minas Gerais often refer to supernatural personages called *tutus, calungas,* and *quimbundos*—all words of Bantu origin (Castro 1995:29).

Resistance to Slavery and Quilombos

In his celebrated book *A People's History of the United States*, Howard Zinn (1999:172) asks, "How can slavery be described?" His answer: "Perhaps not at all by those who have not experienced it." Indeed, many slaves in Brazil undertook desperate measures: suicide, murder of their children, and escape (Leal 2001:292). That said, the celebrated Brazilian sociologist Gilberto Freyre argues that slavery in Brazil was not as bad as one tends to think, particularly during the nineteenth century: "[T]aken as a whole, slavery on nineteenth-century Brazilian plantations seems to have been less despotic than slavery in other American areas; and less cruel—if one admits degrees in cruelty—than the regime of labor in industrial Europe during the first terrible fifty years of economic *laissez-faire* which followed the Industrial Revolution. Less cruel, also, than the regime of labor in latter-day Brazil, where the worker's conditions in fields and factories is still a problem very difficult to solve" (Freyre 1971:79, italics his).

Regardless of the conditions to which the slaves were subjected, runaway maroon communities—called quilombos or *mocambos*—were common in Brazil. The word *quilombo* originates from Kimbundu, meaning 'village'; *mocambo* is from Kimbundu or Kikongo, meaning 'hiding place' (Cunha 2001:526, 655). Quilombos were often formed by African-born slaves from military groups. These fugitives typically survived through farming, black-market mining, and robbery. These communities included not only African slaves but also indigenous slaves and even some white peasants (Cadernos do Arquivo 1988:35). In 1930 the word *quilombo* was registered in some 168 places throughout Brazil (*História do Brasil* 1997:79). But in 2001 the *New York Times* reported that more than 700 descendant quilombos existed in all of Brazil (Rohter 2001).[7]

In a Marxist interpretation, a "return to Africa" constituted the psychological basis for resistance (Bastide 1979:195, 199–200; Guimarães 1999). Such resistance contests theories that Africans acculturated to Europeans and formed quilombos solely for economic purposes (e.g., Flory 1979). Thornton (2006:94–95) contends that the enslaved Africans' history of military service and their shared Bantu cultures "would have an impact on their propensity to revolt as well as the effectiveness of their rebellions." As such, quilombos became a symbol of resistance and refuge from slavery: that is, they were centers of African political and social traditions within Brazil (Moura 1987:32–37). Bastide (1979:200) even argues that there was "a resistance of the whole of African civilization, whose memory was only intensified by the harsh regime of slavery."

These quilombos, however, did not go uncontested by the Portuguese colonial authorities. Escaped slaves were frequently hunted down and killed in military campaigns or by bounty hunters known as *capitães do mato* (captains of the bush). For example, according to the writings of an eighteenth-century Catholic historian, Diogo de Vasconcellos, the then-governor of Minas Gerais, José Antônio Freire de Andrade, ordered the extermination of all escaped slaves living clandestinely in quilombos (Vogt and Fry 1996:237–38).[8]

The End of Slavery in Brazil

Following Brazil's independence in 1822, Brazilian emperor Dom Pedro I signed a treaty and trade agreement with Britain, which called for the end of slave trafficking to Brazil by 1830. Brazil, however, by and large did not respect this law and continued to import more than fifty thousand slaves per year through the 1840s, purchased especially by wealthy landowners on sugarcane and coffee estates. In 1849–1850 the British navy vowed to seize all slaving ships, which effectively ended slave trafficking to Brazil by the mid-1850s (Keen 1996:210–11, 214–15).

By the 1860s slavery in Brazil was becoming politically and socially unacceptable. With the abolition of slavery in the United States, antislavery political activism began in Brazil. For example, writers such as the poet Antônio de Castro Alves and the journalist José do Patrocínio were influential abolitionists. Finally, in May 1888 the Brazilian parliament officially abolished slavery, the last country in the Americas to do so. In 1890 the minister of fazenda, Ruy Barbosa, declared that all documentation related to slavery in Brazil was to be burned for the honor of the patria (Carneiro 2005:96–97).

The end of slavery in Brazil resulted in increased industrialization and urbanization, which spurred much internal migration of the rural population to large cities, particularly Rio de Janeiro and São Paulo. Such migrations gave rise to slums, precursors of the *favelas* that developed in the late nineteenth and early twentieth centuries. Moreover, the Brazilian government enacted campaigns to attract European workers to Brazil. Such campaigns had the goal of "improving" the racial composition of Brazil, which was viewed as "too black" at the time (Santos and Maio 2002:176–77). Former slave jobs were handed over to the many thousands of European migrants—particularly Italians—leaving former slaves with only the worst-paying jobs or forcing them to accept continued enslavement for survival (Keen 1996:236–39).

For their part, landowners typically did not observe abolition. By and large, most worker relationships remained in the form of master-slave, and socially Afro-Brazilians were denied access to education and the right of landownership. Clandestinely held slaves continued to labor for the coffee economy in the states of Rio de Janeiro, São Paulo, and Minas Gerais into the twentieth century. For instance, according to a 2005 interview with Calunga speaker Tadeu de Barros, some former slave owners were still alive then in Patrocínio, Minas Gerais, and thereabouts. In short, it needs to be underscored that Brazil, since the arrival of the Portuguese in

1500, has only recently begun a relative normalization of its racial relations.

According to Castro (1995:24), Brazil needs to be examined within three spaces: as South American in its geographic space, Eurocentric in its economic and technological space, and African in its cultural space. She concludes that the African space is the most important in regard to Brazilian nationality and identity: carnaval, samba, Candomblé, congados, capoeira, cuisine, and instruments—like the *berimbau* and the *cuíca*—all have African roots and are mainstays of Brazilian culture (26). That is, Brazil would not be the Brazil we know today without its interconnected history with Africa.

Nevertheless, much remains to be understood about the African contribution to Brazil, a problem articulated recently by Affonso Romano de Sant'anna (2010), a sociocultural columnist for the Belo Horizonte newspaper *Estado de Minas*. Arguing that, in general, the question of Brazil's historical and cultural connections to Africa has not been an issue of great importance, he writes, "Em geral, o Brasil nunca se preocupou com a África. Era uma espécie de mãe ou irmã longínqua. África era assunto de baianos, a Bahia era uma nação africana dentro do Brasil, e basta" (In general, Brazil never worried about Africa. It was a type of distant mother or sister. Africa was an issue for Bahians, Bahia was an African nation within Brazil, and that's it).

But such a perspective is changing somewhat. In 2003 the Brazilian government mandated the teaching of African and Afro-Brazilian history and culture in public schools (Brazilian Law 10.639). This law has had some tangible results. To cite just one example, a recent elementary history textbook used in the public schools of Minas Gerais, *Contos e encantos mineiros* (Oliveira and Assis 2008), has a chapter dedicated to the cultural and historical contributions of Africa and Africans in Brazil.

One topic that scholars have largely overlooked, however, is the contribution of African languages to Brazil and to Brazilian Portuguese. That is the focus of chapter 3.

CHAPTER THREE

Linguistic Overview

Um estudo dessas vozes d'África, e das tribos indígenas do Brasil seria trabalho, além de curioso, de evidente utilidade, para se conhecer não só a influência que exerceram sobre a nossa sociedade os elementos negro e indiano, como também a direção que vai seguindo a língua portuguesa falada no Brasil.

(A study of African words, and of words from indigenous tribes of Brazil, would be a task, besides being curious, of evident usefulness, in order to know not only the influence that these black and indigenous elements exert on our society, but also the direction in which the Portuguese language spoken in Brazil is heading.)

—Antônio Joaquim de Macedo Soares,
nineteenth-century Brazilian lexicographer
(quoted in Alkmim and Petter 2008:147)

This chapter examines the linguistic context in which Calunga evolved by reviewing linguistic literature on: (1) contact between Portuguese and African languages, (2) African languages spoken in Brazil and Afro-Brazilian speech communities, (3) possible African contributions to Brazilian Portuguese, (4) theoretical models for analyzing Afro-Brazilian language and the African contribution to Brazilian Portuguese, and, briefly, (5) Afro-Hispanic language in the Americas.

INITIAL CONTACT BETWEEN PORTUGUESE AND AFRICAN LANGUAGES

Portuguese has a long history of contact with the languages and cultures of Africa. For example, from the early eighth to the eleventh century AD the southern region of Portugal was occupied by Arabic-speaking Moors.

Following the reconquest of western Iberia, the Moors remained in Portugal for some time (Naro and Scherre 2007:26).

Beginning in the fifteenth century Portuguese voyages, expansion, and subsequent slaving practices shaped Lusophone varieties throughout the world: on Atlantic islands (Madeira, the Azores), in Africa (Guinea-Bissau, Angola, Mozambique) and on nearby islands (Cape Verde, São Tomé and Príncipe), and in South America (Brazil), India (Diu, Daman, Goa), China (Macao), Indonesia (East Timor), and Malaysia (Malacca) (Holm 1989:259–63). Portuguese creole was even used as a lingua franca into the early nineteenth century in parts of Asia (Reinecke 1975:75). Furthermore, Portuguese linguistic traces can be found on virtually every continent, ranging from place-names and lexical items to dialects and a spectrum of creoles. The Portuguese word *crioulo* (creole), for instance, originally was used to categorize an African slave born in Brazil (Holm 1988:9).

The early Portuguese explorers came into contact with a large diversity of languages along the African coast. According to recent estimates, there are more than two thousand languages spoken on the African continent, averaging thirty-five to forty languages in each of the contemporary fifty-five African nation-states and territories (Batibo 2005:14). In a recent study on the state of African languages, Batibo classifies language families and subfamilies (tables 3.1, 3.2).

Table 3.1. African languages and language families

Family	Subfamilies	Number of languages
Niger-Congo (including the Bantu languages)	Kordofanian, Mande, Atlantic, Ijoid, Dogon, Kru, Gur (Voltaic), Adamawa-Ubangi, Kwa, Benue-Congo	1436
Afro-Asiatic	Berber, Chadic, Egyptian, Semitic, Cushitic, Omotic	371
Nilo-Saharan	Songhay, Saharan, Kuliak, Maban, Fur, Central Sudanic, Berta, Kunama, Eastern Sudanic	196

Family	Subfamilies	Number of languages
Khoesan	Northern Khoesan, Southern Khoesan, Central Khoesan (Khoekhoe, Western Khoe, Eastern Khoe), East African Khoesan, Khoesanoid	35

Source: Adapted from Batibo 2005:5–9.

Table 3.2. Niger-Congo languages

Language subfamily	Countries where spoken	Sample languages
Kordofanian	Western Sudan	Koalib, Logol, Tiro, Dengebu, Tegali
Mande	Mali, Côte d'Ivoire, Guinea, Sierra Leone, Liberia	Manding, Susu, Kpelle, Mende, Soninke, Gban
Atlantic	Senegal, Gambia, Liberia, Mali, Guinea, Sierra Leone	Wolof, Fulfude, Diola, Serer, Temne, Basari, Konyagi
Ijoid	Nigeria	
Dogon	Mali, Burkina Faso	Toro, Kamba, Duleri, Bangeri, Yanda, Oru Naya
Kru	Côte d'Ivoire, Liberia, Burkina Faso	Kouye, Ware, Bassa, Klao, Seme
Gur (Voltaic)	Mali, Côte d'Ivoire, Ghana, Togo, Benin, Burkina Faso	Guma, Lobi, Gurunsi, Gan, Viemo
Adamawa-Ubangi	Nigeria, Cameroon, Chad, Central African Republic, Gabon, Democratic Republic of Congo, Congo Republic, Sudan	Mumunye, Nimbari, Mbum, Longuda, Gbaya, Banda, Ngbaka, Zande, Sango

Language subfamily	Countries where spoken	Sample languages
Kwa	Côte d'Ivoire, Ghana, Togo, Benin, Nigeria	Akan, Anyi, Baule, Ga, Logba, Avatime, Ewe, Gen, Fon
Benue-Congo	Nigeria, Central African Republic, Cameroon, all countries south of the equator	Yoruba, Igbo, Nupe, Idom, Jukun, Mambila, all the Bantu languages

Source: Adapted from Batibo 2005:5-9.

Portuguese Pidgins and Creoles in the Atlantic and Brazil

Early Portuguese explorers relied on Arabic translators to communicate with African peoples. As the explorers advanced farther south, African languages became unintelligible to the translators. To solve this problem, Henry the Navigator ordered that captured Africans be shipped to Portugal for Portuguese-language instruction in order to serve as future translators (Holm 1989:268). This policy, along with the development of the Atlantic slave trade, resulted in many Africans living in Portugal and the use of a Portuguese pidgin.

Literary evidence of Afro-Portuguese language appears as early as 1516 in *Cancioneiro geral* by Garcia de Resende. Lipski (2005:52) notes that Resende's book includes a poem with pidgin characteristics, dated 1455, by Fernam da Silveira. "If this [1455] dating is accurate, it means that an Afro-Lusitanian pidgin was already in use only a few decades after Portugal had begun exploration of the sub-Saharan African coast." However, the Portuguese dramatist Gil Vicente provides the major literary evidence of *fala de preto* (black speech), also known as *falar guinéu* (Guinean speech) or *língua de preto* (black language), among slaves in Portugal.[1] The fala de preto, according to Naro and Scherre (2007:27, 29), was a reconnaissance language of pidgin characteristics that the Portuguese later used during their explorations of Africa and with African slaves. But Kihm views the fala de preto differently, describing it as an "artfully devised pidgin (his 'reconnaissance language') that the Portuguese deliberately taught the slaves in order to first communicate with them, then use some of them as interpreters (*linguas*) in subsequent expeditions. . . . [W]hat the slaves learnt was in fact a foreigner talk variety of Portuguese which they then used for communication between themselves" (Kihm 1994:3, italics his). Lipski (2005:55) further notes that "Vicente's texts provide the earliest examples of a realistic Afro-Lusitanian pidgin, complete with phonetic, grammatical, and lexical traits reflecting both the imperfect acquisition of Portuguese by adult speakers of other languages, and direct interference from African areal characteristics." He argues that the literary evidence "suggests that an Afro-Portuguese pidgin was evidently used in continental Portugal at least through the early part of the eighteenth century, although the most publicly visible manifestations had disappeared a century earlier" (62).

The first varieties of pidgin Portuguese documented in the literature cited above developed in or near feitorias along the West African coast in the latter half of the fifteenth century and thereafter (Holm 1989:270). In these settings Portuguese came into contact with different African languages. In particular, languages from the Kwa subfamily (spoken in Ghana, Togo, Benin, Nigeria) and Bantu languages (spoken in Gabon, Congo, Angola) had prolonged contact with Portuguese (Castro 2001:46). In some areas Portuguese pidgins evolved into creoles; in other areas the pidgin persisted for some time but later disappeared, leaving its mark on the local vernacular or being co-opted by other European-based creoles. For instance, West African varieties of French and English have a number of Portuguese-derived words (Holm 1989:268, 271).

Portuguese colonizers known as *lançados* (outcasts), in particular, were important middlemen between speakers of African languages and Portuguese and may have acted as catalysts for the evolution of Portuguese pidgins and creoles (Couto 1992b; Holm 1989:270–71). Such middlemen were a vital part of the Portuguese trade along the African coasts, in both goods and people, into the seventeenth century and beyond (Holm 1989:271). Megenney (1984:179), for example, writes that the Portuguese lançados "were instrumental in promoting easier access to black Africans in many sectors" and "taught their African friends and neighbors how to speak the Portuguese-based reconnaissance language." Moreover, many lançados took African wives, effectively creating biracial, bilingual, and bicultural communities.

There are two classes of Portuguese-based creoles to note: Upper Guinea creole Portuguese, spoken on the Cape Verde archipelago and on the African mainland of Guinea-Bissau, and Gulf of Guinea creoles, spoken on the archipelago of São Tomé and Príncipe (Holm 1989:272–84). Upper Guinea creoles were restructured by West Atlantic and Mande languages; Gulf of Guinea creoles were restructured by Kwa and Bantu languages. Of these Portuguese creoles, Morais-Barbosa (1975:136) concludes, "One could equally well consider these creoles [Cape Verde, Guinea-Bissau, São Tomé and Príncipe] to be dialects of their African languages which contributed toward their formation." Ferraz (1975:153), however, contends that from the historical record it is unclear where the slaves originated from, and it is therefore difficult to explain how the different creoles could have evolved. And Kihm (1994:3) argues that Gil Vicente's língua de preto "shows striking, if limited, similarities with the present Portuguese Creoles of West Africa." He concludes that, "given the back and forth traffic that existed between Portugal and West Africa, it is conceivable, then, that this Portuguese Pidgin served as a basis for at least the proto-creoles of the Cape Verde Islands and Senegambia" (4).

The Portuguese began colonization of the uninhabited archipelago of the Cape Verde Islands in 1462. Since the islands' dry soils were not well suited for sugarcane cultivation, the Portuguese used the archipelago as a way station for explorers. The Portuguese also used it as an "administrative center" for Africa (Holm 1989:272). There, Cape Verde and Guinea-Bissau maintained contact and traded slaves under Portuguese control; however, as Africans from Guinea-Bissau were relocated, ties to their traditional cultures were severed, giving Cape Verde a stronger Portuguese element. Holm (1989:273), for instance, observes that "the Afro-European ambiance of the Cape Verde Islands seems almost Caribbean in comparison to the very African culture of Guinea-Bissau."

On the African mainland a Portuguese creole is spoken on the Atlantic coast of Guinea-Bissau and in the Casamance province of Senegal. This creole developed from a Portuguese pidgin, but it is not known if it first evolved on the Cape Verde Islands or in Guinea-Bissau. Kihm argues, "Traditional wisdom had it that creolization first took place on the Cape Verde Islands—indeed a prototypical setting for this process—whence the creole was then carried over to the continent. Agents of such transference would have been the *lançados* ('castaways') or *tangos-mãos* (?). . . . Contemporary descriptions depict them settled in villages of the interior, with women and children, acclimatized and socially integrated. . . . One thing, apparently, they did not give up, namely their language (or a variety thereof) which they transmitted around them and to their progeny" (Kihm 1994:4, italics his). However, in terms of grammar, Kihm (19) notes that "the grammatical differences between Kriyol and Cape-Verdean as a whole, particularly in the Tense-Aspect and determiner systems, are far-reaching enough that no assimilation appears to be feasible. Kriyol, with its varieties, and Cape-Verdean, with its varieties, do constitute a sub-group within Portuguese-based creoles—let us call it Senegambian Portuguese Creole, for instance—but they are distinct languages by all usual criteria."

It should be added that, unlike in the more Afro-Portuguese culture of Cape Verde, the people of Guinea-Bissau identify themselves with their native ethnolinguistic groups first and foremost; Kriyol is instead spoken as a second language by a large majority of the population. That said, Guinea-Bissau's 1961–1974 war of independence against Portugal brought a widespread usage of this Portuguese creole because of the many ethnic languages spoken there. In this context, Kihm (1994:6) notes that Kriyol "became both a practical tool for linguistic unification . . . and a symbol of the new Bissau-Guinean nationality." However, people in eastern Guinea-Bissau speak mostly ethnic Atlantic and Mande languages.[2]

Farther south, Gulf of Guinea Portuguese creoles are found on the islands of São Tomé and Príncipe, which the Portuguese encountered circa 1471. The first settlers arrived on these previously uninhabited islands in 1485, primarily Portuguese lançados, exiled Jews from Spain, and Africans. The African slaves sent there by the Portuguese were largely from the Elmina feitoria (contemporary Ghana), the Kingdom of Benin (contemporary Nigeria), and the Congo Kingdom (Maurer 2009:2). As with Upper Guinea Portuguese creoles, it is believed that a society of Portuguese men and African slave women were instrumental in the evolution of Gulf of Guinea Portuguese creoles, albeit with different African substrate languages (Holm 1989:278). In addition, as with Cape Verde, São Tomé and Príncipe served as a stopover to provision Portuguese exploration ships and to provide slaves to the Americas. Unlike Cape Verde, however, São Tomé had fertile soils for sugarcane, which resulted in the construction of large colonial plantations. But frequent attacks by French and Dutch pirates and internal slave revolts caused many Portuguese colonizers to abandon their plantations in favor of the new Portuguese colony in South America. In fact, in Brazil some of the earliest sugar planters and their slaves originated from São Tomé (Holm 2004:51).[3] Due to this mass departure of the Portuguese from São Tomé and Príncipe to Brazil, Gulf of Guinea Portuguese creoles have maintained "an unusually high degree of substrate influence" (Holm 1989:279).[4]

One interesting case is the Angolares on the southern tip of São Tomé. According to Bonvini (2008a:32), Angolar evolved originally from a pidgin spoken by Angolan slaves who shipwrecked on São Tomé en route to the Americas. Today the Angolares speak a Bantu-influenced Portuguese creole mostly among themselves and as a form of "secret language."[5]

On the island of Príncipe, the migration of a number of Cape Verdeans has taken a toll on the usage of Principense (known as Lung'Ie [language of the island] by the speakers [Maurer 2009]). "Therefore," writes Maurer (2009:4), "the most widespread language on Príncipe nowadays, after regional varieties of Portuguese, is Cape Verdean Creole."

The first colonizers of Brazil, arriving in the 1530s—largely uneducated men or lançados who spoke differing regional varieties of European Portuguese—came into contact with indigenous Brazilians who spoke varieties of Tupi-Guarani. Acculturation took place between the native Brazilians and the Portuguese colonizers, including intermarriage with indigenous women and the adoption of indigenous foods and customs (Mello 1997:60–62). A language labeled Língua Geral (general language) emerged as a koine version of Tupi-Guarani as a result of migratory movements of indigenous Brazilians after the arrival of the Portuguese (Mello 1997:59). Reinecke (1975:119) argues that Língua Geral spread widely throughout Brazil due to the explorations of the bandeirantes from the mid-sixteenth to the mitdeighteenth centuries and the work of Jesuit missionaries there. Moreover, Rodrigues (1996:10) notes that there were two varieties of Língua Geral spoken along the coast where the Portuguese had established plantations: the Tupi variety, spoken along the Paulista Coast, and the Tupinambá variety, spoken from Rio de Janeiro to the Amazon River.

On the first sugarcane plantations of the Brazilian northeast Portuguese was probably the dominant language, though there was an initial state of linguistic complexity (Mello 1997:59). Mello (1998:74) writes, "Nas áreas agrícolas . . . o cenário lingüístico era complexo . . . : línguas africanas faladas pelos escravos recém-chegados da África, línguas de contato do tipo pidgin, crioulos, além do português reestruturado falado como primeira língua pelos escravos nascidos no Brasil. Tal complexidade está associada à diversidade étnica e lingüística dos escravos trazidos da África. Muitos deles além de falarem suas línguas maternas, provavelmente tinham também conhecimentos mais ou menos avançados de algum pidgin ou crioulo de base portuguesa." (In the agricultural areas . . . the linguistic scene was complex . . . : African languages spoken by slaves recently arrived from Africa, pidgin-like contact languages, creoles, in addition to a restructured Portuguese spoken as a first language by slaves born in Brazil. Such complexity is associated with the ethnic and linguistic diversity of the slaves brought from Africa. Many of them, besides speaking their mother tongues, probably also had more or less advanced knowledge of a type of pidgin or creole of Portuguese base.)

The first waves of African slaves in Brazil worked alongside indigenous slaves and therefore may have learned Língua Geral (Mello 1997:72). But some studies suggest that Portuguese Jesuits, not the general population, actually spoke Língua Geral (Holm 2004:52). Or, as Megenney (2002:589) argues, Língua Geral was likely spoken most among indigenous Brazilians. With the arrival of increasing numbers of African slaves in Brazil, however, Língua Geral was pushed to the margins of the Brazilian territory, such as the Amazon region (Mello 1997:76).[6]

African-born slaves were very likely multilingual, just as many Africans are today (Dimmendaal 2011:225). When these slaves arrived in Brazil, they most likely spoke their native African languages and possibly a type of pidgin or creole that they had acquired in the Portuguese feitorias on the West African shores or on the Portuguese Atlantic islands (São Tomé and Príncipe, Cape Verde). Lipski (2005:62), for instance, notes that "Africans taken to Brazil . . . spoke a Portuguese pidgin during the first stages of their language acquisition, and many of the features of the pidgin documented for Portugal probably arose in Brazil as well." In particular, Sãotomense was likely spoken in Brazil: "It seems reasonable to assume that, whatever the West African pidgin and creole input in the Brazilian linguistic situation, Sãotomense was likely to have been a representative part of it. Coincidentally, the Sãotomense substrate is composed of the language groups that would have played this role in any Brazilian Portuguese, that is, Kwa languages from the Bight of Benin and Bantu languages from the Kongo" (Mello 1997:231–32).

However, a widespread creole was probably not maintained in Brazil (Holm 2004:47; McWhorter 2000:28; Megenney 2002), though early creoles or semi-creoles were possibly spoken for a few generations in certain regions of the colony.[7] Reinecke (1975:111) nonetheless argues that the question of whether creoles were spoken in Brazil "cannot be regarded as closed," listing three theoretical scenarios for pidginization/creolization during the colonial era: (1) creolization of Portuguese, Tupi, or both where Língua Geral was most spoken; (2) pidginization of Portuguese along the border settlements of Portuguese colonization and in indigenous Brazilian areas; and (3) creolization of Portuguese in dense African settlements, later followed by decreolization.

Mello (1997:260–62) hypothesizes that, by the end of the seventeenth century, a partially restructured Brazilian Portuguese vernacular had developed, which was likely the native language of Brazilian-born slaves and the target language of African-born slaves. Furthermore, Holm (2004:47) adds that "certain features of the nonstandard variety [of Brazilian Portuguese] indicate the influence of Amerindian, African, and creole languages."

Contact among Portuguese and African and indigenous languages in Brazil persisted into the nineteenth century, introducing several lexical items and possibly some grammatical influences in Brazilian Portuguese. For example, recent scholarship has estimated that there are as many as four thousand words derived from African languages in Brazilian Portuguese—an estimate less than the number of words derived from Tupi-Guarani (Bonvini 2008a:54, 2008b:101). According to Bonvini (2008b:117), such Africanisms entered Brazilian Portuguese by means of code-switching speakers of various African languages and Portuguese.

AFRICAN LANGUAGES IN BRAZIL

Despite the many varieties of African languages that Portuguese (and other European) slave traders encountered, Castro (1967:27) points out that there were three major African regions that provided significant numbers of slaves to Brazil: Ghana to Nigeria, central Angola, and northern

Mozambique. Among these regions it was the Bantu languages—particularly Kimbundu, Umbundu, and Kikongo (which were labeled as "congo-angola" by the Portuguese)—that exerted the greatest influence in Brazil (Castro 2002:198). Typologically homogenous, Kikongo was spoken by the Bakongo people of the former Congo Kingdom; Kimbundu by the Mbundu (or Ambundu) people of central Angola; and Umbundu by the Ovimbundu people near the port of Benguela (Bonvini and Petter 1998:73; Castro 2001:34–37).[8]

As reviewed in chapter 2, during the seventeenth and eighteenth centuries, Angola was the primary provider of slaves to Brazil, mostly from the Ndongo Kingdom (Kimbundu speakers) in the north and the Benguela Kingdom (Umbundu speakers) in the south. Understanding this past Angola-Brazil nexus is essential not only in regard to the African languages spoken in Brazil but also in regard to the possible African influence in Brazilian Portuguese beyond lexical items (see Lipski 2008b). Castro (2002:39–43) argues that the predominant presence of speakers of Kimbundu, Umbundu, and Kikongo in colonial Brazil was due to the extended period of slave exportation (some four centuries), the demographic density of the regions where these languages were spoken in Africa, and their extensive geographic distribution in Brazil. For instance, Castro's study of Bahian Portuguese—excluding the liturgical language of Candomblés—indicates that 77.3 percent of African lexical items originate from Bantu languages (Castro 1981:4). Bahia, of course, received many Africans from West Africa—speaking languages such as Yoruba, Ewe-Fon, and Akan—in addition to Bantu speakers.

Nevertheless, as reviewed previously, a great number of languages were likely spoken during Brazil's colonial period: indigenous languages, African languages, (restructured) Portuguese, pidgins and/or creoles, and intertwined varieties. Such a multilinguistic situation raises an important question: Exactly *what* was spoken—and to and by *whom*—in colonial Brazil? The answer to this question is likely hidden in the depths of time, but there must have been linguistic diversity, bilingualism, and/or multilingualism.

Needless to say, very little is actually known of the varieties of African languages spoken during the colonial period of Brazil. In fact, there are only two primary sources. The first, *Arte da língua de Angola*, a text of forty-eight pages, was written by the Jesuit priest Pedro Dias and published in Lisbon in 1697 (Bonvini 2008a:33–39).[9] Interestingly, Pedro Dias had served as a priest in Angola, where he learned Kimbundu, later moving to Brazil after the Dutch invasions of Angola. The objective of this publication was to provide the Jesuits with a resource to learn Kimbundu in order to communicate with Africans in both Angola and Brazil. In a letter dated 1694 to Padre Geral Tirso Gonzales of Bahia, Pedro Dias writes, "Estão à espera dela muitos novos e até velhos [jesuítas], que trabalham com estes miserabilíssimos e ignorantíssimos homens, e não se acha nenhuma Gramática desta língua [quimbundu] nem no Brasil nem no Reino de Angola. . . . Assim se acabará a dificuldade em aprender esta língua." (Quoted in Bonvini 2008a:34; The very new and even old [Jesuits], that work with these very miserable and very ignorant men, are waiting and do not have a Grammar of this [Kimbundu] language neither in Brazil nor in the Kingdom of Angola. . . . Thus the difficulty of learning this language will end.)

Bonvini argues that this publication provides evidence that Kimbundu was used by the Jesuits in Brazil, possibly even as a common language among Jesuits and African slaves: "Outros dados permitem induzir que o *quimbundu* era utilizado pelos jesuítas em outros lugares do Brasil e que o critério do conhecimento ou da prática dessa língua condicionava a designação do pessoal, testemunhando assim, desde essa época, o verdadeiro estabelecimento de uma política lingüística em grande escala." (Bonvini 2008a:36, italics his; Other data permit us to deduce that Kimbundu was used by the Jesuits in other places of Brazil and that the criteria of knowledge or practice of this language conditioned the designation of the personnel, such as this testament, from this era, of the true establishment of a large-scale language policy.)

A second text comes from Ouro Preto, Minas Gerais, in the eighteenth century: *Obra nova de Lingoa g.al de mina* by Antônio da Costa Peixoto (1731/1945). This text documents the Mina-Jeje language, or more specifically languages of the Kwa family—such as Yoruba, Ewe-Fon, and Akan—as spoken by African slaves in and around the mining city of Ouro Preto. Essentially this text is a vocabulary manual of 831 African terms that was designed to help Portuguese slave owners communicate with their African slaves. According to Castro (2002:68–69), who has studied the text in detail, 82 percent of the words Peixoto collected originate from Fon, a language of contemporary Benin.

Of further interest are reports of the language of the Palmares quilombo that existed from 1605 to 1695 in the contemporary Brazilian state of

Alagoas. Reports from the Portuguese authorities of this "African Troy" claim that some type of Bantu language was spoken there, possibly even the one described by Pedro Dias (Boadi-Siaw 2007:168; Bonvini and Petter 1998:75; Moura 1987:46–47). Francisco de Brito Freire, a seventeenth-century governor of Pernambuco, noted that what was spoken in the Palmares quilombo was their own "new language," which seemed sometimes as if it was from Guinea or Angola, other times as if it was from Portuguese and Tupi (Moura 1987:46–47). This "new language" of the Palmares quilombo has also caught the attention of creolist Derek Bickerton (2008:136): "What did they speak? Nobody knows, but the Portuguese had to use interpreters in their negotiations. Was it an African language, or a koine . . . of several African languages, or a Creole too deep to be mutually intelligible with Portuguese?" His answer: "We may never know."

In the nineteenth century African languages were still spoken in Brazil, although their use was in decline. Languages such as Kimbundu and Yoruba coexisted with Portuguese within some Afro-Brazilian speech communities. Following the abolition of slavery in 1888, however, there was a geographical redistribution of African-born Brazilians and Afro-Brazilians from rural areas to major cities, which resulted in an almost immediate decline in the speaking of African languages in Brazil (Bonvini 2008a:50).

Today varieties of African languages have been maintained in certain social groups under the auspices of Afro-Brazilian religions (e.g., Candomblé) and as cryptolects (e.g., Calunga, Cupópia, Língua do Negro da Costa). Afro-Brazilian liturgical languages, according to Bonvini (2008a:51), are pidginized forms derived from various African languages: Nagô-queto (= Yoruba), Jeje (= Ewe-Fon), Angola (= Kimbundo-Kikongo). Cryptolects, also analyzed as pidginized forms by Bonvini, are found in isolated areas of former slave communities and are possibly the linguistic results of former quilombos, though this is a speculative hypothesis.

STUDIES ON AFRO-BRAZILIAN LANGUAGES AND CULTURES

The beginning of Afro-Brazilian studies is largely attributed to Raimundo Nina Rodrigues, a lauded professor of the Faculty of Medicine in Salvador, Bahia. He conducted groundbreaking fieldwork in Afro-Brazilian topics in

Bahia at the end of the nineteenth century, particularly regarding the influence of Yoruba in Bahia's liturgical languages, although his findings were not published until 1932, more than twenty-five years after his death. According to Arthur Ramos, a twentieth-century Brazilian social psychologist and anthropologist, Nina Rodrigues launched two influential ideas. First, to understand African cultures in the New World, it is fundamental to understand African cultures in Africa. Second, New World contact between Africans and other cultures led to processes of cultural shift and acculturation that must be understood (cited in Carneiro 2005:17). Moreover, Bonvini and Petter (1998:76) note that Nina Rodrigues raised two important language-related questions: (1) What were the African languages spoken in Brazil? and (2) What influence did African languages have on Brazilian Portuguese? In fact, Nina Rodrigues (1932/1977:122) argued that the African languages spoken in Brazil underwent substantial alterations due to the slaves' acquisition of Portuguese and as African languages melded into lingua francas. However, as Castro (2001:52) points out, Nina Rodrigues's major shortcoming was overlooking the Bantu influence and concluding that Yoruba was the most significant language in the formation of Afro-Brazilian language and culture in Bahia and in Brazil generally.

In Bahia, which historically has been a focal point for Afro-Brazilian language and cultural research, perhaps the best studies are from Yeda Pessoa de Castro. Her *Falares africanos na Bahia* (2001), for example, is an essential scholarly source in this area. The book details the history of African languages in Brazil and the history of research on this topic by outlining five different sociolinguistic levels wherein African influence may be found in terms of the lexicon, phonology, and morphosyntax of the speech of Bahia and Brazilian Portuguese generally. Another noteworthy study on this topic is Megenney's *A Bahian Heritage: An Ethnolinguistic Study of African Influences on Bahian Portuguese* (1978). Recently, Ajayi (2002), a native Nigerian, has written a dissertation on the Yoruba influence in Bahia, analyzing its general impact on Brazilian speech in Bahian liturgical languages and on culture, such as cuisine, music, and dance. In southern Bahia the speech of Helvécia—an isolated community formed by Africans, Francophone Swiss, and Germans—has shown traces of creolization. Ferreira (1985) published the first linguistic study of this community, with Baxter (1992) and Baxter and Lucchesi (1993) providing the most recent descriptions and analyses. Baxter and Lucchesi conclude that the dialect of Helvécia presents traits of irregular language acquisition on par with creole languages, particularly in the verbal system, but is now in a process of decreolization.

In Rio de Janeiro, Bonvini (2000) has described the creole-like speech of the *pretos velhos* (old blacks) of Afro-Brazilian liturgical ceremonies, arguing that it provides evidence of language contact between Portuguese and African languages. He points out that the phonological, morphological, and lexical characteristics of this liturgical speech present characteristics similar to Brazilian Portuguese vernacular, but he does not argue that African languages necessarily influenced such characteristics.

There also have been noteworthy studies of Afro-Brazilian language in Minas Gerais (see map 1). In the 1930s, for his book *A influência social do negro brasileiro*, Dornas Filho (1943) documented some two hundred words and expressions of an Afro-Brazilian language known as "Undaca de Quimbundo" (Kimbundu language)—what he also calls "dialeto congoês" (Congo dialect)—in the village of Catumba (municipality of Itaúna). Dornas Filho offers the following linguistic observations of this "Kimbundu language," albeit somewhat puzzling ones:

> O quimbundo, ou "undaca de quimbundo," que conhecemos, é um dialeto congoês que, em presença do novo meio onde se expandiu, há de ter se modificado bastante em relação à pureza original. Mas é justamente por êsse motivo que êle mais nos interessa. Por essa transformação operada com o fim de servir de expressão num ambiente extranho àquele em que se gerou, adaptando-se e vinculando à língua do Brasil. . . .
>
> Língua de formação bem rudimentar ainda, o congoês, pelos seus dialetos, não possue os atributos e as flexões que apresentam as línguas mais evoluídas como o português. Por isso, o quimbundo que surpreendi em Minas [Gerais] recorre sempre ao português nos casos em que o dialeto não possue recurso para a expressão. (Dornas Filho 1943:71, 73)

(The Kimbundu, or Undaca of Kimbundu [Kimbundu language], that we know is a Congo dialect that, in the presence of the new environment where it expanded, was largely modified in relation to its original purity. But it is exactly for this reason that it interests us. Because of this operated transformation, with the goal of serving the expression in an environment different from the one where it was originated, it adapted and connected itself to the language of Brazil. . . .

A language of quite rudimentary formation, the Congo language, because of its dialects [?], does not possess the attributes and inflections that are present in more evolved languages such as Portuguese. Therefore, the Kimbundu that I observed in Minas [Gerais] always resorts to Portuguese in cases where the dialect does not possess the resources for the expression.)

In northern Minas Gerais, Machado Filho (1943/1985) produced an important study of an Afro-Brazilian language in the São João da Chapada community (municipality of Diamantina) that he traced largely to "puro ambundo" (i.e., Kimbundu) (Alkmim and Petter 2008:154). Machado Filho (1943/1985:14) hypothesizes that this Afro-Brazilian language was the remnant of a "dialeto crioulo de negros bantos" (creole dialect of black Bantus) of Minas Gerais, which has since survived in the form of sixty-five songs known as *vissungos*. Moreover, he poignantly asserts that "de agora em diante, já não cabe dizer que somente existiu, no Brasil, o dialeto dos negros nagôs da Bahia" (14; from now on, it cannot be said that there only existed, in Brazil, the dialect of the Negros Nagôs [Yoruba] of Bahia). In other words, other areas of Brazil, such as Minas Gerais, also have a strong African heritage in terms of culture and language, of which the Bantu were an integral part. Nascimento's (2003) master's thesis provides updated interviews and songs from actual speakers and singers of this Afro-Brazilian community.[10] Also in northern Minas Gerais, the Belo Horizonte newspaper *Estado de Minas* reported in 1983 that residents of the community of Chapada do Norte did not speak fluent Portuguese but instead used a Bantu-based language.[11]

In Ouro Preto, Castro (2002) has examined the lexical items and history of the Mina-Jeje language collected by Peixoto (1731/1945). Also in Ouro Preto, Pereira and Gomes (2003:105–6) have documented the Língua de Jongo, arguing that it is a "secret language" either related to or derived from Nego Nagô (i.e., Yoruba-based). In Bom Despacho, Queiroz (1998) has researched the Afro-Brazilian speech of the Tabatinga community.

This community speaks a "secret language" known as Língua do Negro da Costa that is derived lexically from Bantu and has reduced morphosyntactic structures. Queiroz (100, 104–5) concludes that this Afro-Brazilian cryptolect is the resultant evolution of a pidgin or creole, featuring a "Portuguesement" of the phonology and morphosyntax and an "Africanization" of the lexicon. Finally, near Belo Horizonte, Gomes and

Figure 3.1. Afro-Brazilian village of Quartel de Indaiá, near São João da Chapada, Minas Gerais. Photograph by Steven Byrd, 2002.

Pereira (2000) have studied the Afro-Brazilian culture known as Os Arturos. The culture's ritual language and songs present elements of Bantu-influenced traditions such as congados and reisados.

Within the state of São Paulo, Vogt and Fry (1996) and Andrade Filho (2009) have studied in depth the Cafundó speech community and its Afro-Brazilian speech known as Cupópia. Vogt and Fry (1996:278) conclude that its lexicon is the remnant of an African pidgin spoken in Brazil, probably a descendant of Kimbundu. In addition, Vogt and Fry (234–55, 283–341) devote a section to a comparison of Cupópia and Calunga, including a lexical comparison. Likewise, Andrade Filho (2009:358) classifies Cupópia as the remnant of an Afro-Portuguese pidgin. He offers comparative linguistic data, primarily lexical, of Cupópia, Língua do Negro da

Costa (citing the research of Queiroz [1984]), and Calunga (citing the research of Batinga [1994]) (Andrade Filho 2009: chap. 16).

AFRICAN INFLUENCE IN BRAZILIAN PORTUGUESE

Perhaps the most studied and debated topic regarding African languages in Brazil is the African influence in Brazilian Portuguese. Bonvini and Petter (1998:79) note that studies on this topic tend to focus on two categories: research into the African lexical component in Brazilian Portuguese and the development of phonological and morphosyntactic features through possible creolization, semi-creolization, or decreolization of Brazilian Portuguese vernacular. Debates have largely centered on Brazilian versus European Portuguese and African influence versus the possible (semi-)creolization of Brazilian Portuguese (Bonvini 2008a:21, 2008b:102). However, Bonvini (2008a:50, 59–60, 2008b:102) concludes that such debate has been inadequate and that new theoretical frameworks need to be modeled in order to better understand the history of African languages spoken in Brazil and their contribution to Brazilian Portuguese.

The first written reports of Portuguese spoken by African slaves in Brazil date to the 1820s and 1830s (Bonvini 2008a:49; Bonvini and Petter 1998:77). Unfortunately, these reports are "lamentable" and too "impressionistic" for objective linguistic analysis (Bonvini 2008a:49). It was not until the late nineteenth century that more systematic efforts to analyze the African influence in Brazilian Portuguese would begin. In 1880, for example, Brazilian lexicographer Macedo Soares argued that all types of alterations in Brazilian Portuguese were due to the influence of African languages spoken in Brazil; moreover, he called for studies on indigenous and African elements of Brazilian language and culture in order to better understand their influence in Brazilian Portuguese (cited in Alkmim and Petter 2008:147). Likewise, a study from creolist Adolfo Coelho (1880/1967:37–44) listed comparable creole characteristics in the phonetics/phonology and morphosyntax that composed popular Brazilian speech. Among the characteristics, he noted word-final loss of /-r/ (e.g., *cantá* < *cantar* 'to sing,' *senhô* < *senhor* 'sir') and bare plurals (e.g., *as casa*). However, in two later studies, Coelho (1882/1967:117, 1886/1967:160) noted that Brazilian Portuguese should not be considered a "português degenerado" (i.e., creole Portuguese) but rather should be classified as a dialect of Portuguese that has drifted from its European roots due to ethnic mixing and language contact, especially with African languages. Dialectologist J. Leite de Vasconcellos (1883, 1901:158–62) provided a description of the Brazilian dialect in terms of its grammar and lexicon, identifying the Brazilians themselves as a mixture of indigenous, European (mostly Portuguese), and African descent. In terms of morphology, he identified bare plurals as characteristic of Portuguese creoles, following Coelho's classification (Vasconcellos 1901:160). Also in the late nineteenth century, Ribeiro (1897/1906:219) argued, in a chapter titled "Negro, Elemento," that all types of changes in the lexical and grammatical aspects of "linguagem brasileira" (Brazilian speech) were due to African languages.

In the early decades of the twentieth century a number of publications on regional dialects of Brazilian Portuguese appeared. These synchronic studies, which were based on field research, often registered African terms in the corresponding dialects, even though they are not always identified as such (Alkmim and Petter 2008:151). Some notable publications from this period are: Miranda (1905/1936), which documented peculiar terms in the Amazon region and on the island of Marajó; Amaral (1920/1976), which studied the Caipira Portuguese of São Paulo state; Nascentes (1922), which studied the dialect of Rio de Janeiro; Marroquim (1934), which documented the northeastern dialect; Costa (1937), which registered peculiar terms from the state of Pernambuco; and Teixeira (1938, 1944), which documented the speech of Minas Gerais and Goiás.

The 1930s, in particular, featured published studies pertinent to today's scholarship on the evolution of Brazilian Portuguese and the African contribution. The linguistic scholarship of this decade, largely ideologically driven, was concerned with differentiating Brazil from Portugal, especially in terms of a "national language" (Bonvini 2008a:16–17). Nonetheless, Bonvini and Petter (1998:68) mark this decade as the beginning of the debate on the influence of African languages in Brazilian Portuguese. In addition to Nina Rodrigues (1932/1977), there were two other noteworthy books: *A influência africana no português do Brasil* by Renato Mendonça (1933) and *O elemento afro-negro na língua portuguesa* by Jacques Raimundo (1933). Mendonça attempts to systematize the aspects of vocabulary, phonetics, and syntax of Brazilian Portuguese that he claims were the result of contact with African languages, including a glossary of 375 terms of African origin. Raimundo provides an inventory of 309 words and 132 place-names that he considers of African origin, although Castro (2001:55–56) argues that many etymologies he proposes are questionable. Following these books was the first Congresso Afro-Brasileiro in Recife in 1934, which published two volumes of papers entitled *Estudos afro-brasileiros* (1939). These papers study various African contributions to Brazil in areas such as history, politics, culture, religion, food, and language. Also in the 1930s, Dante de Laytano published *Os africanismos no dialeto gaúcho* (1936), which examines 173 terms mostly of Bantu origin found in the southern state of Rio Grande do Sul and in the neighboring areas of Uruguay and Argentina. And Nelson de Senna published *Africanos no Brasil* (1938), which looks at the African influence in language and customs, including folkloric terms traced to Bantu languages.

In the 1940s and 1950s the idea of "língua portuguesa" (instead of "língua brasileira" or "linguagem brasileira") dominated the scene in the Brazilian education system and raised the idea of "unidade na diversidade" (unity in diversity) in linguistic research (Bonvini 2008a:17). Studies on the African influence in Brazilian Portuguese continued, but new ideas regarding the African contribution were emerging. For example, works by Sílvio Elia (1940/1979, 1965), Gladstone Chaves de Melo (1946/1971), and Serafim da Silva Neto (1950/1986) revisited theories of African influence in Brazilian Portuguese. Elia introduced the idea of Brazilian Portuguese as derived from a semi-creole from indigenous Brazilians, African slaves, and people of mixed race: "uma linguagem rude de gente inculta, denominada *crioulo*, ou *semicrioulo* pela lingüística moderna" (Elia 1965:247, italics his; a simple speech of uneducated people, called *creole*, or *semi-creole* by modern linguistics). Melo (1946/1971:75) echoes the semi-creole argument, writing that "se deve ter formado na boca de africanos natos um dialeto crioulo de tipo iorubá e outro de tipo banto, os quais se foram graditivamente dissolvendo, pelas gerações sucessivas, no meio lingüístico português [no Brasil]" (there must have formed in the mouth of the African-born people a creole dialect of Yoruba type and another of Bantu type, which gradually dispersed, throughout successive generations, within the Portuguese language [in Brazil]). He further argues that African influence in Brazilian Portuguese is present in the verbal and nominal morphology in popular speech. On the other hand, Silva Neto denies the existence of African or indigenous influence in Brazilian Portuguese, except lexically. Instead, he argues that the linguistic base of Brazilian Portuguese is a conservative, archaic European Portuguese. But he believes that Africans' imperfect acquisition of Portuguese did produce some phonological and morphosyntactic deviations. Furthermore, Silva Neto raises the issue that language and social status in Brazil, differences among regions (i.e., urban vs. rural), and social occasions may have been factors for differences in Brazilian Portuguese.

Since the 1960s one of the leading scholars of Afro-Brazilian linguistic studies and African influence in Brazilian Portuguese has been Yeda Pessoa de Castro. In addition to her research on falares africanos, she has written extensively on the African influence in Brazilian Portuguese. In particular, she has argued that in Brazil there was an "africanização do português" (Africanization of Portuguese) and an "aportuguesamento dos africanismos" ("Portuguesement" of Africanisms) over a preexisting indigenous base (Castro 1997:57, 2001:125). Moreover, she emphasizes that Portuguese was *imposed* as a foreign language on a majority population of African speakers over more than three centuries, which resulted in differences in Brazilian Portuguese; and that African languages in Brazil were not simply confined to secretive religious ceremonies or other marginalized areas without ever having contact with the general Portuguese-speaking population (Castro 1997:58–59). In Bahia, for instance, Castro (1983:82) has identified five sociolinguistic levels in Bahian Portuguese, from greater to lesser African influence: (1) Candomblé liturgical speech in a religious context, (2) the speech of the Candomblé faithful in an intergroup context, (3) popular Bahian speech, (4) educated Bahian speech, and (5) general Brazilian Portuguese. Among these levels, Castro (86–95) believes that the liturgical speech of the Bahian pretos velhos (old blacks) constitutes a creolized Portuguese that was spoken by Africans during the period of slavery (cf. Bonvini 2000). But some possible African linguistic characteristics that are present across the spectrum of the sociolinguistic levels are: bare plurals (e.g., *as casa*), loss of /-r/ in verbal infinitives (e.g., *falar* [fa.'la]), and vocalization of /l/ in syllable-final position (e.g., *mal* [maw]) (Castro 1983:95–96).

In terms of lexical items, a number of publications have examined the etymologies of African languages in Brazilian Portuguese. The first lexicographer to note the importance of classifying African words in Brazilian Portuguese was A. J. de Macedo Soares (Alkmim and Petter 2008:147). In an 1880 paper titled "Sobre algumas palavras de origem Africana introduzidas no português falado no Brasil," Macedo Soares addressed the necessity of documenting African and indigenous terms in order to better understand the roots of Brazilian Portuguese. Since then, particularly in the late twentieth and early twenty-first centuries, a number of dictionaries have been published that examine African etymologies of Brazilian terms. Some popular examples are Cacciatore (1988), Cunha (2001), Lopes (2003), and Schneider (1991). However, as Castro (2001:58–60) has reviewed, these dictionaries contain etymological and citation errors and should be consulted with scrutiny. To date, perhaps the most comprehensive and trustworthy publications of African lexical items in Brazil are from Castro (e.g., 2001, 2002).

Brazilian Portuguese Vernacular: A Semi-creole?

One highly debated topic in the linguistic literature is whether or not Brazilian Portuguese vernacular (BPV) is derived from a semi-creole. The term *Brazilian Portuguese vernacular* (also called Popular Brazilian Portuguese or vernacular Brazilian Portuguese) refers to the common, colloquial Portuguese of Brazilians. This dialect employs certain grammatical features that are widely considered wrong or uneducated in certain sociolects. But even educated persons of all ethnicities engage in BPV in certain sociolinguistic contexts. "It is apparent," writes Azevedo (1989:862), "that rules considered typical of the [Brazilian] vernacular are present in the native linguistic repertory of educated speakers, who acquire the standard [Brazilian Portuguese] largely through normative coaching." He further notes that "whereas educated speakers have a choice, lower-class speakers of the vernacular do not" (868). And, as Guy (1989:227) argues, educated speakers of standard Brazilian Portuguese (SBP) are "a tiny minority"; speakers of BPV instead "form a substantial majority." Today the poorest social classes of Brazil, in which Afro-Brazilians are the majority, form the largest body of BPV speakers (Guy 1989:228; Holm 2004:58). Given this sociolinguistic reality, Guy (1989:228) raises an important question: "Can [BPV] be understood as having had, to some extent, a creole history?"

The origins of BPV are not really understood, but some theories have traced it to a semi-creole, a post-creole, or a process of multiple origins (i.e., dialect leveling, influence from African and indigenous languages, language shift, language borrowing [Mello 1997:6, 269–71]). Other theories discard the semi-creole hypothesis in favor of internal linguistic changes of European Portuguese. Guy summarizes well the view of BPV as having originated from a semi-creole:

> On the linguistic side, . . . BPV includes many words of African origin, and the grammar includes a number of features that are either similar to other creoles or reminiscent of the African languages spoken by the original Afro-Brazilians. . . .
>
> On the social side, . . . Brazilian history exhibits all of the characteristics elsewhere associated with the development of creole languages, together with dramatic African influences on the popular culture of modern Brazil. . . .
>
> On all of these dimensions the Brazilian situation seems to have favored the development of a language that is not as divergent from the superstrate as, say, Haitian Creole. But neither is this language purely European. Rather, [BPV] has roots not only in the Romance languages of its European colonizers, but also in the African languages spoken by millions of the first Brazilians. (Guy 1989:240–41)

As reviewed in the previous section, the idea of Brazilian Portuguese as derived from a semi-creole was established by Elia in the 1940s (Bonvini and Petter 1998:69). The semi-creole was a preparatory linguistic state for a creole: that is, a grammatical simplification of Portuguese. More recently, Guy (1981, 1989) and Mello (1997, 1998) have advocated for BPV as stemming from some type of creole past. Likewise, a chapter by Mello, Baxter, Holm, and Megenney (1998) also presents various aspects of lexical, phonological, and morphosyntactic patterns in BPV that may have possible influences from African languages. Baxter (1998:97, 101) argues that there was irregular linguistic transmission in rural dialects of colonial Brazil, which today feature morphosyntactic characteristics that are typologically similar to creole languages. He highlights the following characteristics of rural BPV that have parallel characteristics in creole languages:

Noun phrase characteristics

Lapses in gender agreement (e.g., *aquele coisa*)

Bare and invariant plurals (e.g., *uns quatro mês; patrão não trabalha hoje*)

Subject pronouns as object pronouns, with few occurrences of reflexive and passive pronouns (e.g., *ele matou ele mesmo*)

Relative clause with *que* as a multifunctional pronoun (e.g., *era uma mulher que o marido dela era meio apexiado*)

Verb phrase characteristics

Lapses of subject-verb agreement (e.g., *nós fala, eles fala*)

Greater frequency of subject pronouns with verbs (due to reduced verbal morphology)

Infrequency of subjunctive mood (e.g., *tudo os patrão quer que nós vai trabalhar*)

Pluperfect expressed as *já* + preterite (e.g., *ele já falou*)

Future tenses realized as analytic (*ir* + infinitive: e.g., *vou comer*) instead of synthetic (e.g., *comerei*), and absence of conditional tenses

Infrequency of passive structures

Verb *ter* with existential qualities (e.g., *tem comida*)

Other characteristics

Double negation (e.g., *não vou não*) and post-verbal negation (e.g., *vou não*)

Non-inverted questions (e.g., *que você quer?*) and inverted questions (e.g., *você mora onde?*)

The preposition *em* with the function of locative and goal (e.g., *estou em casa; vou em casa*)

(Adapted from Baxter 1998:101–7)

Another important advocate for the semi-creole hypothesis is Holm (1987, 1992, 2004). As a specialist in creoles, he argues that the grammatical characteristics found across the spectrum of creoles—particularly among Portuguese-based creoles—are also found in BPV. Instead of full creolization, however, semi-creolization (or "partial restructuring") occurred with

BPV.[12] Holm (2004:135–46) concludes that both social and linguistic factors were involved in partially restructuring BPV. The major social factor is "demographic imbalance" between native and non-native speakers during the first century of colonial settlement. He writes that "Africans constituted a considerable proportion of the small total population of Brazil at this linguistically crucial early stage (numbering only a few tens of thousands), making it more susceptible to influence from the fully creolized Portuguese brought to Brazil from Africa" (50).

Linguistic factors, however, are more difficult to generalize. Like Mello (1997:269–71), Holm (2004:143) believes there was a convergence of factors that led to partial restructuring: language drift, primary leveling, imperfect language shift, language borrowing, and secondary leveling. Regarding specifically such linguistic factors, Holm (1992, 2004) and Mello (1997) list grammatical parallels (phonological and morphosyntactic) between BPV and São Tomé and Príncipe Portuguese, as well as other creoles from several locations where African slaves arrived in Brazil. Such parallels, listed below, are justified by the fact that many of the first slaves and slave owners from the sixteenth century migrated to Brazil from São Tomé and Príncipe to establish sugarcane farming (Holm 2004:51):

> Post-verbal negation (e.g., *vou não*)[13]
>
> Consonant-vowel syllabic structure (e.g., *negro* > *nego* 'black'; *dizer* > *dizê* 'to say'; *flor* > *fulô* 'flower')
>
> Palatalization (e.g., *tio* ['tʃi.u] 'uncle'; *quente* ['kẽn.tʃi] 'hot')
>
> Reduction of verbal inflections and lapses of subject-verb agreement (e.g., *nós vai*)
>
> Use of *ta, tava* (from *estar*)
>
> Bare plurals (e.g., *duas casa*)
>
> Subject pronouns as clitics (e.g., *ela chamou eu*)

Also of note, Guy (1989:233) compares data from BPV, Cape Verde creole, and *bozal* Spanish from Cuba, all of which present similar forms of bare plurals. And Lipski (2008b) has outlined possible linguistic connections between BPV and Angolan Portuguese vernacular—especially the speech of the *musseque* neighborhoods of Luanda—and other Afro-Hispanic varieties of Latin America. Among these possible connections are:

> Bare plurals, which are possibly a consequence of language contact or pidginization of Portuguese in the Atlantic sphere
>
> Use of third-person verbal conjugations as default forms (e.g., *nós/eles trabalha*), possibly a result of language-learning errors
>
> Double negation, which is possibly an influence from Bantu languages
>
> Inverted questions (e.g., *você vai onde?*), possibly a trait carried over from pidginized Portuguese
>
> Null definite articles (e.g., *vai acabar [o] mundo*), likely a result of language contact with African languages, which typically do not have definite articles
>
> Paragogic and epenthetic vowels (e.g., *flor* > *fulô* [fu'lo])
>
> (Adapted from Lipski 2008b)

However, there are also opponents of the semi-creole hypothesis of BPV. In the 1960s, for example, Révah (1963) asserted that changes in Brazilian Portuguese were the result of general linguistic tendencies present in other western European languages. Mattoso Câmara (1972:21–22) also denied any African influence in SBP but admitted that the possibility could exist in the phonology and grammar of the popular dialects of Brazil. Tarallo (1993) also has found the (semi-)creolization hypothesis to be highly unlikely, since European and Brazilian Portuguese grammars have too much in common, particularly in the written form. He argues that the (semi-)creolization theory is based largely on speculative historical factors. But perhaps the strongest opponent of the (semi-)creole hypothesis is Anthony Naro. In a collection of essays on the origins of Brazilian Portuguese, Naro concludes that "o português do Brasil sempre foi o português" (the Portuguese of Brazil always was Portuguese) and that there is no empirical basis to derive BPV morphosyntactic and phonological patterns from African or indigenous languages spoken in Brazil, nor is there any empirical basis for a creole hypothesis to explain such patterns (Naro and Scherre 2007:179). Naro and Scherre (2007) support this conclusion through comparative analyses of grammatical patterns in dialects from Brazil and Portugal as well as other languages. They agree that there was irregular linguistic transmission in Brazil but that the grammatical characteristics of BPV are the result of diachronic internal change—tendencies that have occurred in Portuguese and in other Romance languages, as well as in Indo-European languages generally.

Likewise, Rougé (2008), in his comparison of grammatical patterns between the speech of the Tongas on the island of São Tomé and BPV, contends that Brazilian Portuguese did not break typologically from Portuguese into a creole. Yet he does raise an interesting question (albeit one similar to Guy's [1981:309]): "Questão que, para o mundo lusófono, pode ser assim enunciada: por que existem crioulos na Guiné, em Cabo Verde, em São Tomé e não no Brasil?" (Rougé 2008:63; The question, for the Lusophone world, can be thusly stated: why do creoles exist in Guiné, in Cape Verde, in São Tomé and not in Brazil?)[14]

Lastly, Azevedo (2005:215–22) also has examined the historical development of Brazilian Portuguese as a dialect of Portuguese, arguing that its linguistic base is the result of dialect leveling among the Portuguese settlers. In his analysis of the semi-creole hypothesis, he writes that "even if there never was a generalized creole spoken all over colonial Brazil, there may have existed small creole-speaking pockets which, before vanishing completely, had some effect on [BPV]. This resulting partially restructured variety, neither a creole nor a semi-creole but bearing some creole-like features, would be constantly under pressure from the standard language, made mandatory in education and public administration in 1758 . . . , and reinforced by the arrival of the Portuguese court in 1808" (252–53). Azevedo further notes, "Throughout the nineteenth century (and in some regions into the twentieth as well) many White children had Negro wet-nurses and played with children of African or mixed ancestry. Even nowadays, in small towns children of all socioeconomic groups attend public schools where the teachers' standard or semi-standard Portuguese coexists with vernacular varieties. It is in such schools that children have traditionally been initiated into the art of switching from 'classroom Portuguese,' which they come to associate with school, books, and formal learning in general, to the various levels of Brazilian Portuguese spoken at home and in most other situations" (253).

In short, whether or not BPV has semi-creole features is an open question, but it is an interesting debate.

Anti-creole

An interesting theoretical framework for an analysis of Afro-Brazilian speech is what has been termed "anti-creole." According Couto (1992a, 1997, 2002), anti-creole is defined as *"uma língua com pelo menos parte do léxico da língua original (língua dominada) usado com a gramática da língua dominante envolvente"* (Couto 2002:48–49, italics his; a language with at least part of the lexicon from the original language (dominated language) used with the grammar from the involved dominate language). Couto (1997:100–101) theorizes that anti-creoles may have originated among slaves in Brazil as "línguas gerais africanas" (i.e., lingua francas). He further notes that Brazilian anti-creoles "revela[m] uma mescla de africanidade e de caipiridade" (Couto 1992a:73; reveal a mixture of "Africanness" and "Caipira-ness"). That is, anti-creoles have adopted their phonology and morphosyntax from BPV but have maintained a somewhat Africanized lexicon.

Lipski (2009b:381) further notes that anti-creoles are similar to cryptolects, "although the typological boundaries between anti-creoles and cryptolects are not always clear." He continues, "Known anti-creoles tenaciously retain a core lexicon derived from an ancestral community language closely tied to ethnic identity . . . ; there is no other deliberate introduction, invention, or manipulation of lexical items beyond those already established in the anti-creole."

In contrast, Petter (1999) questions the use of the term *anti-creole*, viewing it as imprecise. But she concedes that, given the grammatical, lexical, and sociolinguistic nature of this type of Afro-Brazilian speech, such varieties cannot be classified as creoles either. Nevertheless, Petter concludes that research on the speech patterns of such Afro-Brazilian and indigenous communities is vital for evaluating how Portuguese was historically acquired and if there was a process of creolization—and later decreolization—of Brazilian Portuguese in these communities. She writes, "Parece provável que tenham existido várias línguas francas, nas diferentes regiões do país, no entanto, não se encontram evidências empíricas de tal fato. O que se sabe é que grande parte dos escravos aprendiam o português, com diferentes graus de proficiência, em função de sua posição no quadro social da época.... O estudo das comunidades afro-brasileiras isoladas permitirá recuperar, na fala dos mais idosos, traços do encontro de línguas e culturas ocorrido no passado e oferecerá subsídios para que se avaliem prováveis processos de crioulização e atual descrioulização, a partir de fatos morfossintáticos identificados." (Petter 1999:104–5; It seems probable that there have existed various lingua francas in different regions of the country; however, there is no empirical evidence of such a fact. What is known is that a great part of the slaves learned Portuguese with different levels of proficiency, according to their social position of the era. ... The study of isolated Afro-Brazilian communities can recover, in the speech of the eldest, traces of language and culture that occurred in the past and will offer subsidies to evaluate probable processes of creolization and actual decreolization from identified morphosyntactic data.)

In addition to Calunga, the anti-creole framework can be applied to the Afro-Mineiro Tabatinga community of Bom Despacho and to the Cafundó community of São Paulo state. Interestingly, Mello (1997:14–19) notes that the grammatical structures of the Afro-Brazilian varieties of Bom Despacho and Cafundó are analogous to BPV grammar, but their unintelligibility to speakers of Portuguese "is guaranteed by the frequency of nouns and adjectives of African origin" (19).

Mixed (or Intertwined) Languages

Another theoretical framework to consider for an analysis of Afro-Brazilian speech is mixed languages. *Mixed language* is a descriptive term that refers to the intertwining of grammars with peculiar linguistic results (Thomason 1995). This term, however, has been labeled "pejorative" and "racist" and is often discarded in favor of the term *intertwined languages* (Bakker 2002:81–82; Dimmendaal 2011:238; Gilbert 2002:2). Dimmendaal (2011:238) adds, "An additional reason for not using the term 'mixed language' of course relates to the fact that virtually all languages are mixed, i.e. influenced one way or another by other languages. As a taxonomic label for a specific type of language, the concept of 'mixed language' therefore is not very enlightening." Critical of both the terms *mixed language* and *intertwined language*, Dimmendaal instead prefers the term *syncretic languages*, which "is supposed to show that the two languages which were emblematic for two different social identities were brought together . . . , and also resulted in a fusion of social identities of the speakers" (238).[15]

Terminological problems aside, the grammatical and lexical structure of mixed languages is not any different from natural processes of language contact and language change, including pidginization and creolization. Bakker and Mous (1994:5) offer the following definition: "A very rough approximation is that a mixed language has its lexicon and grammar from different sources. On the basis of the lexicon one would classify such languages as belonging to one language family and on the basis of the morphology, syntax and general grammatical characteristics one would classify them as belonging to another language family." Furthermore, Bakker and Muysken (1995:41) note that "[t]hey are not creoles or pidgins in the strict sense, but they may shed light on the genesis of these languages as well." Sebba adds, "Mixed languages by contrast [to pidgins and creoles] retain the grammatical complexity of their 'grammatical host' language, but replace all or part of the vocabulary with items from another, unrelated language, through a process which has been termed *relexification*" (Sebba 1997:265, italics his). Interestingly, mixed languages, like anti-creoles, tend to feature a strong lexical component rather than a grammatical one. For instance, Bakker and Muysken (1995:50) argue that speakers of a secret language "will always use the grammatical system of the language of the immediate surroundings. . . . Furthermore, a lexicon is remembered longer than a more intricate grammatical system, and for this reason too the decaying language is a more likely candidate for supplying the lexicon."

These peculiar varieties tend to emerge from unique social circumstances and can be categorized as "secret codes," which are foreign to the dominant community. However, one candidate for being a mixed language is Swahili, which is not a secret code but instead is often described as a lingua franca. This language possesses much Arabic vocabulary and eroded Bantu grammatical patterns (Wald 1990).

Theoretical problems aside, mixed languages tend to be "rare" and "exotic" due to their somewhat distinct grammatical structures and social context. Thomason explains, "The distinction has to do with whether the mixed language is that of a persistent ethnic group or that of a new social group (sometimes ethnic, sometimes multiethnic, sometimes a subgroup within a community). The most obvious nonlinguistic correlate of this distinction is time: mixed languages in *persistent* ethnic groups develop through long, slow processes of language change, with or without eventual language shift; mixed languages in *new* ethnic groups, by contrast, emerge relatively rapidly, sometimes within a single generation" (Thomason 1995:17, italics hers).

The structural generalization of mixed languages is grammatical borrowing from the morphosyntax and phonology of the dominant language. Different from pidginization or creolization, which are typically born in a state of "linguistic chaos," mixed languages tend to arise in situations of solid bilingual contact. In addition, mixed languages typically demonstrate a significant sense of linguistic and social resistance, even an autonomous social identity (Thomason 1995:16, 19). Of course, resistance to the dominant social norm is partially futile since the minority social group must operate within it; nevertheless, such resistance often leads to the rise of these mixed languages. The usual result is the striving for a social identity and solidarity within a minority community. In this context, mixed languages are more the product of overt or covert sociohistorical circumstances than purely internal linguistic change.

Thomason (1995) provides three examples of "slow" mixed languages: Kormakiti Arabic, spoken on the island of Cyprus; Ma'a, spoken in Tanzania; and Caló, spoken in Spain. Kormakiti was originally the Arabic language of Maronite Christians who migrated to Cyprus in the twelfth century AD. Today, Cyprus Greek morphosyntax and phonology have percolated into all areas of the Kormakiti grammar, including some 38 percent of the lexicon. But Arabic lexical and grammatical structures, including the phonology, have remained largely intact despite being in a Greek-dominated community for over eight hundred years. Ma'a, originally a Cushtic language, has been in contact with Pare and Shambaa languages—both Bantu—for over three centuries. Unlike Kormakiti, Ma'a has almost entirely Bantu grammar at all levels with basic Cushitic lexical items. In a sense, Ma'a has been "less successful" in terms of resistance than Kormakiti. Caló, also known as Spanish Romani, is a language of the Spanish Gypsies. It features a number of Romani grammatical patterns equivalent to Spanish, though lacking regularity. Caló song lyrics show differing amounts of Spanish grammar; a number of Romani features are also found. Caló may be in the process of language shift from Romani to Spanish, with relexification of Romani words (Thomason 1995:19).

"Fast" mixed languages are the result of quickly developed speech communities, typically new ethnic communities or subgroups within a larger speech community. Thomason (1995:20) notes four examples: Michif of the Turtle Mountain Indian Reservation of North Dakota; Mednyj Aleut of Copper Island, Russia; Media Lengua of central Ecuador; and pidgins and creoles. Michif is a mixture of Cree with French lexical and grammatical structures. Mednyj Aleut is essentially Aleut with Russian finite verb inflections, including Russian pronouns in the past tense. Media Lengua is mostly regional Quechua grammar with Spanish lexical items. Finally, pidgins and creoles typically adopt their lexicons from the dominant language, while grammatical structures are, generally speaking, the result of imperfect second-language acquisition with varying approximations to first-language patterns.

According to Sebba (1997:268–69), there are some important lessons to be learned from mixed languages. First, the social context of language contact is instrumental in determining the language outcome. Moreover, a new language that develops from language contact cannot necessarily carry the label of "pidgin" or "creole." Second, the need for a distinct ethnolinguistic identity, often in the form of a cryptolect, may lead to the creation and usage of a mixed language. Third, the gender of speakers needs to be taken into account as an important aspect of language contact and language intertwining—an aspect that has been largely ignored.

Thomason (2001:204) offers this poignant conclusion about mixed languages: "[C]ontact-induced language change is fundamentally unpredictable, both because we can never hope to explain how a multitude of major and minor social factors combine to produce a particular change and because speakers can and do make deliberate choices about changing their language. The same is true, and even perhaps more true, of the genesis of bilingual mixed languages."

AFRO-HISPANIC LANGUAGE IN LATIN AMERICA

Even though Brazil was the largest single recipient of African slaves during the Atlantic slave trade, it is important to illustrate the greater panorama of the African diaspora in Latin America. Over a span of more than four centuries, at least eight million Africans were sent to every colonial region of Spanish America: to mining areas, to the pampas, to port cities, to urban areas, and especially to the Caribbean islands and to the Caribbean and Pacific coasts of South America (Lipski 2005:1, 2008a:19). All over Spanish America, Africans influenced music, dance, art, religious traditions, cuisine, and language.

The first Africans to arrive in Spanish America were sailors who accompanied Spanish explorers. To cite one example, a North African slave named Estebanico was part of the ill-fated Narváez expedition (1527–1537) that shipwrecked off the coast of Florida, which is chronicled in Cabeza de Vaca's *Relación* (1542/2003). But the first waves of African slave laborers were sent to mining regions: Peru and Alto Peru (Bolivia), Mexico, Colombia, and Honduras. Little has survived from the language of these Africans except some seventeenth-century songs and poems, although Lipski (2008a) has recently documented and analyzed a traditional dialect of Afro-Bolivian Spanish. In addition to mining areas, the greatest use of African slaves was in urban concentrations of Spanish America (Lipski 2005:49). There they labored as domestic slaves, vendors, artisans, and tradesmen's helpers, among other forms of work. Compared to its use in Brazil, colonial plantation labor was actually a rather small affair in Spanish America. There were some haciendas in areas of coastal Mexico and Peru that cultivated sugarcane and cacao plantations in Venezuela, but nothing on the scale of the Portuguese colonial plantations in Brazil.

Following the Haitian Revolution of the 1790s, Haiti's sugarcane production—it was the world's leader at the time—collapsed, giving Spain and Portugal the opportunity to fill the void. A "new sugar boom" was born in the late eighteenth and early nineteenth centuries. Brazil and Cuba became the largest producers in this boom, giving rise to massive importations of Africans, especially from West Africa and the Congo/Angola region. As a result, African languages and bozal Spanish (i.e., the Spanish spoken by African-born slaves, the word *bozal* meaning 'savage' or 'untamed horse' [Lipski 2005:5]) were spoken in areas of the Caribbean that participated in the boom.

During this time hundreds of African languages arrived in Spanish America. But only a handful from the Congo/Angola region (Kikongo,

Kimbundu, Umbundu) and from West Africa (Yoruba, Efik, Igbo, Ewe-Fon, and Akan) made significant contributions to Spanish American dialects. Like Brazilian Portuguese, the lexicon of Spanish American dialects has incorporated words of African origin and possibly some phonological and morphosyntactic aspects as well. But there is, generally speaking, no distinct dialect of "Black Spanish" spoken in Latin America today (Lipski 2005:5; Perl 1998:4). This is in part because African slaves typically were not marginalized and therefore had to communicate in Spanish throughout the regions of Spanish America where they were sent, though there are some exceptions. What is today considered "Black Spanish" often takes the form of songs or liturgical rituals—for example, among the Negros Congos of Panama (Lipski 1989, 2009b) or Palo Monte of Cuba (Fuentes Guerra and Schwegler 2005)—that possess peculiar phonological, grammatical, and lexical elements (Lipski 2008a:21). Lipski (2005:50) explains, "The cultural encounters between sub-Saharan Africans and speakers of Portuguese and Spanish gave rise to numerous contact vernaculars, ranging from rudimentary jargons and pidgins to stable creoles which continue to be spoken even today. As thousands of Africans and their descendants acquired Portuguese and Spanish in the Iberian Peninsula, Africa, and particularly Latin America, they incorporated characteristics common to all second-language varieties of Ibero-Romance languages. Most of these traits did not survive as descendants of Africans acquired Spanish and Portuguese natively, but in areas of heavy Afro-Latin concentration, partial restructuring may have occurred."

However, scholars of Spanish American dialects have generally rejected the idea that Africans influenced Spanish beyond the lexicon (Perl 1998:4). Yet there was *direct* contact between Spanish and African languages and *indirect* contact through various creoles and partial creoles (Perl 1998:5–6). Furthermore, at some period, there was a type of "rupture," whereby African slaves in the Americas ceased to speak their native African languages and began to speak European languages, without necessarily acquiring and speaking them in the same way that European descendants acquired and spoke their native European languages (Alvarez and Obediente 1998:43).

The evidence of Afro-Hispanic language has come largely in the form of bozal Spanish. Evidence of bozal Spanish comes from two sources:

literary imitations in fifteenth-century Portugal and sixteenth-century Spain and Spanish America (Mexico, Peru, Bolivia, Colombia); and nineteenth-century and early twentieth-century texts from the Caribbean (Cuba and, to a lesser extent, Puerto Rico), Río de la Plata (Buenos Aires and Montevideo), and coastal Peru (Lipski 2005, 2008a:19). Even though the texts should be analyzed with caution since many are literary parodies, they do suggest that distinct varieties of Afro-Portuguese and Afro-Hispanic language existed during the colonial period. In the nineteenth century and early twentieth century, for instance, bozal Spanish was spoken especially in the Caribbean by African-born slaves; however, it is not clear whether or not bozal Spanish was fully creolized and became a native language or to what extent it influenced regional varieties of Spanish (Lipski 2005:12). At any rate, these remnants of Afro-Hispanic language shed some light on the language of Africans in both Spain and Spanish America.

Besides literary evidence, an important source of bozal Spanish has come in the form of linguistic field research in Afro-Hispanic enclaves. These enclaves "offer a glimpse into the final stages of *bozal* speech, and the possible retention of post-*bozal* elements in natively spoken Spanish as used by descendants of Africans," notes Lipski (2008a:21, italics his). Some examples of post-bozal speech communities that have been documented and analyzed in recent scholarly literature are:

> *Colombia:* Chocó (e.g., Schwegler 1991) and San Basilio de Palenque (e.g., Friedemann and Patiño Rosselli 1983; Megenney 1986; Schwegler 1996, 1998)
>
> *Cuba:* Oriente (e.g., Ortiz López 1998) and Palo Monte (e.g., Fuentes Guerra and Schwegler 2005)
>
> *Dominican Republic:* (e.g., Green 1997; Megenney 1990)
>
> *Ecuador:* Chota Valley (e.g., Lipski 1987)
>
> *Mexico:* Costa Chica (states of Guerrero and Oaxaca) (e.g., Althoff 1994)
>
> *Peru:* Chincha, Sama–Las Yaras (e.g., Cuba 1996; Lipski 1994b)
>
> *Venezuela:* Barlovento (e.g., Megenney 1999)
>
> (Adapted from Lipski 2008a:23)

In addition to this list, other enclaves of Afro-Hispanic language that have been documented and studied are the speech of Afro-Yungueños of Bolivia and that of Afro-Paraguayans (communities of Camba Cua, Kamba Kokué, Laurelty) (Lipski 2008a, 2009a).

The examination of bozal Spanish both in literary form and through field research has rendered some controversial theoretical models that have implications for understanding the African influence on Latin American dialects (Lipski 2008a:20). One theoretical model claims that Afro-Hispanic language in the Caribbean region, and possibly elsewhere, evolved into a stable creole. This creole may have had its origins in an earlier Afro-Portuguese pidgin or creole formed in the feitorias of coastal Africa, which can be observed today in the form of creole languages of Cape Verde, São Tomé and Príncipe, Palenquero, and Papiamento. A second model proposes that Afro-Hispanic language may have blended into and influenced respective dialects of Spanish, particularly in the Caribbean region. A corollary proposal is that Afro-Hispanic language, especially Caribbean dialects, can be analyzed as a semi-creole (e.g., Alvarez and Obediente 1998; Holm 2004; Lorenzino 1998b), similar to the semi-creolization theory for BPV.

Some linguistic characteristics of dialects of Latin American Spanish and BPV that have been argued to have a possible African influence are:

> Double negation: e.g., *no hablo inglés no*
>
> Bare plurals: e.g., *las hija esta*
>
> Redundant subject pronouns: e.g., *tú tiene(s) hambre*
>
> Phonological reductions of *ser* and *estar*: e.g., *eh, e(s); tú tá hablando*
>
> Non-inverted questions: e.g., *¿qué tú quiere(s)?*
>
> (Adapted from Perl 1998:6)

Perl (1998:7) further notes that, on the surface, there seems to be some sort of connection between popular Hispanic dialects of the Caribbean, the popular dialects of northeastern Brazil, creole languages of Spanish and Portuguese base, and the languages used along the western coast of Africa. Moreover, historical sources mention that African slaves had some sort of linguistic knowledge of Portuguese or creole Portuguese when they arrived in the Americas. Perl (16–19) notes three historical sources for the latter point: (1) Padre Alonso de Sandoval (1627/1987:140), who referred to the language of the African slaves as "muy corrupto y revesado de la portuguesa que llaman lengua de San Thomé" (very corrupt and based on Portuguese that they call language of San Thomé); (2) the speech of marooned slaves in Surinam in the late eighteenth and early nineteenth centuries; and (3) slaves who arrived in Cuba in the mid-nineteenth century and are reported to have spoken Portuguese or pidgin Portuguese. According to some scholars, a type of Afro-Portuguese pidgin or creole may have had wide distribution along the Atlantic and extended into the Caribbean and South America (Perl 1998:18–19). For example, in Palenquero, Papiamento (spoken in the Dutch Antilles), and Saramaccan of Surinam, Portuguese elements such as *ele* (he, she) are present. Both Palenquero and Papiamento have been intensively studied and are important creoles for evaluating the African influence on the Spanish and Portuguese of the Americas (see especially Maurer [1998], Munteanu [1996], and Schwegler [1996, 1998]).

Some examples of grammatical peculiarities in Afro-Hispanic language of South American dialects that are similar to both BPV and Calunga are the following:

Invariant plurals
- *Los pobre peón trabajaban como burros; yo tenía pánico a los hospital* (Chota, Ecuador)
- *en todah parte hay mujé pa cuaquié hora* (vernacular Spanish of San Basilio de Palenque, Colombia)
- *Los patrón y loh mayordomo no dejaba que venía polecía; todito lu mujé* (traditional Afro-Bolivian Spanish)
- *Las tropa los camión, lo militar, esos militar que venía uniformao* (Camba Cua, Paraguay)

Bare plurals
- *Se depiertan los lucero* (Chocó, Colombia)
- *Los hermano peruano, los haitiano* (vernacular Spanish of San Basilio de Palenque, Colombia)
- *Las casita eran de paja* (Chota, Ecuador)
- *en idioma antigo di mis abuelo* (traditional Afro-Bolivian Spanish)

Lack of gender agreement
- *loh mujere; é jodido la cosa* (Camba Cua, Paraguay)
- *el casa del difunto; la gente mismo* (Chota, Ecuador)
- *yo tengo un botella; así como lo gente* (vernacular Spanish of San Basilio de Palenque, Colombia)
- *loh persona mayó; las mujeres altos* (traditional Afro-Bolivian Spanish)

Lapses of subject-verb agreement (with third-person default forms)
- *Así eh las cosa* (Chota, Ecuador)
- *Pero si los hijos coge cinco* (vernacular Spanish of San Basilio de Palenque, Colombia)
- *¿De qué nojotro pobre va viví?* (traditional Afro-Bolivian Spanish)
- *Hay muchoh chico quiere ehtudiá y no puede* (Camba Cua, Paraguay)[16]

(Lipski 2009a)

In short, it is important to discuss briefly the greater panorama of the African presence beyond Brazil and Afro-Portuguese creoles of the Atlantic; African linguistic influence stretches into areas of Spanish America as well. From lexical influences to possible restructuring of vernacular dialects, this panorama demonstrates the complexity of trying to understand the linguistic impact of the African diaspora in the Americas. For example, in examining the African lexical items of the Americas, Megenney (1998:75) argues the need for a comparative methodology to apply data from other regions of the Americas—such as Brazil, Colombia, the Dominican Republic, and Cuba—in order to have a more comprehensive understanding of the African lexical influence in Spanish and Portuguese America. The same observation can be made of grammatical data. Of course, many questions will remain unanswered regarding the full extent of the African linguistic influence in the Americas. But these are nevertheless engaging questions that have brought about a decent corpus of scholarship that examines the remnants and influences of African languages in Latin America.

With this is in mind, there are two examples of African linguistic influence that are worthy of illustration for this study: the Negros Congos of Panama and Palenquero of Colombia. The speech of the Negros Congos has been documented and analyzed by Lipski (1989, 2009b). Palenquero, because of its creole status, has received ample attention from scholars (e.g., Friedemann and Patiño Rosselli 1983; Megenney 1986; Moñino and Schwegler 2002). The following section will focus solely on the field research of Schwegler (1996, 1998).

Palenquero

The small Colombian town of El Palenque de San Basilio is a community of former escaped slaves from Cartagena. Besides the vernacular Spanish of the region (called Kateyano 'Castilian' by the speakers), there is also a creole spoken, known simply as Lengua (language), or as Palenquero by scholars. According to Schwegler (1998:220), the grammatical characteristics of Palenquero are very similar to a former Afro-Portuguese pidgin or creole that was spoken by bozales and their descendants in the Caribbean during the sixteenth and seventeenth centuries. Schwegler explains its importance for Spanish dialects of the Caribbean:

> Hoy, un número creciente de especialistas concuerda en que el habla palenquera no es, como solía pensarse, el resultado de una evolución esencialmente local, sino el producto de contactos lingüísticos con raíces en un pidgin AFROPORTUGUÉS, traído a Cartagena y otras áreas del Caribe afrohispano por esclavos africanos arrojados de las vastas zonas del litoral occidental africano (esencialmente de Senegambia hasta Angola), donde los portugueses mantuvieron . . . un prolongado monopolio sobre el flujo de esclavos hacia América. Bajo esta perspectiva, el palenquero moderno sería pues, el último resto de un habla pidgin afrocaribeña que habría influido de manera significativa en la trayectoria evolutiva de varios dialectos populares hispanocaribeños. (Schwegler 1996:29, emphasis his)

> (Today, a growing number of specialists agree that Palenquero is not, as it could be thought of, the result of an essentially local evolution, but instead the product of linguistic contacts with roots in an AFRO-PORTUGUESE pidgin, brought to Cartagena and

other areas of the Afro-Hispanic Caribbean by African slaves taken from vast zones of the West African coast (essentially from Senegambia to Angola), where the Portuguese maintained . . . a prolonged monopoly of the slave traffic to the Americas. Under this perspective, modern Palenquero would be then the last remnant of an Afro-Caribbean pidgin that would have significantly influenced the evolution of various popular dialects of the Spanish Caribbean.)

During Colombia's colonial period Cartagena was a key port of entrance for African slaves coming to South America. The origins of the African peoples who arrived there were quite varied, and Cartagena was a multiethnic and multilingual port city, especially during the seventeenth century, when El Palenquero de San Basilio was founded (Schwegler 1998:224).[17] Spanish, African languages, and Afro-Portuguese pidgin were likely spoken in Cartagena at the time (Lipski 2005:122), with Africans from the Congo/Angola region dominant both socially and numerically in Cartagena (Schwegler 1998:225).

During the first century after settlement of El Palenque de San Basilio, circa 1650–1750, an Afro-Portuguese pidgin evolved into a creole that was spoken among escaped slaves (Schwegler 1996:35). Schwegler (1998:245) believes that the inhabitants of colonial Palenque spoke a mixed Afro-European speech that, with the passage of time, has evolved into its present form, which today has relatively few grammatical and lexical elements from African languages. This creole was the primary language of the inhabitants of Palenque well into the mid-twentieth century (Schwegler 1996:37; Triana y Antorveza 1997:428). During the 1990s, however, the situation was quite different: a large percentage of Palenque youth neither spoke nor understood Palenquero (Schwegler 1996:42, 1998:242).

In terms of some salient grammatical characteristics of Palenquero, note the following examples, accompanied with standard Spanish translations:

Pronominal system
- *i* 'I'   *suto, ma hende* 'we'
- *bo* 'you'   *utere* 'you' (pl.)

- *ele* 'he, she'   *ané* 'they' (masc. or fem.)
- <u>I</u> *a-ten ambe* 'I am hungry' (Spanish: '(Yo) tengo hambre')
- <u>Ele</u> *a-ten ambe* 'He/She is hungry' (Spanish: '(Él/Ella) tiene hambre')

Lack of gender agreement with adjectives, with the masculine, singular as a default form
- *Akí Palenge suto a-ten baria* <u>familia riko</u> 'In our Palenque there are various rich families' (Spanish: 'En nuestro Palenque hay varias familias ricas')

No definite article in the singular
- <u>Ombe</u> *ta echo p' eso nu* 'Man is not made for that' (Spanish: 'El hombre no está hecho para eso')

Bare plurals
- *I a-kumé un ma* <u>tre pan</u> 'I ate some three breads' (Spanish: '(Yo) comí unos tres panes')
- *Ele a-tené* <u>ndo muhé</u> 'He has two women' (Spanish: 'Él tiene dos mujeres')[18]

Double negation
- *I* <u>nu</u> *bae ayá* <u>nu</u> 'I am not going there (no)' (Spanish: '(Yo) no voy allá')[19]

Prenasal stops
- <u>n</u>*doló* < *dolor* 'pain'
- <u>n</u>*gande* < *grande* 'big'

Consonant-vowel syllable structure
- *kabá* < *acabar* 'to end'
- *kiene* < *quien* 'who'
- *aggo* ['a.go] < *algo* 'something'

Lambdacisms
- aló < arroz 'rice'
- ngalá < agarrar 'to grab'

(Adapted from Schwegler 1998:254–67)

Also noteworthy in El Palenque de San Basilio is a funeral ritual known as *lumbalú* (from Kikongo *lu-mbalu* 'melancholy, memory, recollection'). According to Schwegler (1996:3), lumbalú brings together various elements of African-influenced dance, trance, language, and music—somewhat similar in nature to Haitian Voodoo and Brazilian Candomblé. Like the latter examples, lumbalú is not purely African but rather a syncretism of African form and European content. Lumbalú ceremonies are important cultural and philosophical expressions, including the use of a past Afro-European speech. Different from the speech of the Negros Congos of Panama, which represents a parody of a former Afro-Panamanian speech, the speech used in lumbalú rituals is viewed by the Afro-Colombian practitioners as an ancestral African language or return to Africa (Lipski 1997:159–61).

Schwegler (1996:114) notes that typically the language of the *lumbalúes* is a mixture of Spanish and the local creole, though there are texts purely in Spanish and purely in creole. The eldest singers of lumbalúes believe that an "authentic" lumbalú should always have Africanisms, often with a cryptic sense (Schwegler 1998:246). In fact, lumbalúes typically possess a greater presence of Africanisms than Palenquero, in which Africanisms account for less than 1 percent of its lexical items in daily speech (Schwegler 1998:268). Observe, for example, the use of the Africanism *kalunga* in lumbalú no. 2, documented and translated into standard Spanish by Schwegler (1996:283):

Lumbalú no. 2	Spanish translation[20]
kalunga lunga si fue;	el muerto, el muerto es tuyo [= es tu hijo/hija]
kala si e iguá;	tu cara es igual [= la cara del muerto es igual a la de la mamá del muerto];
María, arió;	María, adiós;

kalunga lunga si fue;	el muerto, el muerto es tuyo;
adió, mamá; ¿pogké parí mon' eli? eee;	adiós, mamá; ¿por qué [= para qué] parió a su hijo?
kalunga lunga si hué;	el muerto, el muerto es tuyo;
kala si e iguá;	tu cara es igual [a la de la mamá];
María; ri ó é,	María; tuyo es [= el muerto es tu hijo],
kalunga lunga si fue	el muerto, el muerto es tuyo.

In this example, which is in traditional Palenquero, *kalunga* means 'dead person,' though, according to Schwegler (1996:53), it is now a ritualistic word with no contemporary meaning. Schwegler (284–85) further notes that the word is derived from Kikongo *ka-lunga* 'lake, sea, ocean,' and that *kalunga* is a common word throughout other areas of the Americas that have had an African presence: Brazil, Venezuela, Jamaica, Cuba, and the United States, often with the meaning of 'aquatic' or 'death' (285–86).[21]

Schwegler (1998:284) concludes that Palenquero is of key importance for rethinking the African influence in Latin American dialects. He argues that scholars who outright reject any African influence beyond the lexicon must take into account the existence of a multilingual situation among Africans and Afro-descendants in the colonial period of the Spanish Caribbean and South America. Their linguistic patterns were very likely a determining factor not only in the formation of the lexicon but also in the grammar, as is evidenced by Palenquero. Hence the study of Palenquero should bring about a theoretical revision of the origins of Spanish dialects in the Caribbean and coastal areas of South America that takes into account the African contribution in both the lexicon *and* the grammar.

Negros Congos of Panama

Panama was part of Colombia until the twentieth century but remained largely autonomous. Recall that the Colombian port city of Cartagena was the principal entry for African slaves arriving in South America throughout the colonial era (Lipski 2005:120). Panama, for its part, "was the site of one of the most prolonged Afro-Hispanic demographic contacts, since almost all slaves destined for the Pacific coast of Spanish America passed through Panamanian ports" (Lipski 2005:123). Like Colombia, Panama received many slaves from the Congo/Angola region, as is evidenced by the speech of the Negros Congos.

In *The Speech of the Negros Congos of Panama*, Lipski argues that this speech is the remnant of an earlier Afro-Hispanic pidgin or bozal Spanish. "It is evident," he writes, "that this dialect, spoken only by Afro-colonial Panamanians, is in some way related to the linguistic situation which obtained among black slave and free groups in colonial Panama, particularly in the 16th and 17th centuries, when the slave trade through Portobelo was at its peak" (Lipski 1989:67). He hypothesizes that the speech, which has been maintained as a historical relic by Afro-Panamanians, "constitutes a true window into the linguistic past, blurred and distorted . . . , but still worthy of excavation and rebuilding" (72).

From his field research for the book Lipski ascertained that Congo is primarily spoken by Afro-Panamanian communities of the Costa Arriba, Costa Abajo, and some towns of the interior. Often the speech is a family tradition that is learned from parents, siblings, or relatives (Lipski 1989:70). It is spoken with grammatical and semantic exaggeration, distortions, and ridicule in order to reenact the history of African slavery in colonial Panama. In comparing the speech of the Negros Congos with Palenquero, Lipski observes,

> [The] *congo* dialect has been retained as a folkloric artifact, which has been reduced in usage to Carnival season, and to explicit artistic and cultural affirmations of Afro-colonial heritage. The fact that Colombian *palenquero* has survived among older residents as a nostalgic link with the past, and that Panamanian *congo* dialect has been transformed into a humorous component of Carnival season with a high rate of deliberate distortion does

not imply an essentially different origin for the two dialects. In Palenque de San Basilio, Colombia, rich Afro-American ceremonies continue to exist, in a purer form than among the Panamanian *congos*. . . . The *negros congos* of Panama were more thoroughly assimilated into regional cultural patterns, and . . . never separated themselves completely from Spanish colonial society and its postcolonial continuation. (Lipski 1989:74–75, italics his)

Lipski (1989:69–114) argues that the exaggerated grammatical characteristics of the Negros Congos have their roots in an earlier Afro-Hispanic language (i.e., bozal Spanish). He supports this hypothesis by comparing the grammatical tendencies of various Afro-Iberian creoles (e.g., Palenquero, Papiamento, Guinea-Bissau creole, Cape Verde creole, Annobon creole), Afro-Hispanic dialects (e.g., Samaná of the Dominican Republic, Chota of Ecuador, Equatorial Guinean, Cuban bozal Spanish, Puerto Rican bozal Spanish, Peruvian bozal Spanish), and Golden Age literary examples of bozal Spanish and *boçal* Portuguese. Of course, grammars vary significantly among the examples mentioned above, but Lipski (76) highlights the following "general categories":

> Reduction of pronominal forms, often realized as a single form for subject, object, and possessive
>
> *(a)mí* 'I, me, my'   *nos* 'we, us, our'
>
> *bo(s)* 'you, your'
>
> *e(le)* 'he, him, his'
>
> Reduction or elimination of verbal inflections, with aspectual particles as commonplace
>
> *mi ta hablá* 'I talk, I am talking' (Cuban bozal Spanish)
>
> *mi ta papia* 'I talk, I am talking' (Papiamentu)
>
> Lapses of noun-adjective agreement
>
> Reduction of prepositions
>
> Postposition of possessive and object pronouns
>
> Canonical patterns for interrogative, negative, and exclamatory sentences

To illustrate further, observe the following comparative table:

Table 3.3. Comparison of Afro-Hispanic dialects and Afro-Portuguese creoles

Feature	Golden Age bozal Spanish/ boçal Portuguese	Afro-Portuguese creoles	Nineteenth-century Caribbean bozal Spanish	Panamanian Congo
conjugated verbs	some	no	few	some
Temporal/aspectual particles (e.g., *ta*)	no	yes	some	no
Form of *vos* as second-person singular pronoun	some	yes	some	no
Pronominal leveling/disjunctive variants (e.g., *(a)mí* = 'I, me, my')	some	yes	some	rare
Nominal inflection	unstable	none	unstable	unstable
Reduction of prepositions	frequent	frequent	frequent	frequent
Reduction of articles	frequent	frequent	frequent	frequent
Fusion of *ser/estar* (e.g., *sa, ta*)	frequent	yes	frequent	rare
Avoidance of embedded constructions	frequent	frequent	frequent	frequent
Subject pronoun as possessive form	some	yes	some	no

Feature	Golden Age bozal Spanish / boçal Portuguese	Afro-Portuguese creoles	Nineteenth-century Caribbean bozal Spanish	Panamanian Congo
Postposed possessives	no	frequent	rare	no
Tener/ter as existential verb	some	yes	frequent	rare
Invariant interrogative syntax (e.g., *qué tú quieres?*)	some	yes	frequent	frequent
Use of *bai* for 'to go' (from Portuguese *vai*)	some	yes	occasional	no
/Cl/ > /Cr/	frequent	yes	frequent	occasional

Source: Adapted from Lipski 1989:91–92.

Finally, note the following excerpt of Congo speech as recorded, transcribed, and translated by Lipski (1989:146–52):

> Tigrillo: vamo a diadogado entre Juan de Dio y Tigrillo ... en e cadajosón ... queda fueda de venfrún de ello nojotro deno un triago ... pedo ... yo te vo a decí ... una cosa ahoda mihma ... porque fue ... con enojo pode oda ... de otedía ... yo no te dije a ti Juan de Dio e diabro no ehtá tacando, nojotro noh fuimo a bocadita ... qui tu cogihte podaí mima ... e padio, deja, pon ete red fueda de agua, sabiendo lo que tú no tronía ...
>
> Juan de Dios: Tú ta doca, yo no vine a jugá pada po da causa de otria con da, con ...

(Spanish translation)

Tigrillo: Vamos a dialogar entre Juan de Dios y Tigrillo, y en el corazón, vamos a darnos un trago, pero ahora mismo te voy a decir una cosa, porque fue con enojo en la lotería, te dije a ti Juan de Dios que el diablo nos está tocando, fuimos a Bocadita, tú fuiste ahí mismo, dejaste la red en el agua, sabiendo que tú tenías . . .

Juan de Dios: Estás loco, yo no fui a jugar la lotería con . . .[22]

In a recent article Lipski has refined his conclusions on the speech of the Negros Congos. He explains that he "initially felt that the fundamental basis for *Congo* speech was an earlier Afro-Hispanic pidgin once spoken by African-born *bozales* . . . , that may have coalesced into a semicreole or creole language in colonial Panama, much as occurred with Papiamentu on Curaçao and with Palenquero in San Basilio de Palenque, Colombia" (Lipski 2009b:385, italics his). Following new field research conducted in 2007–2008, however, he reached "the conclusion that Congo speech is neither a simple continuation of colonial Afro-Hispanic pidgin nor a completely invented language, but rather a richly textured amalgam of elements representing both spontaneous and deliberately manipulated speech" (386). In addition, as with Calunga, Lipski notes that the speech of the Negros Congos is a cryptolect that was historically employed "for the purpose of concealing inter-slave communication from the colonial masters" (395). To those ends, Congo speech comprises four components:

> Semantic distortions of words and phrases (e.g., *vivi* 'alive' for *muerto* 'dead')
>
> Phonetic distortions of Spanish (e.g., *güene* < *bueno/buena* 'good')
>
> Elements of an earlier Afro-Hispanic language or Afro-Iberian creole (e.g., *elle* 'he/she/they,' *utene* 'you' (pl.))
>
> Regional isoglosses in the phonetics and lexicon (e.g., *chakere* 'house, dwelling' [Costa Abajo], *cudancho* 'house, dwelling' [Costa Arriba])
>
> (Adapted from Lipski 2009b:387)

Lastly, Lipski (2009b:398–402) hypothesizes a single locus of origin for the Negros Congos in the central portion of the Costa Abajo. He bases this hypothesis on regional phonetic variation and historical data, which point to the Costa Abajo as a prime area of maroon communities in Panama. The speech then advanced throughout the communities of the coastal region.

Part Two

LINGUISTIC DESCRIPTION

CHAPTER FOUR

Sociolinguistic and Sociohistorical Considerations of Calunga

Nós aprendemos [Calunga] com os pais porque na época, na nossa época, a escravidão ainda era assim mais próxima. Então, nossos pais, nossos avós, falavam demais a calunga.

(We learned [Calunga] with our parents because at that time, in our time, slavery was still much closer. So, our parents, our grandparents, spoke Calunga a lot.)

—Calungador Senhor Cabrera, circa 1980
(quoted in Vogt and Fry 1996:253)

During the eighteenth and nineteenth centuries Minas Gerais became heavily populated with slaves of African descent (African- and Brazilian-born), constituting up to 80 percent of the state's total population during those centuries (Barbosa 1970:315–16). As a result of this influx of slaves into Minas Gerais, African languages, pidgins and/or creoles, (restructured) Portuguese, and intertwined varieties were likely spoken within colonial plantations, mining communities, urban areas, and fugitive slave communities known as quilombos.

In attempting to piece together the historical and linguistic puzzle that is Calunga, it must be underscored that many pieces are missing. On the one hand, it is evident that Calunga's linguistic roots stem from colonial Minas Gerais and its ties to the Atlantic slave trade, particularly slaves from the region of Congo and Angola. On the other hand, *how* Calunga evolved is not presently known. Calunga informants trace its origins simply to "a língua dos escravo" (the slave language) or "a língua dos preto (velho)" (the [old] black language). From Calunga's Bantu lexicon, which is examined in chapter 5, it is evident that these slaves were speakers of Kimbundu, Umbundu, and Kikongo. However, Calunga's phonology and morphosyntax, which are discussed in chapter 6, are on par with contemporary rural Brazilian Portuguese vernacular. Hence, traveling historically and linguistically "from there to here" is not a straightforward endeavor.

In order to provide some understanding of the problems listed above, this chapter examines the sociolinguistic aspects of the Calunga speech community and considers hypotheses regarding the historical origins of Calunga.

OS CALUNGADORES: A SOCIOLINGUISTIC PROFILE

It is not currently known how many Calunga speakers there are in and around the Triângulo Mineiro. Based on interviews conducted by Daniela Bassani Moraes and this author from 2003 to 2005, a possible estimate is in the hundreds. But this figure is not verifiable. This is in large part because members of the Calunga speech community are evasive: that is, many people who know Calunga deny knowledge of it. It is therefore difficult to provide a comprehensive sociolinguistic profile of this speech community. Nevertheless, interviewees tended to agree on a general profile of the calungadores in Patrocínio and thereabouts.

Calunga informants came from all backgrounds, though typically they were cowboys, farmers, and miners who worked around the city of Patrocínio; other informants were urban construction workers who spoke Calunga on the job in Patrocínio. Many Calunga speakers were former *tropeiros* who ran cattle to the states of São Paulo and Goiás. In fact, many white Calunga speakers claimed to have learned Calunga from fellow Afro-Brazilian tropeiros while driving cattle. The most fluent Calunga speakers of the community were Afro-Brazilian men over forty years of age; the very best speakers were typically over seventy years of age.

In particular, the elder Calunga speakers were regarded within Patrocínio as the most knowledgeable of Calunga. Indeed, these speakers understood Calunga's sociohistorical and sociolinguistic links to Africa and the past regime of slavery in Brazil. For example, Joaquim Luís linked Calunga to slavery in the Triângulo Mineiro and explained that it was spoken primarily as a "secret language." He also recited "fantastic" stories in Calunga that spoke of the struggle and perseverance of Afro-Brazilians in the region (see his excerpted dialog in chapter 1).

Another elder Calunga speaker, Inácio de Souza, reiterated stories similar to those of Joaquim Luís. Here he explains how he learned Calunga, along with its social function:

> Eu aprendi essa língua desde menino, trabalhando com os pais. Ia para a roça, o pai lá enrolava a língua com o companheiro e a gente lá escutando. De vez em quando o pai mandava a gente fazer alguma coisa, mandava na *calunga*. E assim, a gente foi aprendendo. Até hoje eu me lembro um dia que ele mandou eu buscar umas cana. Tinha dois canavial. Tinha um que era de um sujeito rico e um de um sujeito pobre. O canavial do mais pobre era melhor, as cana era melhor. Então, falou comigo: "Vai lá buscar uns *viango* pra nós tomar na *mucota*. Vai lá naquele *camano* mais *ôa* que é melhor. Você vai naquele *camano* mais *ôa* e não naquele mais *aprumado*." Eu já sabia que era para ir buscar a cana do mais pobre. A cana era melhor. Assim eu fui aprendendo, né? . . .
>
> Na *calunga*, nós pode xingar vocês todos e vocês não sabem que estamos xingando. Na língua deles, dos pretos de antigamente, eles podia falar o que quisessem, podia estar falando "bom dia," "boa tarde," podia estar xingando e ninguém entendendo nada. Assim que era língua desses preto de antigamente. (Quoted in Vogt and Fry 1996:246, 248–49, italics theirs)
>
> (I learned this language as a child, working with my parents. I used to go to the plantation, my dad there rolling out the [Calunga] language with a friend, and we there listening. Once in a while Dad used to send us to do something, and he would tell us in Calunga. And so we learned. Even today I remember a day that he sent me to get some sugarcane. There were two sugarcane fields. There was one that was of a rich guy and one of a poor guy. The sugarcane field of the poorer one was better; the sugarcane was better. So, he told me [in Calunga]: "Go there and look for some *viango* [sugarcane] so that we take to the *mucota* [mouth]. Go there to that *camano* [man] more *ôa* [poor] which is better. You go to that *camano* [man] more *ôa* [poor; poorer man] and not to that more *aprumado* [rich (man)]." So I knew that it meant to go look for sugarcane of the poorer man. The sugarcane was better. That is how I learned, right? . . .

> In Calunga, we can insult all you and you don't know that we are insulting [you]. In their language, the blacks of long ago, they could say what they wanted to, could be saying "good morning," "good afternoon," could be insulting and no one would understand anything. That was the language of those blacks of long ago.)

What Inácio refers to as "the language of those blacks of long ago" was traditionally a speech that slave descendants utilized to communicate in secrecy so that they would not be understood by people of authority—a theme commonly articulated by other Calunga speakers interviewed for this study.

Here Senhor Cabrera reflects on his speaking of Calunga in Patrocínio. Observe how he links the speaking of Calunga to slavery: "Nós aprendemos com os pais porque na época, na nossa época, a escravidão ainda era assim mais próxima. Então, nossos pais, nossos avós, falavam demais a calunga. Eles vinham sempre falando. Então a gente aprendeu, mas agora nós já quase não falamos. Então, os filhos nem aprenderam com a gente. Que isso eles não aprendem na escola. A gente aprende conversando." (Quoted in Vogt and Fry 1996:253; We learned [Calunga] with our parents because at that time, in our time, slavery was still much closer. So our parents, our grandparents, spoke Calunga a lot. They would always be speaking. So we learned, but now we don't speak [Calunga] as much. So the children didn't even learn from us. That they do not learn in school. We learn conversing.)

Contemporary Calunga conversations usually take place among Afro-Brazilian men in certain social situations, such as on the job, or especially at Galera's Bar in Patrocínio, where calungadores like to get together to drink cachaça (white rum) and speak Calunga. In the present social context Calunga is a symbol of friendship and working-class solidarity among men. In the past, however, its purpose as a cryptolect was more prominent, as expressed by the elder calungadores above. Interestingly, today many working-class white speakers sometimes use Calunga in order to hide potentially damning information from worksite authorities. But white Calunga speakers are clearly not as fluent and furthermore recognize that Afro-Brazilians are the primary source. "Os preto calunga mais" (blacks speak Calunga more/better [than whites]), emphasized Tadeu de Barros when asked about the difference between white and black calungadores.

Figure 4.1. Calunga is frequently spoken at Galera's Bar in Patrocínio. Photograph by Steven Byrd, 2005.

Another aspect of the Calunga speech community is that it appears to be gender specific (i.e., more male than female speakers) rather than race specific. Belarmindo, for example, when asked if there were women who spoke Calunga, said, "Tem, tem ocaio que calunga tamém. Tem sim, mai num é muitas não." (There are, there are women that speak Calunga too. Yes, there are, but there are not many.) When asked why there were not more women who spoke Calunga, José de Barros said, "Porque num viajava, né? Na época eas num viajava, né?" (Because they didn't travel, right? In those days women didn't travel, right?) In other words, women were not present during trips to transport cattle, which kept them from learning Calunga.

The fact that there are not many female speakers of Calunga is somewhat of a mystery. Although no one in Patrocínio could truly identify why this is, perhaps the answer can be found within contemporary Brazilian society. That is, speaking Calunga is no longer a societal necessity in a world with education and mass communications available to most Brazilians. Calunga has instead become a sort of masculine slang related to work, drink, sex, and obscenities, which might explain why women do not want to be associated with this speech community. Another potential reason is that relatively few African women were sent to the Americas generally or to Minas Gerais specifically. Hence, there was perhaps simply a predominance of male speakers of African languages and later of Calunga.

Although there are some fluent female speakers who, like other calungadores, learned Calunga from their parents, women who speak—or even know of—Calunga are few and far between in and around Patrocínio. Most women who have any knowledge of Calunga can recognize no more than a handful of lexical items and demonstrate little interest in speaking it. Moreover, many women rumored to speak Calunga would often deny knowledge of it, only acknowledging its existence within the community.

Only three women spoke Calunga openly in interviews, even though more women among our interviewees were rumored to speak Calunga. All three—Denga Cabrera, Glauce de Souza, and Ângela Ferreira—recall speaking Calunga as children, including with their mothers. Of the three women, only Ângela was able to hold a fluent conversation in Calunga and was willing to affirm that she truly was a "calungadora." Ângela also discussed Calunga as linked to African cultures and languages, a fact that changed the way she views its historical importance. However, Ângela, too, referred to Calunga as a "masculine language" reserved for men to speak in certain social situations, especially those requiring group secrecy. Her husband, Marlenísio Ferreira, a speaker and researcher of Calunga, believes this gender-specific trait of Calunga may stem from an African custom in which only men were granted access to certain "secret information."[1] Denga do Cabrera (daughter of Senhor Cabrera) mentioned in two interviews that her father and mother spoke fluent Calunga with each other and with their eldest daughter, particularly in situations when they did not want to be understood by others outside of the family. After the death of her father and sister, however, Calunga was no longer spoken much in the house. Even though Denga admits to understanding Calunga, she has difficulty producing fluent sentences, restricting her usage to isolated lexical lists. But she vividly recalled one incident when a white friend came to their house and wanted to put together money to drink beer with her father. Senhor Cabrera asked his wife in Calunga in front of the guest: "O camano mavero tem os zipaque?" (Does the white man have any money?) Glauce de Souza, granddaughter of Inácio de Souza, also mentioned that she understands most Calunga but not all. She emphasized that she has little or no interest in speaking it, believing it is for men to speak.

Other women interviewees in Patrocínio, who elected anonymity for this study, had similar answers: "I understand but I don't speak it"; "I used to speak with my father but I don't speak it anymore"; "I always heard Calunga at home but I never spoke it"; or, even more emphatically, "Calunga is not for women to speak." This denial does not necessarily reflect a lack of knowledge of Calunga but a general lack of acceptance by women.

Generally speaking, many people of Patrocínio are not at all familiar with the history of the calungadores. That is, it seems that the society of Patrocínio does not view Calunga as a language with a history and culture worthy of study and preservation. In fact, in the 1980s Senhor Cabrera believed that Calunga was going to die out because the youngest generations and their parents were not speaking it, nor were they very interested in learning it (Vogt and Fry 1996:253). This reality, indeed, puts Calunga in a very precarious situation for the future. But some calungadores, such as Marlenísio Ferreira, who has created *O injó da calunga* (The house of Calunga), are currently active in preserving and teaching about this unique Afro-Brazilian speech within the community. There is also a samba recently composed by Patrocínio singer-songwriter Agnaldo França in homage to the popular Patrocínio politician Sebastião Elói, which is sung partially in Calunga.

Even though predictions cannot be made with absolute certainty, the fact that there are so few speakers—and that efforts to salvage the speech seem small—suggests a grim future for Calunga. At the very least, perhaps some of the lexical Africanisms will remain within the local dialect of Brazilian Portuguese. But a full-scale revival of Calunga seems highly unlikely.

SOCIOHISTORICAL CONSIDERATIONS

One fundamental question to address is, how did Calunga evolve in Minas Gerais? As noted in chapter 3, little is known about the African linguistic heritage in Brazil. Nevertheless, an attempt will be made to add some insight to this problem in a sociohistorical context.

Bandeirantes traveled through the contemporary Brazilian territory labeled Minas Gerais (general mines) from Bahia and São Paulo in the sixteenth and seventeenth centuries using indigenous trails (Resende 2007b:26–27). The motives of the bandeirantes' explorations are not completely understood, but Resende postulates three possible objectives: to search for "negros da terra" (blacks of the land, i.e., indigenous slaves), to perform reconnaissance expeditions in the Brazilian interior, and to exterminate rebellious groups, such as the indigenous Tapuias and fugitive African slaves living in quilombos (26). During a 1693 expedition led by Antônio Rodrigues Arzão through the modern-day cities of Viçosa, Piranga, Ouro Preto, and São João del Rei, gold was discovered (27, 29). Thereafter Minas Gerais became one of the most important territories for the Portuguese. It was widely rumored that a "new Eldorado" had been discovered, which attracted many Portuguese to Brazil. Moreover, at the time of the gold discovery the Portuguese Crown was in a deep economic crisis, adding another reason to invest its efforts in the territory (Resende 2007a:20, 2007b:27).

Ironically, before earning its title of the new Eldorado, Minas Gerais was known as the *sertão:* a hostile land of enemies, diseases, and dangerous animals (Venâncio 2007:87). In truth, much is unknown regarding the region of Minas Gerais before the arrival of the Portuguese bandeirantes. Recent archaeological researchers have speculated that, before Portuguese colonization, humans had been living in Minas Gerais as of eleven to twelve thousand years ago, consisting of anywhere from 11 to 177 ethnic groups and with an estimated total population of 90,000 to 160,000 (Venâncio 2007:88, 90). A Portuguese report from the sixteenth century by Gabriel Soares de Souza offers the following description of the indigenous peoples living in Minas Gerais at the time: "Não vivem estes bárbaros em aldeias, nem em casas, como o gentio, nem há quem lhas visse nem saiba, nem desse com elas pelos matos, dormem no chão sobre folhas . . . mantêm-se dos frutos silvestres e da caça que matam, a qual comem crua ou mal assada." (Quoted in Venâncio 2007:90; These barbarians do not live in villages nor in houses like our people, nor was there anyone who has seen or known them, nor having met them in the forest, they sleep on the ground on leaves . . . they live on fruits from the forest and from hunting, which they eat raw or poorly cooked.) Further Portuguese exploratory reports also mention cannibalism and other practices labeled as "barbarian" (Venâncio 2007:90).

After gold was found in the region and the decision was made to colonize, the Portuguese naturally turned to slavery for their labor force. Interestingly, the decision to use African slaves was made despite the availability of indigenous peoples they could exploit. Historian Tarcísio Botelho (2007:403) explains, "[Q]uando da descoberta do ouro na região . . . de Minas Gerais, houve uma 'opção natural' pela escravidão negra, ainda que existisse uma parcela razoável de escravos de origem indígena nas primeiras décadas da empresa mineradora. A área inicial de mineração esvazia-se, em parte, de população autóctone, expulsa para suas margens ou aculturada ao longo das décadas anteriores, momento em que expedições paulistas a percorreram em busca de 'negros da terra.' Em menos de um século, a importação de cativos transformou as Minas Gerais na principal região escravista do império português." (With the discovery of gold in the region . . . of Minas Gerais, there was a "natural option" for black slavery, despite the existence of a reasonable quantity of slaves of indigenous origin in the first decades of the mining efforts. The initial area of mining partially decimated the autochthonous population, who were expelled to marginal areas or acculturated during the previous decades when the expeditions of the São Paulo bandeirantes went in search of "blacks of the land." In less than a century the importation of slaves transformed Minas Gerais into the principal slave region of the Portuguese Empire.)

Even though gold and precious stones were the principal reason for the colonization of Minas Gerais, the territory's economy was not based solely on mining. Agriculture, urban infrastructure, and various goods and services were also part of its overall development. However, whether in mining, agriculture, or urban development, most of the work in colonial Minas Gerais was performed by slaves of African origin (Guimarães 2007:439).

It is not known how many African slaves arrived in Minas Gerais, but estimates are that roughly ten thousand were in the area circa 1750 (Libby 2007:414). During the second half of the eighteenth century Minas Gerais had the largest slave population in Brazil, and the state's residents may have purchased the largest volume of African slaves in Brazil during the nineteenth century as well (428). Statistics analyzed by Libby (419–20) are revealing: in 1786 African slaves constituted 48 percent of the population of Minas Gerais; in 1805, 46.4 percent. In contrast, the white population was 18.1 percent of the total in 1786 and 19.2 percent in 1805. The remaining portion of the population was freed slaves.[2] In addition to the racial imbalance of blacks to whites in Minas Gerais, there was also a gender imbalance, particularly among Africans: two to four African men for each African woman (416).

The origins of the African slaves in Minas Gerais are sketchy. Libby (2007:431) notes that, until 1730, most shipments of goods into Minas Gerais, including slave shipments, entered through the port of Salvador. Up to the 1740s a prominent slave group was the Minas—speakers of Kwa languages, such as Ewe-Fon and Akan from West Africa—who likely were shipped to Minas Gerais via Salvador, many of whom ended up in Ouro Preto. With the consolidation of the Caminho Novo (New Road) in the 1730s, however, Rio de Janeiro became the principal entrance port for shipments to Minas Gerais. As a result, Bantu slaves from west central Africa—namely "Angolas," "Benguelas," and "Congos"—constituted the three primary groups sent to Minas Gerais during the eighteenth century. These Bantu groups provided the most significant African presence in Minas Gerais during the nineteenth century as well (431–32).

Patrocínio

Before the arrival of the Portuguese, indigenous peoples lived in the Triângulo Mineiro, which was the scene of some conflicts in the region. For instance, Portuguese reports note a battle between the Tremembés and Kayapós that forced the latter group into the Triângulo Mineiro (Venâncio 2007:93). The Araxá (or Araxué) and Cataguá natives are also mentioned in Portuguese reports from the region.

Bandeirantes coming from São Paulo via the Tietê River first explored the Triângulo Mineiro and the Paranaíba River, lying near Patrocínio, during the explorations of the interior in the seventeenth century. In that area a basic town was formed that served primarily as a resting point for the explorations of bandeirantes traveling from Pitangui, Minas Gerais, to Anhangüera, Goiás. In the Patrocínio area they discovered some precious stones and metals, but they initially referred to the region as "o sertão da farinha podre" (the backlands of the rotten flour) (Sampaio 1904).

During the early years Portuguese settlement in the Triângulo Mineiro attracted few commercial interests and only a small number of explorers and priests. The Kayapós, in particular, were opposed to the Portuguese presence and resisted their colonization efforts (Venâncio 2007:98–99). As the Portuguese presence in the area increased, the Kayapós were largely devastated by slavery and European diseases.

A monograph by the municipality of Patrocínio credits Captain Inácio Oliveira de Campos as the founder of Patrocínio. Interestingly, he initially came to the Triângulo Mineiro to hunt down fugitive slaves: in 1771 the Count of Valadares—the Portuguese captain general of Minas Gerais—ordered that Captain Oliveira de Campos seek and destroy quilombos in the region of the Triângulo Mineiro.[3] In 1772, again by decree of the Count of Valadares, Captain Oliveira de Campos founded the first estate near Patrocínio and dedicated it to cattle ranching and farming. This settlement was to be a rest area for the bandeirantes who were exploring the captaincy of Goiás at the time. The first permanent settlers arrived circa 1793, coming from areas such as Ouro Preto, Paracatu, and Diamantina, and some large colonial fazendas began to sprout in the region.[4] The first chapel was erected at the beginning of the nineteenth century, and the town came to be known as Arraial da Senhora do Patrocínio (village of the lady of protection).[5]

Figure 4.2. Stone wall built by slaves to divide colonial fazendas in the Boqueirão region near Patrocínio. Photograph by Steven Byrd, 2005.

The abundance of the Paranaíba River allowed settlers to establish themselves sufficiently to initiate commercial activities such as fluvial mining, farming, logging, and cattle ranching—all of which depended on African slavery (Sampaio 1904:16). The mining of iron, gold, diamonds, and semiprecious stones was somewhat profitable, though Portuguese estate owners and their slaves also cultivated crops—such as rice, beans, and corn—and ranched cattle for meat and milk. Later they established fruit cropping (such as bananas), coffee cultivation, fishing, and hunting (Sampaio 1904:11–12). In 1852 a substantial demographic increase occurred in the Triângulo Mineiro due to the discovery of a large diamond known as "a estrela do sul" (the southern star). Miners, farmers, sertão cowboys, and bandits began to flock to the region. Within this context Patrocínio developed as a rural mining and agricultural town.

In the early twenty-first century Patrocínio remains a rural Brazilian town sustained mostly by coffee and agricultural farming, cattle ranching, and basic commerce. As part of an exodus from nearby fazendas in the second half of twentieth century, many speakers of Calunga have come to live in Patrocínio. Most of the contemporary calungadores have been either cowboys running cattle to the states of São Paulo and Goiás or farmers and ranch hands on nearby fazendas.

Figure 4.3. Cattle fazenda just outside of Patrocínio. Photograph by Steven Byrd, 2003.

Possible Origins of Calunga

In a sketchy anthropological study of Calunga, Batinga (1994:54) hypothesizes that it originated in some of the major mining areas of Minas Gerais: Araxá, Diamantina, Serro, Conceição do Mato Dentro, and Rio Vermelho. However, he does not explain how Calunga could have evolved linguistically into its present state nor why it is today concentrated around Patrocínio. Even so, his is one of the few attempts at providing a sociohistorical explanation of Calunga.

Before Batinga's study, one of the best sources on Calunga's history was Sebastião Elói, a popular Patrocínio politician (now deceased). According to Elói, Calunga was "o dialeto do nosso povo" (the dialect of our people) that has since been lost. He laments not learning more about Calunga in an interview with Vogt and Fry circa 1980: "Os negros africanos [de Patrocínio] foram morrendo; eles tinham um vocabulário grande [de Calunga] que foi se perdendo e a gente não cuidou disso. A 'língua africana' foi ficando diminuída, de poucas palavras, e a gente sem perguntar a eles por que usavam essa linguagem, esse dialeto." (Vogt and Fry 1996:252; The blacks [of Patrocínio] were dying out; they had a large vocabulary [of Calunga] that was being lost and we did not take care of it. The "African language" became diminished, of few words, and we did not ask them why they used that speech, that dialect.) Historically, Elói sees Calunga as a symbol of African identity, even as an instrumental force for rebellion: "Antigamente o negro falava que os portugueses judiavam deles porque eles conversavam a *calunga*. Os portugueses reprimiam eles, punham eles a ferro, eles conversavam uns com os outros e ninguém sabia se era para fazer uma sedição. Aqui o nosso município aqui [de Patrocínio] conheceu muitas sedições. . . . Eram sedições do povo com os negros. (Vogt and Fry 1996:251, italics theirs; In the past blacks said that the Portuguese would treat them bad for speaking Calunga. The Portuguese repressed them, put them in shackles, they talked to each other but nobody knew if it was to make a rebellion. Here our municipality [of Patrocínio] was familiar with many rebellions. . . . There were popular rebellions among the blacks.)

When asked about the history of Calunga, informants interviewed for this study unanimously identified it as "a língua dos escravo" (the language of the slaves) or "a língua dos preto (velho)" (the language of the

[old] blacks), but they did not elaborate. Instead, informants typically explained *when* one speaks Calunga. To cite one example, white calungador José Dinamérico, when asked about the history of Calunga, expressed that it was always spoken by tropeiros along the São Paulo–Minas Gerais–Goiás cattle routes on which he journeyed. In addition to speaking Calunga on cattle runs, which was rather common among the informants interviewed for this study, other calungadores mentioned that they had learned it on urban construction sites and/or during local farming work with Afrodescendants in the Patrocínio region over the past fifty or so years. While such interviews were interesting, given that many enjoyed sharing their stories about fellow calungadores, very little was learned about the history and origins of Calunga from contemporary speakers.

One hypothesis regarding the origins of Calunga is that it evolved within the quilombos of Minas Gerais (Vogt and Fry 1996:236). Indeed, there were some notable quilombos in the region. For instance, historian Waldemar de Barbosa (1970:312) notes, "Com relação ao Triângulo Mineiro, . . . há uma particularidade digna de nota: foi a região onde mais proliferaram os quilombos e onde tiveram a mais longa duração. O Quilombo do Ambrósio ou Quilombo Grande durou mais de trinta anos." In relation to the Triângulo Mineiro, . . . there is a peculiarity worthy of note: it was the region where quilombos proliferated most and where they had the longest duration. The Quilombo of Ambrósio or Quilombo Grande lasted more than thirty years.) Historian Roger Bastide (1979:193) adds, "The quilombos of Minas were well organized and were the largest except for Palmares. They had the population of about twenty thousand Negroes, who had flocked from every corner of Brazil, from São Paulo, and from Bahia; these were joined by a number of mulattoes, criminals, and brigands; the inhabitants were divided among dozens of different villages, four of these being larger than the rest and fortified: Ambrosio, Zundu, Gareca, and Calaboca, all located near Sapucahy."

Archaeologist Carlos Magno Guimarães (1983:52) estimates that there were some 127 quilombos throughout Minas Gerais between 1710 and 1798; historian Richard Price (1999:248) notes some 160 quilombos in the area during the eighteenth century. But, even though these numbers seem impressive, historian João José Reis (2001:301) explains that "most quilombos in Minas [Gerais] and elsewhere involved few fugitives, often very few, for the colonial government defined a quilombo as the gathering

Figure 4.4. Area of former Ambrósio quilombo near Patrocínio. Photograph by Steven Byrd, 2005.

of five or more fugitive Africans or Afro-Brazilians settled in an unpopulated area."

For all intents and purposes, the languages spoken within the quilombos are unknown, though there are some speculative ideas. For example, there is some anecdotal evidence of a "linguistic syncretism" in the Palmares quilombo: African languages, Portuguese, and Tupi (see chapter 3, "African Languages in Brazil"). Likewise, Couto (1997:100–101) hypothesizes that anti-creoles may have originated among slaves in Brazil as "línguas gerais africanas" (i.e., lingua francas), perhaps within quilombos. That said, he concedes that there are no concrete data regarding the language(s) of the quilombos. But a common language—such as an anti-creole, pidgin, creole, or even (restructured) Portuguese—would have been essential for the organization and survival of the quilombo. Couto argues, "Não dispomos de informações seguras sobre as relações sociais existentes nessas comunidades de escravos fugitivos. As autoridades da época tinham por único objetivo exterminá-las, não se dando ao luxo de dar informações sobre sua organização, muito menos de sua linguagem. No entanto, ... parece poder detectarem-se alguns dados que comprovam que pelo menos em alguns quilombos deve ter havido anti-crioulos, quando não um pidgin ou até mesmo um crioulo." (Couto 1992a:78; We do not have solid information about the existing social relations in those communities of escaped slaves. The authorities of the era had only the objective of exterminating them, not giving in to the luxury of providing information about their organization, much less about their language. However, . . . there seems to be some detectible data that may prove that at least in some quilombos there may have been anti-creoles, a pidgin, or even a creole.)

Dornas Filho (1943:72) also notes that the quilombo setting was fundamental to the "Kimbundu" language and the associated "African village" of Catumba, Minas Gerais: "E é coisa curiosa a examinar o povoado do Catumba, que se me afigura às ruinas de considerável quilombo. Ainda hoje só é habitado por pretos que só falam entre si o quimbundo, e levam ainda a vida meio aventurosa de quilombo, salteando e roubando as imediações. A ignorância do povo lhes atribue práticas tenebrosas de feitiçaria, o que os isola inteiramente no seu reduto, onde vivem à lei de uma cubata africana." And it is something interesting to examine the village of Catumba, which appears to me as being the ruins of a considerable quilombo. Even today it is inhabited only by blacks who speak among themselves Kimbundu and have a somewhat adventurous quilombo life, moving around and stealing from nearby places. The ignorance of the village attributes dark practices of witchcraft to them, which isolates them entirely within their space, where they live according to the law of an African village.) Machado Filho (1943/1985:57–59) likewise notes that the quilombos of Minas Gerais maintained their Bantu language and customs during the time of his field research.

Colonial documentation from Minas Gerais highlights that within a single quilombo there were many nações (nations), which were roughly equivalent to African ethnic groups (Guimarães 2007:445). For example, Barbosa (1964:25) has highlighted that slaves from the Angola region were likely predominant in many of the quilombos. Bantu languages such as Kimbundu, Umbundu, or Kikongo could thus have been spoken within these quilombos, particularly among African-born slaves.

Regarding Calunga specifically, historian Tarcísio José Martins expressed in a 2003 interview with this author that he believes it evolved as a hybrid pidgin speech comprising Bantu languages, Portuguese, and Língua Geral within the quilombos of the Triângulo Mineiro. However, Carlos Magno Guimarães strongly refuted Martins's claim in a 2003 interview, emphasizing that there are *no available data* regarding the language(s) spoken in the quilombos of Minas Gerais. What was spoken in those quilombos, he stressed, may have been any language—or mixture of languages—but *we simply know nothing* about this question.

Even though the social organization of the quilombos is largely unknown, including the language(s) spoken therein, it seems likely that Portuguese would have been a particularly advantageous language for the marooned slaves to know. For example, in regard to the *quilombolas'* relationships with the Portuguese, Reis writes,

> It is true that in many early quilombos such as Palmares, Africa would be reinvented based on cultural syncretisms involving several different African ethnic groups interacting with one another as well as with local populations. Quilombos, however, were almost never completely isolated from the surrounding society but maintained both conflictive and cooperative relationships with it. Their members raided and kidnapped, but they also traded and kept a network of friends and often lovers with both free people and people still in bondage. Even whites such as farmers and merchants developed friendly relationships with quilombolas. [These] relationships . . . were fundamental to the survival of the quilombos. (Reis 2001:304)

A second hypothesis to consider is that Calunga could have evolved as a rural falar africano in the colonial fazendas of the Triângulo Mineiro. According to this hypothesis, African slaves may have maintained some form of their native African languages beyond a few generations, combined with their eventual acquisition of the regional Portuguese. Given that African slaves made up a large percentage of the population in Minas Gerais, the maintenance of some form of African language for some generations seems a possibility. Also, as noted in chapter 3, in the colonial fazendas of Brazil there was a state of linguistic complexity: African languages, pidgin and/or creole languages, (restructured) Portuguese, intertwined varieties, and Língua Geral. Perhaps a rural falar africano evolved within this linguistic complexity.

While much remains to be understood, it is this author's position that the history of Calunga is hidden amid the linguistic complexity of the colonial fazendas of the Triângulo Mineiro. That is, the fazenda was the center of colonial Brazilian life—the place where most slaves lived and worked—and an Afro-Brazilian language such as Calunga may have been spoken within such a setting. Furthermore, given the lopsided proportion of blacks to whites during the crucial colonial period of Minas Gerais, it would seem logical that slaves of African descent would mostly be speaking to other slaves of African descent within these fazendas. Quilombos, in contrast, were relative anomalies, with the members of these communities being often small in number and frequently hunted down by colonial authorities. Plus, there is no evidence to indicate what was spoken in the quilombos nor how a fugitive community could preserve a "secret language" and then later disseminate it into the larger community outside of the quilombo. That point, coupled with the fact that contemporary calungadores make no reference to quilombos, seems to indicate that fazendas—particularly ones dedicated to cattle ranching, which many calungadores do reference—should be viewed as a more probable candidate for the primary locus of Calunga.

Other Afro-Brazilian Speech Communities

In addition to Calunga, it is worth considering other Afro-Brazilian speech communities located in southeastern Brazil. One that is near Patrocínio is Língua do Negro da Costa in Bom Despacho, Minas Gerais. Queiroz's (1998:98–107) research on this Afro-Mineiro community argues that this speech evolved as a type of pidgin that existed during the era of slavery. She points out that, because of its grammatical and lexical structure, it is not a traditional pidgin: the lexical items are derived largely from Bantu languages, but the grammatical system is essentially Portuguese, quite similar to Calunga. She notes that its lexical items in particular serve as an ethnolinguistic "secret code." Moreover, she aptly points out that it is not a creole language, since it is not anyone's native language, but instead is a pidgin that is acquired among friends, typically when they are between the ages of eleven and twenty. This pidgin was preserved as part of a type of Afro-Brazilian ritual similar to other Afro-Brazilian traditions: that is, congados, folklore, artisanship, cuisine, and so forth. One interesting definition that she provides for Língua do Negro da Costa is, "Língua usada pelos *negros tradicionais antigos* do bairro Tabatinga" (102, italics hers; Language used by the *traditional old blacks* of the Tabatinga neighborhood).

Like Queiroz, Vogt and Fry (1996:278–80) also conclude that, on the basis of their collected lexical data, Cupópia of the Cafundó community of São Paulo state developed from an African pidgin. Cupópia is similar both grammatically and lexically to Calunga and is a possible dialectal counterpart. According to Vogt and Fry, Cupópia is likely the descendant of a Bantu-Portuguese pidgin or creole with a strong Kimbundu and Kikongo lexical base, now found in an advanced stage of decreolization. The basic morphosyntax of the language is composed of rural Portuguese grammar (i.e., Caipira Portuguese), somewhat equivalent to Calunga (see chapter 6).

Also noteworthy are the falares africanos that have existed in Minas Gerais in the Diamantina region (Machado Filho 1943/1985; Nascimento 2003), in the village of Catumba (Dornas Filho 1943), and in Ouro Preto (Castro 2002; Pereira and Gomes 2003:105–6) (see chapter 3, "Studies on Afro-Brazilian Languages and Cultures"). And there are other traces of Afro-Brazilian speech around Minas Gerais and Goiás to take into consideration as well. For instance, in the north of Goiás there are some thirty Kalunga communities that are supposedly the descendants of quilombos of African and indigenous slaves. Unfortunately, no linguistic accounts of Afro-Brazilian speech have been documented there.[6]

Essentially it is not known if all these falares africanos are simply isolated Afro-Brazilian speech communities or if they are all part of the same linguistic "puzzle" in which Calunga is but one piece. More field research is needed to better understand how these Afro-Brazilian speech communities are related, if they are related at all. Amid such uncertainty, what does seem clear is that all these falares africanos have been spoken and maintained for reasons of resistance and identity and especially as a defensive mechanism in the form of cryptolects.

The contemporary Calunga speech community is small and composed essentially of older, Afro-Brazilian men, although there are some white speakers of Calunga as well. When asked about the history and nature of Calunga, the speakers identified it simply as "a língua dos escravo" or "a língua dos preto (velho)." Clearly much remains to be understood about the origins of Calunga. That said, it seems possible that it evolved as some type of Bantu-Portuguese hybrid language amid the linguistic complexity that was commonplace within the colonial fazendas of Brazil generally and within Minas Gerais specifically. But it bears repeating here that the types of languages that Africans and African descendants spoke in Brazil—specifically in Minas Gerais—as well as where exactly these languages were spoken (i.e., within quilombos or fazendas?) and how they evolved into varieties of falares africanos such as Calunga is not well understood. The lexicon and grammar of Calunga, which are addressed in the following chapters, can provide some insight to these questions, but again, how Calunga evolved into its current form is presently unknown.

CHAPTER FIVE

The Calunga Lexicon

Ces langues [africaines au Brésil], déracinées de leur niche écologique, ont été soumises à l'épreuve de diverses ruptures, dont celle sémantique: le sens des mots est devenu brutalement obsolète ou en porte-à-faux, parce que ne reflétant plus la réalité africaine, mais encore sans prise sur la réalité nouvelle faite de notions différentes et de nouvelles dénominations.

(These [African languages in Brazil], uprooted from their ecological niche, underwent various changes, for example in the semantic aspect: the meaning of words became suddenly obsolete or different because they no longer reflected the African reality but were still without referents in the new reality made up of different concepts and different names.)

—Linguists Emilio Bonvini and
Margarida Maria Taddoni Petter (1998:72)

If one asks a Calunga speaker, what is Calunga?, the speaker will typically provide a series of lexical items and translate them into Portuguese rather than explain it as a "foreign language." That is, the key component of Calunga is its lexicon.

In order to better understand the Calunga lexicon, this chapter provides: a glossary of collected Calunga terms with tentative etymologies and an analysis of Calunga terms with lexical items from other Afro-Brazilian speech communities.

CALUNGA GLOSSARY

In the Calunga glossary below are 307 terms with translations and spelling patterns (based on the 1971 standard for Brazilian Portuguese orthography). These terms were collected by this author during in situ interviews between 2003 and 2005 in Patrocínio, Minas Gerais, and thereabouts. Of particular importance for this glossary was calungador José Astrogildo, who, in 2003, provided this author with a list of some one hundred handwritten Calunga terms. The spelling patterns for the Calunga terms herein were based largely on Astrogildo's rendering of them; however, some words have been slightly altered orthographically by this author to better correspond to phonetic patterns of the calungadores. For example, *aprumá(r)*, which was rendered as *aprumar* by Astrogildo, shows that the word-final /r/ is not pronounced in Calunga; the parentheses signal that it is a verbal infinitive.

Because little is known about the history and evolution of Calunga, etymologies and analyses provided herein are tentative and in no means definitive or conclusive. Many etymologies are qualified with "possibly," "uncertain," and/or "etymology undetermined"; in some cases more than one language—or a mixture of languages—may have been a source of the Calunga term in question.[1] That said, some etymologies are clearly more certain than others. For sources cited in the glossary, see the list of abbreviations that precedes the notes.[2]

A (26 TERMS)

adufe. Baker. Possibly related to Arabic *ad-duff* 'tambourine' (N:18; VF:285).
afochê. Shotgun. Etymology undetermined.
aiêto. Big, large. Etymology undetermined.
amera. Face. Umbundu *omela* 'mouth' (J:355); Umbundu *mela* 'mouth' (A:717; VF:293).
amparo. Covering, protection, support. Portuguese *amparar* 'to protect, defend, support' (C:41; N:40).
amparo de conena. Chair. *See* amparo; conena.
amparo de cupia. Hat, cap. *See* amparo; cupia.
amparo de curiá(r). Fork. *See* amparo; curiá.
amparo de cuzeca. Bed. *See* amparo; cuzeca.
amparo de mirante. Glasses. *See* amparo; mirante.
amparo de omenha. Umbrella. *See* amparo; omenha/omeia.
angora. Horse. Kimbundu *ngolo* 'zebra' (VF:309); Umbundu *ngolo* 'zebra'

(A:946); Umbundu *oñgolo* 'zebra' (J:359).

aprumado. Rich, better. Past participle of *aprumá(r)*. Brazilian Portuguese 'better health, luck, or finances; well dressed' (N:57).

aprumá(r). To do, make, happen. Portuguese *prumo* 'iron instrument used to check verticality, prudence' (C:643); Brazilian Portuguese 'to make a better life' (VF:287); Brazilian Portuguese 'to improve one's health or luck, dress well' (N:57).

aprumá(r) banzo. To have sex. *See* aprumá(r); banzo.

aprumá(r) curiá. To eat. *See* aprumá(r); curiá.

aprumá(r) cuzeca. To sleep. *See* aprumá(r); cuzeca.

aprumá(r) mirante. To look, see. *See* aprumá(r); mirante.

aprumá(r) mucota. To eat, kiss. *See* aprumá(r); mocota/mucota/micota.

aprumá(r) omenha. To rain. *See* aprumá(r); omenha/omeia.

aprumá(r) omenha do ganzipe. To urinate. *See* aprumá(r); ganzipe; omenha/omeia.

arangá. Son of a single mother. Etymology undetermined.

ariranha. Cigarette, smoke. Possibly related to Kimbundu *dikanha* 'tobacco' (VF:288).

assungá(r). To come. Possibly related to Kimbundu *sunga* 'to pull' (VF:288); or possibly related to Brazilian Portuguese *sungar* or *assungar* 'to pull up, raise' (N:70; VF:288).

atindundu. Wine. Etymology undetermined.

atuá. Day. Possibly from Portuguese *atual* 'what exists in the present' (C:83; N:73).

B (11 terms)

bacuri. Sound, music, box. Possibly related to Brazilian Portuguese *bacurinho* 'boy' (VF:289); or possibly related to Tupi *bacuri* 'type of tree' (N:81).

bacuri de calunga. Radio, telephone. *See* bacuri; calunga.

bacuri de cumba. Watch. *See* bacuri; cumba.

bambi. Cold. Kimbundu *mbambi* 'cold' (M:314; VF:289); Umbundu *mbambi* 'cold' (A:657); Kikongo, Kimbundu, or Umbundu *(o)mbambi* 'cold' (CA:167).

banga. Charm. Kikongo *banga* 'dear' (LA:18); Umbundu *mbanga* 'intelligent, knowledge' (A:664).

banzo. Sexual relations. Kimbundu *mbanze* 'love amulet' (VF:289); Umbundu *mbasi, mbaysi* 'lover, concubine' (A:667).

berrida. Running. Etymology undetermined.

bungulá(r). To jump. Etymology undetermined.

buraco/buraca. Bag carried on an animal's back for the purpose of travel. Possibly from Umbundu *ombuluaka* 'travel bag' or from Provençal and/or Spanish to Portuguese *burjaca* > *bruaca* (C:128).

buraco de duana. Shirt pocket. *See* buraco; duana.

buraco de nanga. Pant pocket. *See* buraco; nanga.

C (57 terms)

caceba. Old, used. Etymology undetermined. Possibly related to Umbundu *kavisa* 'to make tired, because of boredom' (A:289).

cacimbo. Fog. Kimbundu *kixima* 'water well, source of water' (N:108); Kikongo *kisiwu* or Kimbundu *kisibu* 'fog' (CA:186).

cacunda. Back. Kimbundu *kakunda* 'hump, hunchback(ed)' (N:109); Kikongo or Kimbundu *ka(di)kunda* 'back' (CA:188).

caçutu. Important person. Kikongo or Kimbundu *(ka)Ntutu* 'Bantu divinity (protector from disease)' (CA:188).

cafamo. Clear. Etymology undetermined.

cafangá(r). To leave. Kikongo *kufunga, kavuka* or Kimbundu *nkafunga* 'to leave' (CA:190).

cafifa. Luck (good or bad). Kikongo or Kimbundu *kafufwa* 'that which provokes bad luck, death' (CA:189).

cafofo. White man. Etymology undetermined. In Minas Gerais *cafofo* can mean a place where African slaves were held and sold (N:110). Kikongo or Kimbundu *kafwofo* 'burial, place for dead things' (CA:189).

cafuim. Curly hair. Possibly related to Umbundu *kavuka* 'to roll up, to curl up' (A:289).

caiumba. Soldier, police officer. Etymology undetermined.

caixinha de semá (cemá). Vagina. Portuguese *caixinha* 'little box.' *See* semá/cemá.

calunga. Speech, talk (Calunga). According to some Patrocínio natives the term is derived from Portuguese *(a)cá* + *língua* 'language here' (José Dinamérico, personal interview, 2003). Lopes (2003) argues for a multilinguistic Bantu term: *kalunga* 'God' from the verb *oku-lunga* 'to be intelligent, clever' (L:57–58). In the Ambos and surrounding African peoples it is found with this usage. Or perhaps the word originates from Kimbundu *kalunga* 'sea, dead,' which is a type of secondary god in the Bantu cults (C:142). According to Micha Lindemans (Encyclopedia Mythica, www.pantheon.org), *calunga* (or *kalunga*) is the father of patron god(dess) Musisi—the ancestral god, or supreme being, of creation and death—for the Lunda people of Angola, Zaire, and Zambia. Castro (2001:192–93) presents six options for the origin and meaning of the term; the sixth option argues that *calunga* originated from either Kikongo, Kimbundu, or Umbundu, *kalongela* > *kalonga*, with the meaning 'helper or carrier of the carriage' in Brazil. Interestingly, the *Enciclopédia Luso-Brasilera de cultura* (1963: vol. 4, p. 551) provides one definition of *calunga* as "rapaz auxiliar nas carroças e automóveis de transporte de carga" (auxiliary boy on the wagons and automobiles of cargo transportation). The *Grande enciclopédia portuguesa e brasileira* (1936–1960: vol. 5, p. 536) defines *calunga* as "o transcendente, o incognoscível ou o sobrenatural, na mística dos angolenses" (the transcendent, the unknown, or the supernatural, in the mysticism of Angolans). Also of interest is the Kimbundu word *kilunga*, which means 'cattle' (M:319). Another definition of *kalunga* in Umbundu is 'to shout, speak!,' or a type of special greeting in order to engage in conversation, from the verb *kaluka* (A:258, 1355). A final interesting definition of *kalunga* is 'proper name' or 'clan' (LA:207).

calungá(r). To talk, speak (Calunga). *See* calunga.

camanim. Boy. Diminutive of *camano*.

camano. Man, person. Kimbundu *muana, mona* 'son, daughter' or *kamona* 'of the son' (VF:292).

camano cafamo. White man. *See* cafamo; camano.

camano de outras inglaterra. Foreigner (not necessarily from another country but simply from "somewhere else"). *See* camano; inglaterra.

camano desaprumado. Fool, poor man. *See* camano; desaprumado.

camano maioral. Man of respect, boss, God. Portuguese *maioral* 'great, owner, boss.' *See* camano.

camano ôa. Bad man. *See* camano; oâ.

camano ofú. Black man. *See* camano; ofú.

camboque. Cheese. Etymology undetermined.

candando. Hug (noun). Etymology undetermined.

candango. Bad person, bandit. Possibly related to Kimbundu *kindangi* 'person of bad taste' (CA:195); or possibly related to Kimbundu *kangundun* (diminutive form of *kingundu*) 'villain, bad'—the name that the Africans used to refer to the Portuguese (N:117).

candunga. Sun. Possibly related to Umbundu *ndunga* 'egg yolk' (A:889; VF:294).

cangundo. Mischievous person. Kimbundu *kan-gundu*, diminutive form of *kin-gundu* 'villain, bad person' (L:62).

caputo. Blind. Etymology undetermined.

cauba. Jaguar. Etymology undetermined.

cavanza. Fight. Etymology undetermined.

cazumbi. Spirit. Kikongo *(ka)mvumbi* 'ghost, skinny and pale person' (CA:357–58).

cemá/semá. Hair. *See* semá/cemá.

cheba. Weak. Etymology undetermined. Possibly related to Umbundu *teva* 'shame, sorrow, grief' (A:1473).

chia. Butter. Etymology undetermined.

chicongo. Shadow. Kimbundu *pungo* or *tipungo* 'hat' (VF:296); Kikongo *mpongu* 'hat, cap' (CA:318).

chipoquê/chipoque/tipoquê. Bean(s). Kimbundu *kipoke* 'bean' (VF:335); Umbundu *poke* 'bean' (A:1123).

conena. Anus, butt, excrement. Kikongo or Kimbundu *kunena* 'to defecate' (CA:215; M:167; VF:297).

coteque. Night. Umbundu *teke, uteke* 'night' (A:1447).

cubá(r). To do, make, arrange. Portuguese *cubar* 'to evaluate, measure' (N:177).

cuciá(r). To dawn, wake up. Possibly related to Kikongo *kia* 'dawn,' *kuma kukia* 'the day dawns' (B:52); Kimbundu *kúkia* 'to dawn, wake up' (M:30).

cueto. Companion. Kimbundu *ukueto* 'companion' (M:128); Umbundu *kwetu, ukwetu* 'friend, companion' (A:451).

cumba. Time, hour, sun. Kimbundu *kumbi* 'sun, light, hour' or Umbundu *ekumbi* 'sun' (M:584; VF:300); Umbundu *kumbi* 'sun, hour, day' (A:398).

cumbaca. City, village. Kimbundu *kimbaka* 'city' (M:116); Kimbundu *kumbara* 'in the village' (VF:300).

cumba de indaro. Day. *See* cumba; indaro.

cumba imbuno. Night. *See* cumba; imbuno.

cumba ofú. Night. *See* cumba; ofú.

cumbata. Hut, shack. Kimbundu *kubata* 'house' (M:102); Kikongo or Kimbundu *kibata* 'house' (CA:213).

cupia/cupiá. Head. Possibly related to Kimbundu *ku-pupia* 'to speak' (VF:301); Umbundu *popya* 'to speak, talk' (A:1142).

cupiá(r)/copiá(r). To understand. Kimbundu *ku-pupia* 'to speak' (VF:301); Umbundu *popya* 'to speak, talk' (A:1142).

curiá. Food. Kimbundu *kudia, kuria* 'to eat, food' (M:127; VF:301); Kikongo or Kimbundu *kudiá* 'to eat' (CA:215); Umbundu *kulya* 'to eat, food' (A:396).

curima. Work, job. Kimbundu *kudima, kurima* 'to work' (VF:301); Kikongo *kutima* 'to work,' Kimbundu *kudima* 'to work,' Umbundu *okulima* 'to work' (CA:215).

curimá(r). To work. See curima.

curirá(r). To cry. Kimbundu *ku-dila, ku-didila, kulila, kuririla* 'to cry' (M:115, VF:302).

curitá(r). To sing. Etymology undetermined. Possibly related to Umbundu *kundila* 'to preach' (A:407).

curriola. Group. Etymology undetermined. Possibly related to Portuguese *curral* 'place where cattle are collected' (C:235).

cutá. Ear. Possibly from Kikongo *kutu* 'ear' (M:454); or etymology undetermined (VF:302).

cuzeca. Sleep, tiredness. Kimbundu *kuzeca, kuzeta* 'to sleep, rest, tiredness' (VF:303).

cuzecá(r). To sleep. See cuzeca.

D (14 terms)

dandara/dandará. Child. Etymology undetermined. Possibly related to Kimbundu *ana* 'children' (VF:322); or possibly related to Portuguese *dandá* (distortion of *andar*) 'to walk' in infantile speech (N:181).

dandará ofú. Black child. See dandara/dandará; ofú.

dandará santo. Newly born. See dandara/dandará; santo.

dandarazim. Toddler. Dimunitive form of *dandara/dandará* 'child.'

desaprumado. Bad, sick. Past participle of *desaprumá(r)*.

desaprumá(r). To undo. Antonym of *aprumá(r)* 'to do, make.' See aprumá(r).

duana. Shirt, coat. Etymology undetermined.

duana cafamo. Clear shirt. See cafamo; duana.

duana imbuno. Dark shirt. See duana; imbuno.

duana indaro. Yellow, red shirt. See duana; indaro.

duana mavero. White shirt. See duana; mavero.

duana ofú. Black shirt. *See* duana; ofú.
duana sengo. Green shirt. *See* duana; sengo/sengue/senguê.
duque. Insect. Possibly related to Kikongo *vuku, vuka* 'insect' (M:362; VF:303).

E (5 terms)

ei. Bad. Kimbundu *ei* 'thieves, lack of conscience' (VF:304).
embuá/imbuá. Dog. Kimbundu or Kikongo *imbua, mbua* 'dog' (M:97); Kikongo *mbwa* 'dog' (B:62); Umbundu *mbwa* 'dog' (A:706); Kikongo or Kimbundu *mbwa* 'dog,' or Umbundu *ombwa* 'dog' (CA:252).
engonhá(r). To save time. Etymology undetermined. Possibly related to Umbundu *ngoña* 'indolent, lazy' (A:950).
escutante. Ear. Portuguese *escutar* 'to hear, listen.'
exoa. Foolish. Etymology undetermined. Possibly related to Umbundu *syoha* 'lazy, indolent, late, lethargic' (A:1399).

F (6 terms)

faim. Knife. Etymology undetermined.
fimba. Swimming, diving. Possibly related to Umbundu *fima* 'pool' (A:84).
fojo. Hole. Portuguese *fojo* 'hole' (N:286).
frize. Axe. Etymology undetermined.
fuá. Mess. Kikongo *mfwa(nza)* or Kimbundu *mufufwa* 'uproar, racket' (CA:236).
fuzilo. Lightning. Portuguese *fuzil* 'lightning' (N:298).

G (10 terms)

gamboa. Bird. Etymology undetermined.
ganga. Boss, owner. Kikongo or Kimbundu *nganga* or Umbundu *oganga* 'boss' (CA:240).
ganzipe. Penis. Etymology undetermined. Possibly related to Portuguese *ganzepe* 'notch to connect wood' (N:302).
gatuvira. Coffee. Etymology undetermined.

grimpa. High, up. Portuguese *grimpar* 'to rise, go up' (C:396; N:316).

guaxaúna. Squash. Possibly from Tupi (see C:399 for related flora and fauna Tupi morphemes with *guax-*).

gudunhá(r). To take, grab. Etymology undetermined. Possibly related to Umbundu *nguto* 'spoon' (A:969).

gumbo. Day, today. Possibly from Kimbundu *kuma* 'day' (M:198); or etymology undetermined (VF:307).

gunga. Bell. Kimbundu *ngunga* 'bell' (M:580; VF:307); Kikongo *ngunga* 'bell (of a European pattern)' (B:20); Umbundu *ngunga* 'bell' (A:966).

guriô. Father. Kimbundu *nguri* 'father' (M:458).

I (28 terms)

imabe. Mischievous person. Possibly related to Kikongo *umbiu* 'disobedience, naughtiness' (B:439).

imberela. Meat. Possibly related to Umbundu *mbe* 'sheep, goat' (A:668); or possibly related to Kimbundu *camberera* 'meat' (VF:293).

imberela de omenha. Fish. See imberela; omenha/omeia.

imbuá/embuá. Dog. See embuá/imbuá.

imbuá de sengo. Wolf. See embuá/imbuá; sengo/sengue/senguê.

imbuete. Piece of bread, club, stick. Umbundu *mbweti* 'staff, club, stick, wood' (A:712).

imbuete de indaro. Match. See imbuete; indaro.

imbuno. Dark. Kimbundu *mbundu, mumbundu* 'black' (adj.) (M:440); Umbundu *imbundu* 'the Bundos—name of the peoples from the high plains of Benguela' (A:700).

incaca. Armadillo. Kikongo *nkaka* 'anteater' (B:378).

indaro. Fire, yellow, red. Kikongo *ndalu* 'fire' (CA:347); Kimbundu *ndalu* 'fire' or Umbundu *ondalu* 'fire' (VF:287); Umbundu *ndalu* 'fire, inferno' (A:813–14).

indaro de cumba. Sun. See cumba; indaro.

indaro de cumba imbuno. Moon, star. See cumba; imbuno; indaro.

indarumim. Moon. Possibly related to Kimbundu *mini, muini* 'light' and *ndalu* 'fire' (VF:308); or diminutive form of *indaro*.

ingazeiro. Penis. Etymology undetermined. Possibly related to Kimbundu *nja* 'penis' (J:370); or possibly related to Tupi *ingá* 'common name for legume-type plants' (C:436; N:348).

inglaterra. Region, land. Possibly related to Portuguese *Inglaterra* 'England.'

ingomo/ingombe. Ox, cattle. Kimbundu *ngombe* 'ox, cow' (J:370; VF:309); Umbundu *ngombe* 'ox, cow' (A:948); Kikongo, Kimbundu, Umbundu *(o)ngombe* 'ox, cattle' (CA:254).

ingrimo. Tooth, teeth. Etymology undetermined.

ingugiá(r). To keep watch. Etymology undetermined. Possibly related to Portuguese *vigiar* 'to keep watch.'

inharra. Snake. Kimbundu *nhoka, njíua* 'snake' (M:121); Umbundu *ñoha* 'snake (of any species), serpent' (A:984).

inhoto. Bone. Nhaneca *ontho* 'leg bone' (VF:309).

injequê. Corn, popcorn. Etymology undetermined. Possibly related to Yoruba *onjé* 'food' (CA:308).

injó. House. Kimbundu *inzo, njo* 'house' (M:102); Kikongo *nzo* (B:111; VF:310); Umbundu *ndjo* 'house' (A:857); Kikongo, Kimbundu, Umbundu *(o)nzo* 'house' (CA:348).

injó de banzo. Bordello. See banzo; injó.

injó de grade. Jail. Portuguese *grade* 'fence.' See injó.

injó de marafo. Bar. See injó; marafa/marafo.

injó de zipaque. Bank. See injó; zipaque.

injoquê. Bag, cup. Kimbundu *nzeke* 'bag' (M:555); Umbundu *ndjeke* 'bag' (A:845).

injó santo. Church. See injó; santo.

J (8 terms)

jamba. Diamond. Etymology undetermined.

janga. Small, smaller. Possibly related to Kikongo *ninga* 'to decrease' (B:197).

jangorô. Wall. Possibly related to Kikongo *mongo* 'wall' (VF:311).

jerico. Mischievous person. Brazilian Portuguese *jerico* 'donkey, ass' (N:363); Arabic *jarsh* > Huasa *jaki* 'donkey' + Portuguese *-ico* (CA:258–59).

jibundo. Cry, sadness, lament. Etymology undetermined.

jifeto. Grimace. Etymology undetermined.

jijumba. Tattoo. Kimbundu *jimbumba* 'tattoos' (M:599).

jinguba. Peanut. Kimbundu *nguba, jinguba* 'peanut' (M:32); Kikongo *nguba* 'ground nut' or *dia nguba* 'plant of ground nut' (B:98); Kikongo or Kimbundu *jinguba* 'peanut' (CA:261).

K (2 terms)

kimbo. City, town, village. Etymology undetermined. Possibly related to Kimbundu *kilombo* 'village, settlement' (M:495); or possibly related to Kimbundu *ku-mbara* 'in the village' (VF:300).

kukiá(r)/cuciá(r). To dawn, wake up. Kimbundu *kúkia* 'to dawn, wake up' (M:30); Kikongo *kia* 'dawn,' *kuma, kukia* 'the day dawns' (B:52).

L (2 terms)

lorri. Fish. Possibly Umbundu *loyi* 'bagre eléctrico (a type of fish)' (A:565); or possibly Nhaneca *ohi* 'fish' (VF:312).

lubra. Chest. Etymology undetermined.

M (46 terms)

macura. Fat (noun). Kimbundu *makuria* 'foods' (VF:313).

madubim. Peanut. Etymology undetermined. Possibly a distorted form of Portuguese *amendoim* 'peanut.'

mafuim/mapuim. Flour. Etymology undetermined.

maiaca. Seed. Kikongo *mayaca* 'manioc' (L:133); Kikongo *mandiaka* < Portuguese *mandioca* 'manioc' (CA:271).

maiembe. Medicine. Kimbundu *inhemba* 'medicine' (VF:314).

maioral. Superior, boss, owner. Portuguese *maioral* 'greater, boss, owner.'

malamba. Disgrace. Kimbundu *ma-lamba* 'disgraces' (M:186); Kikongo or Kimbundu *malamba* 'unhappiness, lament' (CA:272).

malambre. Slow, slowly. Kikongo *malembe* 'slow' (M:388).

malara. Orange (fruit). Kimbundu *malalanza* 'orange tree' (M:384; VF:314); Kikongo or Kimbundu *malala* < Portuguese *laranja* 'orange' (CA:272).

malombo/malumbim. Fruit. Kimbundu *malombo* 'fruit of the Jordan palm tree' (VF:314).

malombo de sanjo. Egg. *See* malombo/malumbim; sanjo/sanjô/sanja.

malumbí. Fish. Kimbundu *mulebi, musumbi* 'little fish' (M:471).

malungo. Brother, equal, same. Kimbundu *malungo* 'companion, comrade, of the same condition, adopted brother' (N:396; VF:315); Kikongo or Kimbundu *nkwanlugo* 'brother, companion in the same boat' (CA:273).

mambi. Needle. Possibly related to Umbundu *mbambo* 'nail, peg' (A:658).

mangonheiro. Swindler, mischievous person. Possibly Kimbundu *mangonha* 'a lie' (M:418); Umbundu *mangoña* 'laziness, lethargy, uselessness' (A:643); Kikongo or Kimbundu *mangona* 'indolence, lazy' (CA:276); and Portuguese morpheme -*eiro*.

manjira. Street, road. Kimbundu *njila* 'road' (M:553; VF:315); Kikongo *njila* 'road, path' (B:156).

marafa/marafo. Cachaça, alcoholic drink. Kimbundu or Kikongo *malavu, malufu* 'wine' (B:336; M:650; VF:316); Kikongo or Kimbundu *malafu, maravu* 'alcoholic drink' (CA:272).

marafa de uíque. Beer. See marafa/marafo; uíque.

marafa de vinhango. Cachaça. See marafa/marafo; viango/vinhango.

marangola. Horse, donkey. See angora.

massa de camboque. Cheese bread. Portuguese *massa* 'dough.' See camboque.

massango/massongo/massuango. Rice. Kimbundu *masangu* 'corn, cereal' or Kikongo *ma-nsangu* 'corn' (M:109, 422; VF:317).

mataco. Buttocks. Kimbundu *mataka, mataku* 'buttocks,' plural form of *taku, ditaku* (M:436).

matumba. Foolish. Kikongo or Kimbundu *matumbi* 'rude' (CA:280).

matura. Spell. Etymology undetermined.

mavero. Milk, breast, white. Umbundu *omavele* or Kimbundu *mavele*, both plural forms of *avele* 'milk' (M:387); Kimbundu *mele* 'breasts, milk' is the plural form of *diele* and *avele* (VF:318); Umbundu *vele* 'breast, teat, milk' (A:1651).

milongo. Medicine. Kimbundu *milongo* 'medicine' (M:415); Kikongo or Kimbundu *mi-nlongo* 'medicine' (CA:283).

mirante. Eye. Portuguese *mirar* 'to see.'

missosso. History, story. Kimbundu *musoso* 'history' (M:337).

moca. Coffee. From Moca, a port known for coffee exportation (C:526; N:421).

mocó. Arm, weapon, knife. Umbundu *moko* 'knife, machete' (A:733).

mocó de espirro. Firearm. Portuguese *espirro* 'sneeze.' See mocó.

mocota/mucota/micota. Mouth. Kimbundu *mukoto* 'cow, hoof, paw' (VF:320).

mongo/mungo/mungue. Salt. Kimbundu *mongua, mungua* 'salt' (M:558; VF:321); Umbundu *mongwa* 'salt' (A:741); Kikongo or Kimbundu *mungu, mungwa* 'salt' (CA:293).

monzape. Hand. Etymology undetermined. Possibly a variation of *munzá*; or possibly an Africanized form of Portuguese *mão* 'hand.'

mucafa. Old (fem.). See mucafo.

mucafo. Old (masc.). Kimbundu *mukulo, mukulu* 'old' (M:642; VF:319).

muchinga. Nose. Kimbundu *muxinga* 'end, extremity' (VF:320).

mufete. Fish. Kimbundu *mufete* 'fish' (M:471).

mumbacho. Cigarette. Etymology undetermined.

mumonha. Laziness. Kimbundu *umonha* 'laziness' (M:498); Umbundu *mumunu* 'slow person' (A:751).

munzá. Hand. Etymology undetermined. Possibly a variation of *monzape*; or possibly an Africanized form of Portuguese *mão* 'hand.'

muquifo. Bordello. Etymology undetermined.

murrudo. Big, strong, powerful. Possibly Kimbundu *mundundu* 'big' (M:328; VF:321); or possibly Portuguese *murro* 'fist' (N:431).

muxima. Heart. Kimbundu *muxima* 'heart' (M:146); Kikongo, Kimbundu, or Umbundu *(mu)ntima, nzima* 'heart' (CA:294).

muxito. Forest. Kimbundu *muxitu* 'forest, backwoods, bush country' (M:414).

N (10 terms)

nagoma. Drum. Kimbundu *ngoma* 'drum' (M:598); Kikongo *ngoma* 'drum' (B:64); Umbundu *ng˜oma* 'drum' (A:948).

nanga. Clothes, pants. Kimbundu *nanga* 'cloth' or Umbundu *onanga* 'clothes' (VF:322).

nanga cafamo. Clear clothes. See cafamo; nanga.

nanga imbuno. Dark clothes. See imbuno; nanga.

nanga mavero. White clothes. See mavero; nanga.

nanga sengo. **Green clothes.** See nanga; sengo/sengue/senguê.

nani. Small. Etymology undetermined.

nhoto. Skinny, thin. See inhoto.

niguciê. Cat. Possibly related to Kimbundu *ngatu* 'cat' (derived from Portuguese) and/or to Kimbundu *kisue* or *kisuéia* 'cat' (M:322).

niguciê de sengo. Jaguar. See niguciê; sengo/sengue/senguê.

O (21 terms)

ôa. Bad, nothing, poor, worse. Etymology undetermined. Possibly related to Umbundu *ova* 'stupidity, lethargy, hypocrisy' (A:1034).

ocai/ocaia/ocaio. Woman. Kimbundu *ucai* 'woman' (VF:325); Umbundu *ukãyi* 'woman, wife' (A:291).

ocai de banzo. Prostitute. See banzo; ocai/ocaia/ocaio.

ocai ofú. Black woman. See ocai/ocaia/ocaio; ofú.

ocai santo. Virgin. See ocai/ocaia/ocaio; santo.

ocaizim. Girl. Diminutive form of *ocai.*

odara. Pretty. Yoruba *odárá* 'good, pretty' (CA:300).

ofú. Black. Etymology undetermined.

omenha/omeia. Water, region. Kimbundu *menha* 'water' (M:22); Kimbundu *menya* 'water' (CA:282).

omenha de mavero. Milk. See mavero; omenha/omeia.

omenha de urungo. Gasoline. See omenha/omeia; urungu.

omenha de vinhango. Cachaça. See omenha/omeia; viango/vinhango.

opira. Pretty. Etymology undetermined.

opô. Eye. Etymology undetermined. Possibly related to Portuguese *olho* 'eye.'

orirá(r). To sing. Etymology undetermined. Possibly related to Portuguese *orar* 'to pray'; or possibly related to Yoruba *oro* 'incitement, stimulant' (CA:309).

orofim. Firewood. Etymology undetermined.

orogongi. Egg. Etymology undetermined.

orongoia. (Wood) bridge. Etymology undetermined.

oropemba. Seethe. Etymology undetermined.

ossumba. Fear. Umbundu *sumba* 'to fear, be afraid, fearful, coward' (A:1364).

otaca/otata. Father. Kimbundu *tata* 'father' (M:458).

P (11 terms)

paim. Hoe. Etymology undetermined. Possible variation of Calunga *faim* 'knife.'

pandú. Stomach. Etymology undetermined.

papa rato. Cat. Portuguese *papar* 'to eat' (C:577; N:465); Portuguese *rato* 'rat.'

pegante. Hand, arm. Portuguese *pegar* 'to grab.'

periá. Rabbit. Etymology undetermined.

pixiê. Food. Etymology undetermined.

ponto de conena. Anus. Portuguese *ponto* 'point.' See conena.
ponto de mirante. Eye. Portuguese *ponto* 'point.' See mirante.
ponto de poente. Nose. Portuguese *ponto* 'point' and *poente* 'west, setting.'
ponto pisante. Foot. Portuguese *ponto* 'point' and *pisar* 'to step.'
puco. Rat. Kimbundu *puku* 'rat' (J:371; M:524); Kikongo *mpuku* 'rat' (B:172).

Q (16 terms)

quicumbi. Young person. Kimbundu *kikumbi* 'puberty, celebration of puberty' (M:298, 511).
quijongo. Cricket. Etymology undetermined. Possibly related to Kimbundu *kinzenze* 'cricket' (M:330).
quimba. Stump, piece. Kikongo *kibalanga, kibata* 'testicles' (CA:322).
quimbim. Dead. See quimbimba.
quimbimba. Dead man. Kimbundu *kiambi, kimbi* 'death, cadaver' (M:89; VF:330).
quimboto. Toad. Kikongo *(ki)bototo* 'large toad' (CA:325); Kimbundu *kimboto* '(African) frog' (VF:331).
quimimbá(r)/quimbimbá(r). To die. See quimbimba.
quinda. Container. Etymology undetermined.
quindú. Fat (adj.). Etymology undetermined. Possibly related to Kimbundu *kindukutu* 'obese' (M:326).
quinhama/quinhamba. Leg. Kikongo or Kimbundu *kinama* 'leg, paw' (CA:252); Kimbundu *kinama* 'leg' (M:478).
quinhamá(r). To walk, travel. See quinhama/quinhamba.
quiombô. Wild pig. Kimbundu *ki-ombo* 'warthog' (J:370).
quissanda. Mischievous woman. Etymology undetermined. Possibly related to Kimbundu *kidianzanga* 'prostitute' (M:509).
quitata. Prostitute. Kimbundu *kitata* 'prostitute' (M:509).
quiunda. Anger. Kikongo *kunda* 'anger' (M:521).
quizumba. Party, mess, confusion. Kimbundu *kizomba* 'party, festivity' (M:298); Kikongo or Kimbundu *kizomba* 'party, celebration' (CA:329).

S (15 terms)

sanjo/sanjô/sanja. Chicken, hen. Kimbundu *sanji* 'hen' (M:320); Umbundu *sandji* 'hen' (A:1217).

santo. Pure. Portuguese *santo* 'saintly, holy.'
sarava. Dance. Etymology undetermined.
saravá. Good-bye. Possible Africanized pronunciation of Portuguese *salvar* 'to save' or greeting in Umbundu 'save!' (VF:333); or possibly from Fon *savalu* 'to greet (divinities)' (CA:336).
saravá(r). To dance. *See* sarava.
semá/cemá. Hair. Etymology undetermined.
semá cor de indaro. Blond hair. Portuguese *cor* 'color.' *See* indaro; semá/cemá.
semá de mucota. Mustache. *See* mocota/mucota/micota; semá/cemá.
semá ofú. Black hair. *See* ofú; semá/cemá.
sená/cená/ciamá. Beard. Etymology undetermined.
sengo/sengue/senguê. Forest, green. Kimbundu *sengue* 'forest' (VF:334); Umbundu *senge* 'forest' (A:1258).
sucaná(r). To marry. *See* sucano.
sucano. Marriage, wedding. Kimbundu *ku-sokana* 'to marry' (M:102; VF:334).
sumate. Soup. Etymology undetermined.
suruba. Big party. Possibly from Tupi *surubá* 'good, excellent' (N:607).

T (5 terms)

tamangô. Egg. Etymology undetermined.
tatá. Father, mother, parent. Kimbundu *tata* 'father' (M:458); Kikongo or Kimbundu *taata* 'father, title of honor' (CA:340); Portuguese *tatá* 'dad (infantile form)' (N:616).
tipoquê/chipoquê/chipoque. Bean(s). Kimbundu *kipoke* 'bean' (VF:335); Nhaneca *otuipoke* 'bean' (VF:335); Umbundu *poke* 'bean' (A:1123).
tipune/tipungue/tipungo. Hat. Possibly Kimbundu *kibunga, kibuanga* 'hat' (VF:336).
tunda. Beating. Portuguese *tunda* 'beating' (C:797; N:640).

U (7 terms)

uanjá(r). To cook. Etymology undetermined.
uí. Yes. Etymology undetermined.
uíque. Sugar, sweet, alcohol. Kimbundu *uíki* 'honey' (M:416; VF:337); Kikongo, Kimbundu, or Umbundu *wiki* 'honey, sweet' (CA:347).
umbundu. Black man. Kimbundu *mbundu, mumbundu* 'black' (adj.) (M:440);

Umbundu *mbundu* 'name of the peoples from the high plains of Benguela' (A:700); language of the Ovimbundo people of the former Benguela kingdom (CA:347).

urano. God, heaven. Portuguese *urano* 'heaven' (C:804).

urungo. Vehicle, car. Etymology undetermined.

urungo de omenha. Boat, canoe. See omenha/omeia; urungo.

V (2 terms)

vapora. (Nonsense) discussion. Etymology undetermined.

viango/vinhango. Sugarcane. Possibly from Umbundu *angu* 'hay, herb, straw, wild grass' or Kimbundu *dianga* 'sugarcane' (M:94; VF:339).

X (2 terms)

xaxatá(r). To touch. Etymology undetermined. Possibly related to Kimbundu *xika* 'to touch' (M:613); or possibly related to Kikongo, Kimbundu, or Umbundu *(o)njaya* or Yoruba *ìshaká* 'itch' (CA:258).

ximbado. Drunk. Etymology undetermined. Possibly related to Kimbundu *jimbila* 'to lose' (M:475).

Z (3 terms)

zingrim. Tooth. Etymology undetermined.

zipaque. Money. Possibly from Kimbundu *vipaco* 'gold' (VF:340).

zueira/zoeira. Noise. Kikongo or Kimbundu *zuela* 'to speak a lot' and Portuguese *zoeirar* 'to buzz, make noise' (CA:357).

LEXICAL ANALYSIS

While many Africanisms are present in the Calunga lexicon, there is also a significant influence from Portuguese, a few that are derived from Tupi (or from Língua Geral), and perhaps even a tiny bit of Yoruba. However, it must be underscored that tracking the source languages of Calunga words is not a clear-cut task, which makes a detailed analysis of the lexicon problematic.

That is, as native African languages were uprooted and transplanted to new environments, words underwent varying degrees of phonetic, phonological, morphosyntactic, and semantic changes. Hence any type of lexical analysis of Calunga will present shortcomings and raise further questions regarding the nature of the terms.

With such analytic problems noted, an attempt will be made to examine Calunga terms. First, the terms can be examined according to etymological categories. There are arguably five:

1. *Direct Africanisms.* These terms are typically derived from Bantu languages—Kimbundu, Umbundu, Kikongo—and have basically equivalent meanings in both the African language(s) in question and Calunga.

    curima 'work, job'
    embuá/imbuá 'dog'
    ingomo/ingombe 'ox, cattle'

2. *Metaphoric Africanisms.* These are generally terms that represent similar, but not exactly the same, concepts in the African language(s) in question and Calunga.

    indaro 'fire, yellow, red'
    marafa/marafo 'cachaça, alcoholic drink'
    mavero 'milk, breast, white'

3. *Portuguese.* These terms are derived from Portuguese, often archaic:

    aprumado 'rich, better'
    atuá 'day'
    escutante 'ear'

4. *Hybrid Portuguese-Africanisms.* These periphrastic terms are typically made up of an African language and Portuguese, often with a metaphoric meaning.

amparo de curiá(r) 'fork'
aprumá(r) banzo 'to have sex'
camano maioral 'man of respect, boss'

5. *Tupi-derived* (or *Língua Geral*) *terms*. This lesser category includes lexical items in Calunga derived directly from either Tupi or Língua Geral (or possibly indirectly from the local dialect of Brazilian Portuguese that acquired them from Tupi or Língua Geral).

guaxaúna 'squash'
ingazeiro 'penis'

Second, Calunga lexical items pertain particularly to a category labeled "vocabulário de especialidade" (specialty vocabulary) by Bonvini (2008b:117–20). Different from a "vocabulário comum" (common vocabulary), which is open and unlimited by nature, a vocabulário de especialidade is limited, specific, and exclusive to a given speech community, often with a strong sense of intergroup identity. A typical example is Afro-Brazilian liturgical languages; cryptolects also fit these criteria. Bonvini (120) explains, "Os vocabulários de especialidade . . . [são] essencialmente unidades lexicais completas, que pertencem exclusivamente às línguas africanas empregadas nesses cultos ou nessas comunidades de descendentes de escravos, qualquer que seja seu estatuto lingüístico específico. O funcionamento dessas línguas, com forte valor identitário, permanece paralelo ao da língua portuguesa, que é considerada como se situando num espaço ao mesmo tempo exterior e diferente." (The specialty vocabularies . . . [are] essentially complete lexical units, which pertain exclusively to African languages used in these cults or in these communities of slave descendants whatever may be their specific linguistic stature. The function of these languages, with a strong sense of identity, remains parallel to the Portuguese language, which is considered situated in an exterior and different space at the same time.) On par with Bonvini's definition of vocabulário de especialidade, calungadores typically do not engage in lengthy conversations about daily topics in Calunga; instead, it is usually reserved for a number of select topics (see semantic categories below).

In a similar vein to Bonvini's vocabulário de especialidade is Queiroz's (1998:104–5) analysis of Língua do Negro da Costa as a "língua especial"

(special language). According to her analysis, this type of phenomenon within Afro-Brazilian speech communities is known as "lexical Africanization," which serves the purposes of a "secret language" and re-creates a remote past of a "mythical Africa" where slaves were in control of their destiny. She further argues that this "special language" shows a grammaticalization toward Portuguese—an "aportuguesamento gramatical"—and a lexicalization toward Africanisms—an "africanização lexical" (104).

Castro (2001:125) offers a similar analysis in her research on different levels of African influence in Brazilian speech (from Afro-Bahian liturgical language to popular Bahian Portuguese to Brazilian Portuguese in general), arguing that there occurred a "double interaction" of an "africanização do português" (Africanization of Portuguese) and an "aportuguesamento dos africanismos" ("Portuguesement" of Africanisms).

In terms of some noteworthy semantic categories—following Bonvini's vocabulário de especialidade—Calunga terms roughly fall into certain categories toward which calungadores direct their conversations. The most prominent category is related to "cowboy terms" (i.e., tropeiros): that is, almost all calungadores interviewed were tropeiros who would speak Calunga during their cattle drives. Even one meaning of the word *Calunga* is an 'auxiliary boy on the wagons and automobiles of cargo transportation' (see *calunga* in the glossary on the previous pages). Other collected terms fit more or less into some of the following semantic categories:

1. **Verbs**[3]

   aprumá(r) 'to do, make, happen'
   assungá(r) 'to come, leave'
   bungulá(r) 'to jump'
   cafangá(r) 'to leave'
   calungá(r) 'to talk (Calunga)'
   cubá(r) 'to do, make, arrange'
   cuciá(r) 'to dawn, wake up'
   cupiá(r)/copiá(r) 'to understand'
   curimá(r) 'to work'
   curirá(r) 'to cry'
   curitá(r) 'to sing'
   desaprumá(r) 'to undo'
   engonhá(r) 'to save time'
   gudunhá(r) 'to take, grab'
   ingugiá(r) 'to keep watch'
   orirá(r) 'to sing'
   quimimbá(r)/quimbimbá(r) 'to die'
   quinhamá(r) 'to walk, travel'
   saravá(r) 'to dance'
   sucaná(r) 'to marry'
   uanjá(r) 'to cook'
   xaxatá(r) 'to touch'

2. Tropeiro (cowboy)

angora 'horse'
berrida 'running'
buraco/buraca 'bag'
cuciá(r) 'to dawn'
cumbaca 'city, village'
curriola 'group'
faim 'knife'
ganga 'boss, owner'
imberela 'meat'
imbuá de sengo 'wolf'
indaro 'fire'
inglaterra 'region, land'
ingomo/ingombe 'ox, cattle'
kimbo 'city, town, village'
mangonheiro 'swindler'
marangola 'horse, donkey'
mavero 'milk'
mocó 'arm, weapon, knife'
muxito 'forest'
niguciê de sengo 'jaguar'
omenha/omeia 'water, region'
orofim 'firewood'

3. Food and drink

amparo de curiá 'fork'
aprumar curiá 'to eat'
atindundu 'wine'
camboque 'cheese'
chia 'butter'
chipoquê/chipoque/ tipoquê 'bean'
curiá(r) 'to eat, food'
faim 'knife'
gatuvira 'coffee'
imbuete 'piece of bread, club, stick'
injequê 'corn, popcorn'
jinguba 'peanut'
madubim 'peanut'
mafuim/mapuim 'flour'
maiaca 'seed'
malara 'orange (fruit)'
malombo/malumbim 'fruit'
marafa 'cachaça, alcoholic drink'
marafa de uíque 'beer'
marafa de vinhango 'cachaça'
massa de camboque 'cheese bread'
massango/ massongo/ massuango 'rice'
moca 'coffee'
mongo/mungo/ mungue 'salt'
omenha de mavero 'milk'
orogongi 'egg'
pixiê 'food'
sumate 'soup'
tamangô 'egg'
uanjá(r) 'to cook'
uíque 'sugar, sweet'

4. Flora and fauna

cauba 'jaguar'
duque 'insect'
gamboa 'bird'
imberela de omenha 'fish'
imbuá 'dog'
incaca 'armadillo'
inharra 'snake'
lorri 'fish'
marangó 'donkey'
marangola 'horse, donkey'
mufete 'fish'
niguciê 'cat'
niguciê de sengo 'jaguar'
periá 'rabbit'

puco 'rat'

quijongo 'cricket'

quimboto 'toad'

quiombô 'wild pig'

sanjo/sanjô/sanja 'chicken, hen'

sengo/sengue/senguê 'forest, green'

viango/vinhango 'sugar cane'

5. People and relationships

aprumar banzo 'to have sex'

arangá 'son of a single mother'

banzo 'sexual relation'

camanim 'boy'

camano 'man, he, person'

camano-cá 'I, me'

camano cafamo 'white man'

camano desaprumado 'fool, stupid man'

camano maioral 'man of respect, boss'

camano ôa 'bad man'

camano ofú 'black man'

candando 'hug'

candango 'bad person, bandit'

cangundo 'mischievous person'

cueto 'companion'

dandara/dandará 'child'

dandará santo 'newly born'

dandará ofú 'black child'

dandarazim 'toddler'

exoa 'foolish'

ganga 'boss, owner'

guriô 'father'

imabe 'mischievous person'

malungo 'brother, equal, same'

mangonheiro 'swindler, mischievous person'

matumba 'foolish'

ocai/ocaia/ocaio 'woman'

ocai de banzo 'prostitute'

ocai ofú 'black woman'

ocai santo 'virgin, single woman'

ocaizim 'girl'

odara 'pretty'

otaca/otata 'father'

quicumbi 'young person'

quissanda 'mischievous woman'

quitata 'prostitute'

6. Human body and clothing

amera 'face'

amparo de cupia 'hat, cap'

amparo de mirante 'glasses'

amparo de omenha 'umbrella'

buraco de duana 'shirt pocket'

buraco de nanga 'pant pocket'

cafuim 'curly hair'

caixinha de semá (cemá) 'vagina'

caputo 'blind'

cemá 'hair'

conena 'anus, butt, excrement'

cupia/cupiá 'head'

cutá 'ear'

desaprumado 'bad, sick'

duana 'shirt, coat'

duana cafamo 'clear, white shirt'

duana imbuno 'dark shirt'

duana indaro 'yellow, red shirt'

duana mavero 'white shirt'

duana ofú 'black shirt'

duana sengo 'green shirt'

ganzipe 'penis'

inhoto 'bone'

jifeto 'grimace'

lubra 'chest'

macura 'fat (noun)'

mataco 'buttocks'

mavero 'milk, breast, white'

milongo 'medicine'

mirante 'eye'

monzape 'hand'

muchinga 'nose'

mucota/micota 'mouth'

muxima 'heart'

nanga 'clothes, pants'

nanga cafamo 'clear clothes'

nanga imbuno 'dark clothes'

nanga mavero 'white clothes'

nanga sengo 'green clothes'

opô 'eye'

pandú 'stomach'

ponto de mirante 'eye'

ponto de poente 'nose'

ponto pisante 'foot'

quindú 'fat' (adj.)

quinhama/quinhamba 'leg'

semá (cemá) 'hair'

semá cor de indaro 'blond hair'

semá de mucota 'mustache'

semá ofú 'black hair'

sená (cená/ciamá) 'beard'

tipune/tipungue/tipungo 'hat'

zingrim 'tooth'

7. Work and money

adufe 'baker'

aprumado 'rich, better'

camano maioral 'man of respect, boss'

curima 'work, job'

curimá(r) 'to work'

ganga 'boss, owner'

ingugiá(r) 'to keep watch'

injó de zipaque 'bank'

kimbo 'city, town, village'

kukiá(r) 'to dawn, wake up'

zipaque 'money'

8. Festivities and social life

ariranha 'cigarette, smoke'

atindundu 'wine'

bacuri 'sound, music, box'

curriola 'group'

injó de marafo 'bar'

marafa(o) de uíque 'beer'

marafa(o) de vinhango 'cachaça'

ocai de banzo 'prostitute'

omenha de vinhango 'cachaça'

orirá(r) 'to sing'

quissanda 'mischievous woman'

quitata 'prostitute'

quizumba 'party, mess, confusion'

sarava 'dance'

saravá 'good-bye'

sucano 'marriage, wedding'

suruba 'big party'

ximbado 'drunk'

Third, it is perhaps most interesting to compare and contrast Calunga terms with lexical items documented in other Afro-Brazilian speech communities. For such a lexical comparison, six documented varieties of Afro-Brazilian speech are presented in table 5.1 (pp. 149–65). The basis of the selected terms (i.e., the left-hand column) originates from Calunga. Terms that demonstrate similarities (and differences) in form and meaning to the Calunga terms were then selected from across a spectrum of Afro-Brazilian speech communities in Minas Gerais, São Paulo, and Bahia. The lexical comparison shows that Bantu languages—particularly Kimbundu, Umbundu, and Kikongo—provided lexical items to various forms of Afro-Brazilian speech found throughout the southeast region of Brazil and in the northeastern state of Bahia. It is not known whether such lexical items were introduced via "pure" forms of African languages or via more "corrupted" forms (i.e., pidginized, creolized, or intertwined varieties). It should be noted, however, that none of the selected terms were found to correspond to the eighteenth-century Mina-Jeje language of Ouro Preto, which is understandable given that 82 percent of Mina-Jeje words are derived from Fon (Castro 2002:68–69).[4]

In general, the lexical items from table 5.1 seem to provide some evidence of varieties of African languages or Afro-Brazilian languages that were formerly widespread in the southeastern and northeastern regions of Brazil (see map 1). This makes sense if we take into account that, during Brazil's colonial period, many African- and Brazilian-born slaves were transported to Minas Gerais from major slave ports on the coast, namely from Bahia, Rio de Janeiro, and São Paulo. This might be one conceivable explanation for similar terms being found across a vast geography. That said, given the ample uncertainty about what Africans and African descendants spoke during Brazil's colonial period, no solid conclusions can be reached. But the similarities do provide some evidence of the types of African languages spoken (and still somewhat maintained) in these regions of Brazil and the subsequent linguistic changes they underwent.

As African languages were uprooted and transplanted into a new environment, African lexical items were subject to grammatical and semantic changes. Bonvini and Petter (1998:72) rightly question whether one can really affirm that the African terms that took root in Brazil have the same form and meaning as in Africa (see their quotation at the beginning of this chapter). Even though Bonvini and Petter raise a valid point, it must be noted that the words in table 5.1 generally *did maintain* their original meanings from the African source languages (though there are some exceptions: e.g., *amera, angora, calunga*).

In terms of form, the Africanisms in Brazil underwent morphosyntactic and phonetic/phonological changes. To understand this process, in Bantu languages there is a division of nouns into nominal classes—numbering between ten and twenty—that varies depending on the language in question (Castro 2001:32; Wald 1990:1000). These classes are prefixes that precede the noun stem. Observe, for instance, Swahili with *-ndu* 'place' as the noun stem: *pa-ndu* 'at a place,' *ku-ndu* 'around a place,' *mu-ndu* 'inside a place' (Wald 1990:1001). Furthermore, Bantu languages typically employ phonemic high and low tones (Wald 1990:998). But such characteristics of Bantu phonology and morphology were lost in Brazil, and words were instead reinterpreted as single lexical units. An excellent example of this process can be observed in a word documented by Machado Filho (1943/1985:134): *quimbundo* 'black person,' derived from the word *kimbundu*. In its original sense the Bantu prefix *ki-* denotes the language of the *mbundu* people. However, in Dialeto crioulo sanjoanense the word has been reinterpreted as a sole lexical unit whose meaning has been generalized to designate anyone of African descent. Similarly, in Calunga the term *umbundu* 'black man'—the original meaning being the language of the Ovimbundu people—has also come to designate any man of African descent. Lastly, in some instances there are several pronunciations for a single term across the Afro-Brazilian speech communities—or even within the same speech community (observe, for example, *chipoquê* 'bean(s)' and *coteque* 'night')—which demonstrates how African phonological and morphosyntactic elements underwent what Castro (2001:125) and Queiroz (1998:104) call "aportuguesamento." Also of particular interest is the way Calunga lexical items have phonologically altered—and orthographically represented—Bantu prenasal stops with prothetic vowels following Portuguese phonological patterns: Bantu *mbua* 'dog' > Calunga *embuá* [ẽ^m.bu.'a] or *imbuá* [ĩ^m.bu.'a] 'dog'; Bantu *ngoma* 'drum' > Calunga *nagoma* [nã.'gõ.ma] 'drum' (see chapter 6).

It is further worth noting that the African languages themselves may have undergone processes of dialect leveling since some are more or less mutually intelligible. For instance, Kikongo and Kimbundu were described in the late sixteenth century as being as similar as Spanish and Portuguese;

Umbundu being less similar but with "strong convergences" in vocabulary and grammar to Kikongo and Kimbundu (Thornton 2006:95). As such, a possible koine variety may have formed among speakers of such languages in Africa and/or in Brazil.

The selected words in table 5.1 are largely of Bantu origin—particularly Kimbundu, Umbundu, and Kikongo—that have been altered in varying degrees from their source languages. However, as discussed previously, in many instances it is difficult to know for certain which may have been the actual source language. That is, is the etymology from Kimbundu, Umbundu, or Kikongo? Or is the lexical item the result of some leveled form of those languages? And how much "aportuguesamento" occurred with the item in question? Moreover, in some instances there are variations for a single term, sometimes even within a single speech community (e.g., *angora* 'horse,' *chipoquê* 'bean'). Why is this? Such questions can yield perhaps only tentative answers but are nevertheless worth raising in order to spur discussion regarding the dynamics at play.

The lexical items in table 5.1 move from left to right in a "west to east" scheme (i.e., from the Brazilian interior to the coastal regions): the first four are Afro-Brazilian speech communities from Minas Gerais, followed by São Paulo, and finally Bahia (which is the farthest geographically from Calunga). The table concludes on the right-hand side with a tentative etymological examination. Excluding the etymological column, there are 236 words in the table (minus variations within a single term), with 66 total terms from Calunga. Although not much should be read into the numbers, nor is it an objective here to engage in statistical analysis, it should be noted that 82 percent of the sample can possibly be traced to Bantu languages from the Congo/Angola region, with the remaining 18 percent of another origin or of undetermined origin.[5] Of further note is that Cafundó had the most terms similar to Calunga, with 42; Undaca de Quimbundo was second with 38, Língua do Negro da Costa was third with 36, Dialeto crioulo sanjoanense was fourth with 31, and lastly was Falares africanos na Bahia with 23. While there are many blanks in the table where lexical equivalents were not found in the respective speech community, eight terms had documented varieties in all the Afro-Brazilian speech communities: *curima* 'work,' *embuá* 'dog,' *ganga* 'boss, owner,' *indaro* 'fire,' *ingomo* 'ox, cattle,' *injó* 'house,' *tatá* 'father,' and *uíque* 'sweet.' For sources cited in the table, refer to the abbreviations list that precedes the notes.

The Calunga Lexicon

Table 5.1. Comparison of lexical items documented in Afro-Brazilian speech communities of Minas Gerais, São Paulo, and Bahia

Calunga	Língua do Negro da Costa	Dialeto crioulo sanjoanense	Undaca de Quimbundo	Cupópia of Cafundó	Falares africanos na Bahia	Etymology
afochê 'shotgun'				afoché 'shotgun' (VF: 285)		Undetermined
amera 'face'		omerá 'tongue' (MF:133)				Umbundu omela 'mouth' (J:355); Umbundu mela 'mouth' (A:717; VF:293)
angora 'horse'; marangola 'horse, donkey'	arongó, arangome, aranguão, ingora, orongó, orangó, orongome 'horse' (Q:125, 131)	ongoró 'horse' (MF:133)	orangôlo, n'goro 'horse' (DF:77)			Kimbundu n'golo 'zebra' (VF:309); Umbundu n'golo 'zebra' (A:946); Umbundu oñgolo 'zebra' (J:359)
bambi 'cold'	bambi 'cold' (Q:113)	mbambe 'cold' (MF:132)	mbambe 'cold' (DF:74)		bambi 'cold' (LS) (CA:167)	Kimbundu mbambi 'cold' (M:314; VF:289); Umbundu mbambi 'cold' (A:657); Kikongo, Kimbundu, Umbundu (o)mbambi 'cold' (CA:167)

Calunga	Língua do Negro da Costa	Dialeto crioulo sanjoanense	Undaca de Quimbundo	Cupópia of Cafundó	Falares africanos na Bahia	Etymology
banga 'charm'		mbanga 'penis' (MF:132)				Kikongo banga 'dear' (LA:18); Umbundu mbanga 'intelligent, knowledge' (A:664)
calunga 'speech, talk'		calunga 'sea,' which is sung in the vissungos with various meanings, though 'sea' is the original meaning (MF:127–29)	calunga 'sea, death' (DF:74)		calunga 'sea' (LS), 'salve (hooray)' (LS), 'ornament' (LP), 'small rat' (BA), 'helper or carrier of the carriage' (BR) (CA:192–93)	Castro (2001:192–93) presents six options for the origin and meaning of the term; the sixth option argues that calunga came from either Kikongo, Kimbundu, or Umbundu kalongela > kalonga, with the meaning 'helper or carrier of the carriage' in Brazil.
camboque 'cheese'	aiaque, aiato 'cheese' (Q:112)					Etymology undetermined
camanim 'boy'	camonim, camona, camone 'child' (Q:115)		camoná 'boy, son' (DF:75)	camanaco 'boy' (VF:292)		Kimbundu muana, mona 'son, daughter' or kamona 'of the son' (VF:292)

Calunga	Língua do Negro da Costa	Dialeto crioulo sanjoanense	Undaca de Quimbundo	Cupópia of Cafundó	Falares africanos na Bahia	Etymology
chicongo 'shadow'		quipungo 'hat' (MF:134)	pungo, tipungo 'hat' (DF:78, 79)	chicongo, chipango 'hat' (VF:296)	pungo 'hat, cap' (LS) (CA:318)	Kimbundu pungo or tipungo 'hat' (VF:296); Kikongo mpongu 'hat, cap' (CA:318)
chipoquê, chipoque, tipoquê 'bean(s)'	tipoque, tiproque, tipoquê, tipoquero 'bean' (Q:135)		tipoquê 'bean' (DF:79)	chipoquê 'bean' (VF:296)		Kimbundu kipoke 'bean' (VF:335); Umbundu poke 'bean' (A:1123)
conena 'anus, butt, excrement'	conema 'feces' (Q:117)			conena 'anus'; conenar 'to defecate' (VF:297)	cunema, cunena 'to defecate' (LS) (CA:215)	Kikongo or Kimbundu kunena 'to defecate' (CA:215; M:167; VF:297)
cueto 'companion'	cuete 'man' (Q:119)	ucuêto, vacueto, acuêto 'companion' (MF:135)	ocuêto 'man, monkey' (DF:77)			Kimbundu ukueto 'companion' (M:128); Umbundu kwetu, ukwetu 'friend, companion' (A:451)
curirá(r) 'to cry'				curirar 'to cry' (VF:302)		Kimbundu ku-dila, ku-didila, kulila, kuririla 'to cry' (M:115; VF:302)

CHAPTER FIVE

Calunga	Língua do Negro da Costa	Dialeto crioulo sanjoanense	Undaca de Quimbundo	Cupópia of Cafundó	Falares africanos na Bahia	Etymology
coteque 'night'	*oteque, conteque* 'night' (Q:132)	*otequê* 'day' (MF:134)	*otecame, otéque* 'night' (DF:77)	*téqui, otéqui* 'night' (VF:335); *oturo* 'night' (VF:328)		Umbundu *teke, uteke* 'night' (A:1447)
cumba 'time, hour, sun'	*cumba, pumba* 'sun' (Q:120)	*ucumbi* 'sun' (MF:91)	*cumbe* 'light, fire'; *cumbe de uanja* 'sun' (lit. 'light of day'); *cumbe de otecame* 'moon' (lit. 'light of night') (DF:75)	*cumbe* 'sun' (VF:300)		Kimbundu *kumbi* 'sun, light, hour'; Umbundu *ekumbi* 'sun' (M:584; VF:300); Umbundu *kumbi* 'sun, hour, day' (A:398)
cumbaca 'city, village'	*cumbara, incumbara* 'city' (Q:120)	*combaro* 'inhabited place' (MF:130)	*cumbara* 'city' (DF:75)		*cumbara* 'city' (LS) (CA:215)	Kikongo *kumbanda* 'city' (CA:215); Kimbundu *kimbaka* 'city' (M:116); Kimbundu *ku-mbara* 'in the village' (VF:300)
curiá 'food'	*curiá(r)* 'to eat'; *cureio, cureia curei* 'food' (Q:120)	*curiar* 'to eat'; *curiacuca* 'chef' (*curiar* + *cuca* 'old, ugly woman') (MF:130)	*curiá* 'to eat' (DF:75)		*cuniá, curiá* 'to eat' (LS) (CA:215)	Kimbundu *kudia, kuria* 'to eat, food' (M:127; VF:301); Kikongo, Kimbundu *kudiá* 'to eat' (CA:215); Umbundu *kulya* 'to eat, food' (A:396)

The Calunga Lexicon 153

Calunga	Língua do Negro da Costa	Dialeto crioulo sanjoanense	Undaca de Quimbundo	Cupópia of Cafundó	Falares africanos na Bahia	Etymology
curima 'work, job'	curimba, curimbo, curima, curimo 'work' (Q:121)	curima 'service' (MF:130)	curimá 'service, work' (DF:75)	curimar 'to work, to pray' (VF:301)	curimá 'to work' (LS) (CA:215)	Kikongo kutima 'to work,' Kimbundu kudima 'to work,' Umbundu okulima 'to work' (CA:215); Kimbundu kudima, kurima 'to work' (VF:301)
duque 'insect'			duque 'insect' (VF:303)			Possibly related to Kikongo vuku, vuka 'insect' (M:362; VF:303)
embuá, imbuá 'dog'	cambuá 'dog' (Q:114)	omboá 'dog' (MF:133)	m'boá 'dog' (DF:76)	arambeca, arambuá 'dog' (VF:288)	imbuá 'dog' (LS) (CA:252)	Kimbundu or Kikongo imbua, mbua 'dog' (M:97); Kikongo mbw 'dog' (B:62); Umbundu mbwa 'dog' (A:706); Kikongo, Kimbundu mbwa 'dog' or Umbundu ombwa 'dog' (CA:252)
frize 'axe'				frize 'axe' (VF:305)		Etymology undetermined

Calunga	Língua do Negro da Costa	Dialeto crioulo sanjoanense	Undaca de Quimbundo	Cupópia of Cafundó	Falares africanos na Bahia	Etymology
ganga 'boss, owner'	inganga 'priest' (Q:125)	angananzambi 'god' (MF:121); nganga, uganga 'priest' (MF:132)	unganga 'god, priest, missionary' (DF:79)	ganga inganan- zambe 'god, saint' (VF:309)	ganga 'boss, priest, seer' (LS) (CA:40) ganga 'boss, priest, seer' (LS) (CA:40)	Kikongo, Kimbundu nganga or Umbundu oganga 'boss' (CA:240)
gatuvira 'coffee'	cajuvira 'coffee' (Q:113)		tiuvira, kiuvira 'coffee' (DF:79)			Etymology undeter- mined
guaxaúna 'squash'				guaxaúna 'squash' (VF: 307)		Possibly from Tupi (see C:399 for related flora and fauna Tupi morphemes with guax-)
imberela 'meat'	camberela, camberelo, timbere, timberéia 'meat' (Q:114)			camberéra 'meat' (DF:74)		Kimbundu camberera 'meat' (VF:293); possibly related to Umbundu mbe 'sheep, goat' (A:668)
imbuete 'piece of bread, club, stick'	imbuete 'tree, wood, stick, penis' (Q:124)			imbuele 'stick, wood, tree' (VF:308)		Umbundu mbweti 'staff, club, stick, wood' (A:712)

The Calunga Lexicon   155

Calunga	Língua do Negro da Costa	Dialeto crioulo sanjoanense	Undaca de Quimbundo	Cupópia of Cafundó	Falares africanos na Bahia	Etymology
imbuno 'dark' (see also umbundu)			quimbundo 'black' (DF:78) (from Kimbundu, language of the Mbundu)	nimbi 'black' (VF:324)		Kimbundu mbundu, mumbundu 'black' (adj.) (M:440); Umbundu imbundu 'the Bundos—name of the peoples from the high plains of Benguela' (A:700)
incaca 'armadillo'				incaca 'armadillo' (VF:308)		Kikongo nkaka 'anteater' (B:378)
indaro 'fire, yellow, red'	anduro 'fire, gold'; unde 'sun' (Q:137)	ondara 'fire' (MF: 121, 133)	andaro, undáro, undarú 'fire' (DF:74, 79)	andaru 'fire' (VF:287)	undaro 'fire' (LS) (CA:347)	Kikongo ndalu 'fire' (CA:347); Kimbundu ndalu 'fire' or Umbundu ondalu 'fire' (VF:287); Umbundu ndalu 'fire, inferno' (A:813–14)
ingomo, ingombe 'ox, cattle'	gombê 'ox' (Q:122)	ngombe 'ox' (MF:132); orongombe 'ox' (MF:133)	orongome, orongombe, 'ox' (DF:77)	ingombe 'ox, cow' (VF:309)	ingombe 'ox, cattle' (LS) (CA:254)	Kikongo, Kimbundu, Umbundu (o)ngombe 'ox, cattle' (CA:254); Kimbundu ngombe 'ox, cow' (J:370, VF:309); Umbundu ngombe 'ox, cow' (A:948)

Calunga	Língua do Negro da Costa	Dialeto crioulo sanjoanense	Undaca de Quimbundo	Cupópia of Cafundó	Falares africanos na Bahia	Etymology
ingrimo 'tooth, teeth'; *zingrim* 'tooth, teeth'				*ingrime* 'drunk, tooth, teeth' (VF:309)		Etymology undetermined
inharra 'snake'		*nhorrã* 'snake' (MF:132)	*inhofa* 'snake' (DF:75)		*nhoca, quinioca* 'snake, serpent' (LP) (CA:326)	Kikongo or Kimbundu *(ki)nyoka* 'snake' (CA:326); Kimbundu *nhoka, njíua* 'snake' (M:121); Umbundu *ñoha* 'snake (of any species), serpent' (A:984)
inhoto 'bone'				*inhoto* 'bone' (VF:309)		Nhaneca *ontho* 'leg bone' (VF:309)
injequê 'corn, popcorn'	*jequê, injequê, jiquê, jiqui, onjequê* 'bag, belly, mouth' (Q:126)	*onjequê* 'corn' (MF:133)	*indiequê* 'small bag' (DF:75)	*injequê* 'bag, receptacle, cup, bowl' (VF:310)		Etymology undetermined

The Calunga Lexicon   157

Calunga	Língua do Negro da Costa	Dialeto crioulo sanjoanense	Undaca de Quimbundo	Cupópia of Cafundó	Falares africanos na Bahia	Etymology
injó 'house'	conjolo, conjor, conjô, canjolo 'house' (Q:118)	onjó 'house, ranch' (MF:133)	injó, undió 'house' (DF:75)	injó 'house' (VF:310)	injó, unzó 'house' (LS) (CA:254, 348)	Kikongo nzo (B:111; VF:310); Kimbundu inzo, njo 'house' (M:102); Umbundu ndjo 'house' (A:857); Kikongo, Kimbundu, Umbundu (o)nzo 'house' (CA:348)
jamba 'diamond'		jambá 'gold' (MF:131)				Etymology undetermined
lorri 'fish'	orufim, orufino, ourofino, urufim 'fish' (Q:131)		orossi, uruxi 'fish' (DF:77, 79)			Possibly Umbundu loyi 'bagre eléctrico (a type of fish)' (A:565); or possibly Nhaneca ohi 'fish' (VF:312)
malara 'orange (fruit)'				malara 'orange (fruit)' (VF:314)	malala 'orange (fruit)' (LS) (CA:272)	Kimbundu malalanza 'orange tree' (M:384; VF:314); Kikongo or Kimbundu malala < Portuguese laranja 'orange' (CA:272)

Calunga	Língua do Negro da Costa	Dialeto crioulo sanjoanense	Undaca de Quimbundo	Cupópia of Cafundó	Falares africanos na Bahia	Etymology
malungo 'brother, equal, same'		malungo 'of the same age' (MF:139)			malungo 'companion, brother in the same boat' (LS); 'black companion embarking from Africa (archaic)' (LP) (CA:273)	Kimbundu malungo 'companion, comrade, of the same condition, adopted brother' (N:396; VF:315); Kikongo or Kimbundu nkwanlugo 'companion, brother in the same boat' (CA:273)
mambi 'needle'				mambi 'needle, thread, knife' (VF:315)		Possibly related to Umbundu mbambo 'nail, peg' (A:658)
massango, massongo, massuango 'rice'	assangue, assango, assengue, imassango, missangue 'rice' (Q:112)		massango 'rice' (DF:76)	massango, massongo, massuango 'rice' (VF:317)		Kimbundu masangu 'corn, cereal' or Kikongo ma-nsangu 'corn' (M:109, 422; VF:317)

The Calunga Lexicon 159

Calunga	Língua do Negro da Costa	Dialeto crioulo sanjoanense	Undaca de Quimbundo	Cupópia of Cafundó	Falares africanos na Bahia	Etymology
mavero 'milk, breast, white'	*mavera, mavero, mavelo, maverda, avera, avero, avelo, aver* 'milk, breast' (Q:128)		*mavéro* 'milk' (DF:76)	*avero* 'milk' (VF:289)		Kimbundu *mele* 'breasts, milk,' the plural form of *diele* and *avele* (VF:318); Umbundu *vele* 'breast, teat, milk' (A:1651); Umbundu *omavele* or Kimbundu *mavele*, both plural forms of *avele* 'milk' (M:387)
moca 'coffee'				*moca* 'coffee' (VF:318)		*Moca*, a port known for coffee exportation (C:526; N:421)
mocó 'arm, weapon, knife'	*moco, moque, muque, muco* 'tool, weapon' (Q:128)		*mocó* 'knife' (DF:76)			Umbundu *moko* 'knife, machete' (A:733)

Calunga	Língua do Negro da Costa	Dialeto crioulo sanjoanense	Undaca de Quimbundo	Cupópia of Cafundó	Falares africanos na Bahia	Etymology
mongo, mungo, mungue 'salt'		omungá 'salt' (MF:133)	mongo 'salt' (DF:76)	mungo 'salt' (VF:321)	mongo, mungo 'salt' (LS) (CA:288, 293)	Kikongo or Kimbundu mungu, mungwa 'salt' (CA:293); Kimbundu mongua, mungua 'salt' (M:558; VF:321); Umbundu mongwa 'salt' (A:741)
muchinga 'nose'				muchinga 'nose' (VF:320)		Kimbundu muxinga 'end, extremity' (VF:320)
murrudo 'big, strong, powerful'	uarrufo, uarrufa, arrufo, uarrubo, arrubo 'strong, powerful' (Q:136)					Possibly from Kimbundu mundundu 'big' (M:328, VF:321); or possibly Portuguese murro 'fist' (N:431)
nanga 'clothes, pants'	urunanga, urundanga, arunanga, arundanga 'clothes' (Q:137)	oronanga 'clothes' (MF:133)	oronanga 'clothes' (DF:77); urunanga 'pants' (DF:79)	nanga 'leaf, skin, feather, clothes' (VF:322)		Kimbundu nanga 'cloth' or Umbundu onanga 'clothes' (VF:322)
nhoto 'skinny, thin' (see also inhoto)				nhoto 'skinny, hard' (VF:324)		Nhaneca ontho 'leg bone' (VF:309)

The Calunga Lexicon

Calunga	Língua do Negro da Costa	Dialeto crioulo sanjoanense	Undaca de Quimbundo	Cupópia of Cafundó	Falares africanos na Bahia	Etymology
niguciê 'cat'	*mingüé* 'cat, jaguar' (Q:128)					Possibly related to Kimbundu *ngatu* 'cat' (derived from Portuguese) and/or to Kimbundu *kisue* or *kisuéia* 'cat' (M:322)
ocai, ocaia, ocaio 'woman'	*ocaia, ocaio, caio* 'woman' (Q:129)		*ocaia* 'woman' (DF:77)		*ocáia* 'concubine, lover' (PS) (CA:300)	Kimbundu *ucai* 'woman' (VF:325); Umbundu *ukãyi* 'woman, wife' (A:291)
omenha, omeia 'water, region'	*omenha, omém* 'water, rain, urine, blood' (Q:130)	*omenhá, menhá* 'water' (MF:133)	*omenha* 'water, lake, swamp, wet' (DF:77)		*menha* 'water, stream' (LS) (CA:282)	Kimbundu *menha* 'water' (M:22); Kimbundu *menya* 'water' (CA:282)
orofim 'firewood'				*orofim* 'firewood' (VF:326)		Etymology undetermined
otaca, otata 'father'	*tata, otata* 'father' (Q:133)	*otata* 'father' (MF:134)	*tatá* 'father' (DF:79)	*tata* 'father' (VF:334)	*tata, tatá* 'father,' title of respect (PS) (CA:340)	Kikongo or Kimbundu *taata* 'father,' title of respect (CA:340); Kimbundu *tata* 'father' (M:458)

Calunga	Língua do Negro da Costa	Dialeto crioulo sanjoanense	Undaca de Quimbundo	Cupópia of Cafundó	Falares africanos na Bahia	Etymology
quimboto 'toad'		quimboto 'toad' (MF:134)		quimboto 'toad' (LP) (CA:325)		Kikongo (ki)bototo 'large toad' (CA:325); Kimbundu kimboto '(African) frog' (VF:331)
quinhama, quinhamba 'leg'	tinhame, quiname 'leg' (Q:133)		quinhama, vinhama 'foot' (DF:78)	quinamba 'leg, foot' (VF:331)	quinama, inama 'foot, leg, paws' (LS) (CA:252, 325)	Kikongo or Kimbundu kinama 'leg, paw' (CA:252); Kimbundu kinama 'leg' (M:478)
periá 'rabbit'				periá 'rabbit' (VF:329)		Etymology undetermined
puco 'rat'		npuco 'rat' (MF:133)				Kikongo mpuku 'rat' (B:172); Kimbundu puku 'rat' (J:371, M:524)
sanjo, sanjô, sanja 'chicken, hen'		orossanje, ossange 'hen' (MF:133)	ossange 'bird, chick,' ossange-ocaia 'hen' (lit. 'chick-woman'), ossange-ocuêto 'rooster' (lit. 'chick-man') (DF:77, 78)	sanje 'bird' (VF:332); sanjo 'chicken, hen' (VF:333)		Kimbundu sanji 'hen' (M:320); Umbundu sandji 'hen' (A:1217)

Calunga	Língua do Negro da Costa	Dialeto crioulo sanjoanense	Undaca de Quimbundo	Cupópia of Cafundó	Falares africanos na Bahia	Etymology
sengo sengue, senguê 'forest, green'	sengue, sengo 'forest' (Q:133)	senguê 'forest' (MF:135)	ossenguê, senge 'forest' (DF:77, 79)	sengue 'forest' (VF:334)		Kimbundu sengue 'forest' (VF:334); Umbundu senge 'forest' (A:1258)
sucaná(r) 'to marry'; sucanado 'married'	cassucará(r) 'to marry'; cassucarado, sucarado 'married' (Q:116)					Kimbundu ku-sokana 'to marry' (M:102; VF:334)
tatá 'father, mother, parent' (see also otaca)	tata, otata 'father' (Q:133)	otata 'father' (MF:134)	tatá 'father' (DF:133)	tata 'father' (VF:334)	tata, tatá 'father,' title of respect (PS) (CA:340)	Kikongo or Kimbundu taata 'father,' title of respect (CA:340); Kimbundu tata 'father' (M:458)
uíque 'sugar, sweet, alcohol'	uíque, uígue 'sugar, sweet' (Q:136)	oique rapadura 'hard sugar' (MF:133)	uique 'sugar, sweet' (DF:79)	uíque 'sweet, sugar' (VF:337)	uíque 'honey, sugar, sweet' (LS) (CA:347)	Kikongo, Kimbundu, or Umbundu wiki 'honey, sweet' (CA:347); Kimbundu uíki 'honey' (M:416, VF:337)

Calunga	Língua do Negro da Costa	Dialeto crioulo sanjoanense	Undaca de Quimbundo	Cupópia of Cafundó	Falares africanos na Bahia	Etymology
viango, vinhango 'sugarcane'	*vianjê* 'sugarcane' (Q:137)		*vienguê* 'sugarcane' (DF:80)			Possibly Umbundu *angu* 'hay, herb, straw, wild grass' or Kimbundu *dianga* 'sugarcane' (M:94; VF:339)
umbundu 'black man' (see also *imbuno*)				*vimbundo* 'black' (VF:339)		Kimbundu *mbundu, mumbundu* 'black' (adj.) (M:440); Umbundu *mbundu* 'name of the peoples from the high plains of Benguela' (A:700); language of the Ovimbundo people of the former Benguela kingdom (CA:347)
zipaque 'money'			*vipaco* 'gold' (DF:80)	*vipaque, vipaco* 'money' (VF:340)		Possibly related to Kimbundu *vipaco* 'gold' (VF:340)

African lexical items from Calunga and other Afro-Brazilian speech communities provide valuable data on the varieties of African languages that were formerly spoken and are still somewhat maintained throughout Brazil. Such Africanisms are important "linguistic fossils" that can aid linguists in their attempt to "unearth" the African linguistic past of Brazil. These "fossils" demonstrate that Bantu languages such as Kimbundu, Umbundu, and Kikongo were present in Brazil in one form or another and have been somewhat preserved in various Afro-Brazilian speech communities. These lexical items also demonstrate some possible avenues through which Africanisms entered Brazilian Portuguese.

CHAPTER SIX

Calunga Grammar

A calunga tem só um verbo e um "desverbo," que é *"aprumá(r)."*

(Calunga has only a verb and an "unverb," which is *"aprumá[r]"*)

—Calungador José Astrogildo, personal interview, 2003

This chapter aims to describe and analyze the grammar of Calunga. The linguistic corpus utilized is qualitative and drawn from recorded interviews and empirical observations. In addition to the grammatical description of Calunga, the chapter offers comparative analyses, primarily using the local dialect of Caipira Portuguese, labeled as Brazilian Portuguese vernacular (BPV). Data on BPV were provided via consultation with Daniela Bassani Moraes, a native of southern Minas Gerais and fellow researcher of Calunga, and with Ângela Ferreira and Marlenísio Ferreira (1993), both Patrocínio natives and calungadores. Standard Brazilian Portuguese (SBP), Kimbundu, and other forms of Afro-Brazilian speech are also exemplified for purposes of comparison and contrast.

It is pertinent to highlight, however, that all analyses in this chapter are tentative and primarily for descriptive and comparative purposes. That is, given the lack of historical data regarding African languages in Brazil and Afro-Brazilian speech, it is difficult to draw any solid conclusions from the data. Nevertheless, it is this author's position that the data do offer some insight into the present and former language patterns of Africans and Afro-Brazilians. Whether or not African languages or a (semi-)creole influenced the grammar of Calunga and BPV is considered by this author as an open question, but it is raised nonetheless.

PHONETICS AND PHONOLOGY

Calunga does not have a phonetic system different from Brazilian Portuguese: its sound inventory and sound patterns are also observed in the regional BPV. However, phonological patterns from Calunga's Bantu-derived lexical items do show some phonetic and phonological gaps and peculiarities that are worthy of attention. Note the sounds in tables 6.1 and 6.2.

Table 6.1. Calunga vowels

	Front	Central	Back
High (-nasal)	i		u
(+nasal)	ĩ		ũ
Mid high (-nasal)	e		o
(+nasal)	ẽ		õ
Mid low (-nasal)	ɛ		ɔ
(+nasal)		ɐ̃	
Low (-nasal)		a	
(+nasal)			

Table 6.2. Calunga consonants

	Labials	Labio-dentals	Dento-alveolars	Alveolars	Palatals	Velars	Glottal	Retroflex
Stops (-voice)	p		t			k		
(+voice)	b		d			g		
Fricatives (-voice)		f		s	ʃ		[h]	
(+voice)		v		z	ʒ			
Affricates (-voice)					[tʃ]			

	Labials	Labio-dentals	Dento-alveolars	Alveolars	Palatals	Velars	Glottal	Retroflex
(+voice)					[dʒ]			
Nasals	m			n	ɲ			
Liquids				l, r, ɾ	*ʎ			[ɻ]
Glides					[j]	*[w]		

Note: [lʲ] is the commonly articulated sound of /ʎ/ in SBP but is written as /ʎ/ here. [j̃] is the commonly articulated sound for /ɲ/ in SBP but is written as /ɲ/ here. Square brackets ([]) indicate an allophone.

*Unattested in Calunga data; attested in SBP.

Phonemes and Allophones

Since Calunga has a limited lexicon, it is difficult to illustrate traditional minimal pair groupings of phonemes and allophones, though sporadically they do occur (e.g., *semá* 'hair'—*sená* 'beard'; *sarava* 'dance'—*saravá* 'goodbye'). The examples below attempt to capture traditional phonological descriptions, but bear in mind that gaps exist in the data.

Calunga has seven oral and five nasal vowels on par with SBP. Nasal vowels do not appear to be phonemic, as in Portuguese, but are employed due to regressive nasalization. One or another type of these vowels forms the nucleus of the syllable (e.g., *camano-cá* [ka.mẽ.nũ.'ka] 'I'; *curiá* [ku.ɾi.'a] 'food'). Open and closed mid vowels are typically on an item-to-item basis, though some possible phonotactic patterns—such as unstressed mid-vowel raising—may open and close mid vowels accordingly. One peculiarity, moreover, is the lack of diphthongs in the data. Only one diphthong occurs, albeit in few words: [aj] (e.g., *ocaia* [u.'kaj.a], *ocaio* [u.'kaj.u], or *ocai* [u.'kaj] 'girl'). Another attested diphthong from Portuguese, [ej] (e.g., *brasileiro* [bɾa.zi.'lej.ɾu] 'Brazilian'), is somewhat rare in the data and often realized as a monophthong [e]: *zueira* [zu.'ej.ɾa] > [zu.'e.ɾa] 'noise.'

Plosive stops /p t k/ and /b d g/ realize only at the syllable onset and are always occlusive in Calunga. However, loss of /d/ is typical of the progressive morpheme—*ando* > ['ẽ.nũ], a frequent characteristic of BPV (e.g., *falando* [fa.'lẽ.nũ] 'speaking'). Observe the following examples:

1. *camboque* [kẽᵐ.'bo.ki] 'cheese'
2. *caputo* [ka.'pu.tu] 'blind'
3. *duque* ['du.ki] 'insect'
4. *bacuri* [ba.'ku.ɾi] 'sound, music'
5. *gumbo* ['gũᵐ.bu] 'day'
6. *calungando* [ka.lũŋ.'gẽ.nũ] 'speaking (Calunga)'

Affricate sounds of /t d/ ([tʃ dʒ]) are rare and allophonic if and when they are realized in Calunga. The voiced palatal affricate [dʒ], a common allophone in BPV and SBP (e.g., *dia* ['dʒi.a] 'day'), is unattested in Bantu-derived words of Calunga, though it is attested sporadically in Portuguese-derived words (e.g., *desapruma* [dʒi.za.'p(ɾ)ũ.mẽ] '[he/she/it] undoes'). However, [tʃ] as an apparent allophone is realized in a few Bantu-derived words of Calunga:

7. *tipoquê* [tʃi.po.'ke] 'bean'
8. *mufete* [mu.'fɛ.tʃi] 'fish'

Calunga fricatives /f s ʃ h v z ʒ/, all phonemes in Portuguese, are realized at the syllable onset in Calunga. /s/ may be realized in the syllable coda, but it is realized as [+voiced] ([z]) before a voiced consonant or vowel (see "Phonotactics," p. 172):

9. *semá* [se.'ma] 'hair'
10. *os gumbo* [uz.'gũᵐ.bu] '(the) days'
11. *as ocai* [a.zu.'kaj] '(the) women'
12. *missosso* [mi.'so.su] 'history'
13. *zueira* [zu.'e.ɾa] or [zu.'ej.ɾa] 'noise'
14. *fuá* [fu.'a] 'mess'
15. *ofú* [o.'fu] 'black'
16. *vapora* [va.'pɔ.ɾa] '(nonsense) discussion'
17. *xaxatá(r)* [ʃa.ʃa.'ta] 'to touch'
18. *jifeto* [ʒi.'fɛ.tu] 'grimace'
19. *injó* [ĩⁿ.'ʒɔ] 'house'
20. *lorri* ['lu.hi] 'fish'

Nasal consonants /m n ɲ/ occur in the syllable onset. When nasal consonants appear in syllable-final position, they are not realized as consonants but instead nasalize the proceeding vowel (i.e., regressive nasalization), a characteristic of BPV and SBP as well. Prenasalized stops (e.g., /mb ng/, etc.), common in Bantu languages, are not attested in Calunga data. Calunga has developed various phonotactic patterns to adapt Bantu prenasal stops (see "Phonetic and Phonological Analysis," p. 173). Observe the following examples:

21. *moca* ['mɔ.ka] 'coffee'
22. *nani* ['nẽ.nĩ] 'small'
23. *inhoto* [ĩⁿ.'ɲɔ.tu] 'skinny'
24. *gumbo* ['gũᵐ.bu] 'day'
25. *calungá(r)* [ka.lũᵑ.'ga] 'to speak (Calunga)'

Liquids /l r ɾ/ are somewhat infrequent in the Calunga lexicon, but when they do occur they typically realize at the syllable onset. /r/, written orthographically as *r* or *rr*, is phonetically realized as [h]. Word-final rhotics are generally unrealized, especially in verbal infinitives (e.g., *calungar* > [ka.lũᵑ.'ga] 'to speak [Calunga]'). But syllable- and word-final /r/ can also be realized as a retroflex [ɻ]—a typical trait of the local BPV. Also, when /ɾ/ forms the second segment of consonant clusters, it is subject to deletion. Note some examples of liquids in Calunga:

26. *mavero* [ma.'vi.ɾu], [ma.'vi.ɻu], or [ma.'viɻ] 'white, milk'
27. *calungador* [ka.lũᵑ.ga.'do] or [ka.lũᵑ.ga.'doɻ] 'speaker of Calunga'
28. *calungá(r)* [ka.lũᵑ.'ga] 'to speak (Calunga)'
29. *quinhamá(r)* [kĩⁿ.ɲẽ.'ma] 'to walk'
30. *lorri* ['lu.hi] 'fish'
31. *ricomo* [hi.'ko.mũ] 'knife' (VF:332)
32. *curiá* [ku.ɾi.'a] 'food'
33. *orirá(r)* [u.ɾi.'ɾa] 'to sing'
34. *aprumá(r)* [a.p(ɾ)ũ.'ma] 'to do'
35. *imberela* [ĩᵐ.be.'ɾɛ.la] 'meat'

Phonotactics

The regular syllable structure of Calunga is consonant-vowel (CV). A single vowel, oral or nasal, can be a syllable in Calunga (e.g., *ocaio* [u.'kaj.u] 'girl'; *inhoto* [ĩⁿ.'ɲɔ.tu] 'skinny'); there are no syllabic consonants in the nucleus. Only a few consonants are permitted in the syllable coda: /s/ (e.g., *os camano* [us.ka.'mẽ.nũ] 'the men'), allophonic [z] (e.g., *os gumbo* [uz.'gũᵐ.bu] '[the] days'), and very sporadically an allophonic retroflex [ɻ] (e.g., *mavero* [ma.'vi.ɾu], [ma.'vi.ɻu], or [ma.'viɻ], 'white, milk'). CV syllables are generally maintained through regressive nasalization and resyllabification. Other than a vowel, Calunga allows /s/ in the syllable coda. Between vowels, word-final /s/ is resyllabified and realized as [+voiced] (i.e., /s/ > [z]), even across a word boundary. Observe:

36. *os camano* [us.ka.'mẽ.nũ] 'the men, they'
37. *as ocaio* [a.zu.'ka(j).u] 'the women, they (fem.)'
38. *desaprumá(r)* [di.za.p(ɾ)ũ.'ma] or [dʒi.za.p(ɾ)ũ.'ma] 'to undo'

Vowel raising with mid vowels frequently occurs, especially with unstressed mid vowels. These vowels are written orthographically with *e* and *o* but are realized phonetically as [i] and [u]:

39. *chipoque* [ʃi.'po.ke] or *chipoquê* [ʃi.pu.'ke] 'bean'
40. *mavero* [ma.'vi.ɾu] or [ma.'vi.ɻu] 'white, milk'
41. *orirá(r)* [u.ɾi.'ɾa] 'to sing'

Calunga has few consonant clusters. If they do occur, generally /ɾ/ is the second segment (e.g., /fɾ pɾ bɾ gɾ/). These consonant clusters can be reduced by deletion of their rhotic segment, occurring most frequently with /pɾ/ > [p]:

42. *aprumá(r)* [a.pɾũ.'ma] or [a.pũ.'ma] 'to do'
43. *lubra* ['lu.bɾa] 'chest'
44. *malambre* [ma.'lẽᵐ.bɾi] 'slow, slowly'
45. *frize* ['fri.zi] 'axe'

Stress in Calunga is generally on the penultimate syllable. However, some words do receive stress on the final syllable. Antepenultimate stress (i.e., *cálunga) is unattested in the data:

46. *injó* [ĩⁿ.'ʒɔ] 'house'
47. *imberela* [ĩᵐ.be.'rɛ.la] 'meat'
48. *chipoque* [ʃi.'po.ke] or *chipoquê* [ʃi.pu.'ke] 'bean'
49. *dandara* [dẽⁿ.'da.ɾa] or *dandará* [dẽⁿ.da.'ɾa] 'child'
50. *sarava* [sa.'ɾa.va] 'dance'; *saravá* [sa.ɾa.'va] 'good-bye'

Phonetic and Phonological Analysis

Calunga phonology is on par with BPV, with few peculiarities to highlight. That is, there are no phonetic sounds or phonological patterns that are not also attested in the regional BPV. Furthermore, there are no "foreign" phonemes (i.e., prenasal stops, phonemic tones, etc.) or phonotactic structures in Calunga that are not also attested in the local dialect of BPV. And speakers of Calunga are not associated with any "foreign accent" that could identify them as calungadores or as a distinct speech community of Afro-Brazilians. On the other hand, there are certain gaps in Calunga phonology—that is, some phonemes and allophones that are common in Brazilian Portuguese are generally unattested in Calunga.

First, vowel sounds and vowel variability are virtually the same in both Calunga and BPV. Both systems employ a seven oral vowel system with open and closed mid vowels and five nasal vowels. However, where nasal vowels are phonemic in Portuguese (e.g., *pau* ['paw] 'wood'; *pão* ['pẽw̃] 'bread'), in Calunga there are no such attested cases of minimal pairs in the data. Instead, nasal vowels appear to be allophonic (e.g., *calungando* [ka.lũŋ.'gẽnũ] 'speaking [Calunga]').

As with the phonological processes of vowels, both systems realize regressive nasalization and maintain mostly consistent CV syllables. Calunga, however, appears somewhat more restrictive to CV syllables than BPV, which allows a variety of allophonic consonants in the syllable coda. Calunga does realize the morphological inflection /s/ (and allophonic [z]) and very sporadically some variant of /r/—both from Portuguese—in word-final position (e.g., *os camano* [us.ka.'mẽ.nũ] 'the men,' 'they'; *os gumbo* [uz.'gũᵐ.bu] '[the] days'; and very sporadically [ɻ]: *mavero* [ma.'viɻ] 'white, milk'). Other than these, no other consonantal sounds are permitted in the syllable coda.

Second, in terms of consonantal phonemes and their corresponding allophones, Calunga and BPV show little difference, except in the syllable-final coda, as discussed above. Voiceless and voiced plosive stops are phonetically realized in the same manner and same positions. Unlike BPV, however, affricate phonemes and allophones in Calunga are rare and accounted for as allophones only in few words. Likewise, other palatal sounds, which are realized frequently in BPV and SBP as phonemes and allophones, are less common in Calunga. Calunga does realize palatal consonants /ɲ/ and /ʃ/, but no form of /ʎ/ is attested in the data. The phoneme /r/—phonetically realized as [h], as in the local variety of BPV—is present in few words of Calunga (e.g., lorri ['lu.hi] 'fish'; ricomo [hi.'ko.mũ] 'knife'). In addition, one peculiar /r/ allophone in both BVP and Calunga is the retroflex [ɻ] in syllable-final position (and very sporadically between vowels), which is likely adopted from the regional BPV (e.g., Calunga mavero [ma.'vi.ɻu] 'white'; BPV fazendeiro [fa.zẽⁿ.'de(j).ɻu] 'farmer').

Regarding phonotactics, again both Calunga and BPV are quite parallel. That said, one difference is the behavior of muta cum liquida consonant clusters, which are popular in Portuguese (and Romance languages in general), though they are more restricted in Calunga. Interestingly, the regional variety of BPV—which has a number of consonants clusters—frequently reduces some clusters: /gɾ/ > [g], /tɾ/ > [t], /pɾ/ > [p] (e.g., negro > nego 'black man,' outro > oto 'other,' progresso > pogresso 'pro-gress').[1] In these instances, the second consonant of the cluster must be [ɾ].

On the whole, it is evident that Bantu-derived words underwent a Portuguese (or perhaps an "Iberian Romancesque") syllabification. There is some evidence, albeit little, that some Portuguese-based words may have passed through Bantu resyllabification (e.g., salvar > saravá 'good-bye').

In analyzing words of Bantu origin, there are some noteworthy observations. One is the realization of prenasal stops (e.g., Umbundu o-ngato 'cat' < Portuguese gato 'cat'). In Calunga, Bantu prenasal stops, which are syllable onsets in Bantu languages, appear to have been subsequently reanalyzed by means of a few strategies: (1) an epenthetic vowel (e.g., [na.go] < /ngo/), (2) a prothetic vowel (e.g., [ĩŋ.go] < /ngo/); and (3) deletion of one of the consonantal segments (e.g., [go] < /ngo/ or [no] <

/ngo/). Other instances of prenasal stops are generally realized in Calunga as syllable-final nasals that nasalize the proceeding vowel through regressive nasalization. Observe the strategies employed in Calunga with Bantu prenasal stops (Calunga words are listed first):

51. *imbuete* [ĩᵐ.bu.'ɛ.tʃi] 'stick, wood' < Umbundu *mbweti* 'staff, club, stick, wood'
52. *ingomo* [ĩᵑ.'gõ.mũ], *ingombe* [ĩᵑ.'gõᵐ.bi] 'ox, cattle' < Kimbundu, Umbundu, Kikongo *ngombe* 'ox, cow'
53. *injó* [ĩⁿ.'ʒɔ] 'house' < Kimbundu *inzo, njo* 'house,' Kikongo *nzo*, Umbundu *(o)nzo* or *ndjo* 'house'
54. *nagoma* [na.'gõ.ma] 'drum' < Kimbundu, Kikongo *ngoma* 'drum,' Umbundu *ng͂oma* 'drum'

Bantu glides /j w/, which form the onset or nucleus of the Bantu syllable, were resyllabified as high vowels in Calunga /i u/ or realized as a *yod*-style semi-vowel as part of the diphthong /aj/:

55. *imbuete* [ĩᵐ.bu.'ɛ.tʃi] 'stick, wood' < Umbundu *mbweti* 'staff, club, stick, wood'
56. *maiaca* [maj.'a.ka] 'seed' < Kikongo *mayaca* 'manioc'
57. *ocai* [u.'kaj] / *ocaia* [u.'kaj.a] / *ocaiu* [u.'kaj.u] 'woman' < Kimbundu *ucai* 'woman' or Umbundo *ukāyi* 'woman, wife'

Some Calunga vowels appear somewhat unchanged from their possible Bantu etymology, though some vowel changes and vowel variability likely occurred. First, Calunga's Bantu-derived words are typically penultimate or final stress: *cupia* or *cupiá* 'head'; *dandara* or *dandará* 'child'; *sanjo, sanjô,* or *sanja* 'chicken, hen.' Second, there is a tendency in Calunga to raise mid vowels, typically in unstressed positions. Interestingly, when writing Calunga words the informants used Portuguese spelling norms with *e* or *o*, when historically the letter was possibly a high vowel in the original Bantu: for example, Calunga *imbuete* 'wood' < Umbundu *mbweti*; Calunga *indaro* 'fire, yellow, red' < Kikongo, Kimbundo *ndalu* 'fire' or Umbundo *ondalu* 'fire.'

A number of consonantal changes seem to have occurred from Bantu languages to Calunga. That said, it is rather difficult to assess such changes due to uncertain etymologies. Nonetheless, observe some of the possible consonantal changes from Bantu languages to Calunga:

58. *malara* [ma.'la.ɾa] 'orange (fruit)' < Kimbundu *malalanza* 'orange tree'; or from Kikongo or Kimbundu *malala* < Portuguese *laranja* 'orange'
59. *marafa* [ma.'ɾa.fa] 'cachaça' < Kimbundu or Kikongo *malafu, malavu, maravu, malufu* 'wine, alcoholic drink'
60. *curima* [ku.'ɾi.ma] 'work, job' < Kimbundo *kudima, kurima* 'to work'; Kikongo *kutima* 'to work'; Umbundo *okulima* 'to cultivate, labor'

Lastly, note some possible vocalic changes and stress patterns that Calunga underwent:

Vowel changes
61. *amera* [a.'mɛ.ɾa] 'face' < Umbundu *(o)mela* 'mouth'
62. *massango* [ma.'sẽᵑ.gu], *massongo* [ma.'sõᵑ.gu], *massuango* [ma.su.'ẽᵑ.gu] 'rice' < Kimbundo *masangu* 'corn, cereal' or Kikongo *ma-nsangu* 'corn'
63. *sucano* [su.'ka.nu] 'marriage, wedding' < Kimbundo *ku-sokana* 'to marry'

Vowel prothesis
64. *imbuá* [ĩᵐ.bu.'a], *embuá* [ẽᵐ.bu.'a] 'dog' < Kimbundu or Kikongo *(i)mbua* 'dog'; Kikongo, Kimbundu *mbwa* 'dog'; Umbundu *(o)mbwa* 'dog'
65. *incaca* [ĩᵑ.'ka.ka] 'armadillo' < Kikongo *nkaka* 'anteater'

Semi-vowel changes
66. *maiaca* [maj.'a.ka] < Kikongo *mayaca* 'manioc,' Kikongo *mandiaka* < Portuguese *mandioca* 'manioc'
67. *lorri* ['lu.hi] 'fish' < possibly Umbundu *loyi* 'type of fish'

Stress patterns and variation
68. *chipoque* [ʃi.'po.ke], *chipoquê* [ʃi.pu.'ke] 'bean' < Kimbundu *kipoke* 'bean,' Umbundu *poke* 'bean'

69. *dandara* [dẽⁿ.'da.ɾa], *dandará* [dẽⁿ.da.'ɾa] 'child' < undetermined origin
70. *sarava* [sa.'ɾa.va] 'dance,' *saravá* [sa.ɾa.'va] 'good-bye' < Africanized pronunciation of Portuguese *salvar* 'to save' or greeting in Umbundu 'save!'

MORPHOSYNTAX

Calunga morphosyntax is largely on par with BPV, albeit further reduced in some areas and distinct in others.

Noun phrases (NP) in Calunga are typically formed with a determiner (DET), which is derived from Portuguese: *o(s), a(s), um, uns, uma, umas*:

1. *o camano* '(the) man'   *os camano* 'the men'
2. *a ocai* '(the) woman'   *as ocai* 'the women'
3. *o ingombe* '(the) cow'   *os ingombe* 'the cows'
4. *um camano* 'a man'   *uns camano* 'some men'
5. *uma ocai* 'a woman'   *umas ocai* 'some women'
6. *um ingombe* 'a cow'   *uns ingombe* 'some cows'

Also, the NP is also subject to diminutive conversion through the BPV morpheme *-im* or *-zim*—a reduced form of the Portuguese diminutive morpheme *-inho* (e.g., *pouco* 'a little' > *pouquinho* 'a little bit') or *-zinho* (e.g., *só* 'only' > *sozinho* 'alone'):

7. *imbunim* 'little black boy' (from *imbundo* 'black (man)')
8. *ocaizim* 'little girl' (from *ocai* 'girl')
9. *camanim* 'boy' (from *camano* 'man')

Singular nouns are realized with or without a DET. The formation of plurals is realized morphologically through the plural DET but lacking corresponding inflectional affixation on the NP (i.e., bare plurals):

10. *(a) omenha* '(the) river, (the) water' > *as omenha* '(the) rivers, (the) waters'

11. *(a) marafa* '(the) cachaça' > *as marafa* '(the) cachaças'
12. *camano tem pocas cumba* 'he is young' (lit., 'he has few year')

Gender is generally marked by the DET, though it may be observed in the word-final Portuguese morphemes *-o* or *-a* in some nouns:

13. *a ocai* 'woman'
14. *o camano* 'man'
15. *a ocai sucanada* 'married woman'
16. *a ocai mucafa* 'old woman'

However, observe that the DET does not necessarily correspond to the gender, where a masculine DET may be employed as a type of "default form":

17. *o ocai* 'the woman'
18. *os ocai* 'the women'
19. *oto ocai* 'another woman'

Possession is realized exclusively through analytic means by employing the Portuguese preposition *de* and its variants with the DET (*do[s]*, *da[s]*) for masculine and feminine, respectively. This characteristic is used not only for possessive constructions but also for word creation, generally with a metaphorical sense (see the lexical analysis in chapter 5):

20. *injó* 'house': *injó de zipaque* 'bank' (lit., 'house of money'), *injó de marafo* 'bar' (lit., 'house of cachaça')
21. *zipaque* 'money': *zipaque do camano-cá* 'my money' (lit., 'money of me')
22. *marafo* 'cachaça': *marafo do camano* 'your/his cachaça' (lit., 'cachaça of the man')

Adjectives in Calunga are mostly regular verbal participles derived from Portuguese: *aprumado* 'good, rich,' from *aprumá(r)* 'to do, make'; *desaprumado* 'bad,' from *desaprumá(r)* 'to undo.' Others can be possibly traced to Bantu languages:

23. *ôa* 'bad, nothing, poor, worse'

24. *indaro* 'fire, yellow, red'
25. *mavero* 'milk, breast, white'

Adjectival gender agreement may or may not occur with the NP and systematically lacks number agreement. With Bantu-derived adjectives, gender and number agreement typically do not occur. Observe the following examples:

26. *ingombe desaprumado* 'sick cow'
    os ingombe desaprumado 'sick cows'

27. *ocai aprumada* 'pretty woman'
    as ocai aprumada 'pretty women'

28. *(o) camano mavero* '(the) white man'
    os camano mavero '(the) white men'
    (a) ocai mavero '(the) white woman'
    as ocai mavero '(the) white women'

29. *(o) camano ôa* '(the) bad man'
    os camano ôa '(the) bad men'
    (a) ocai ôa '(the) bad woman'
    as ocai ôa '(the) bad women'

30. *ocai murrudo* 'strong woman'

Also, adjectives may be expressed with copulative verbs *tá/tava* (from *estar* 'to be') or *é/foi/era* (from *ser* 'to be'):

31. *os camanim já tá tudo ôa*
    'the boys are already all finished (i.e., "grown up")'

32. *o camano é sucanado?*
    'are you married?'

Subject and object pronouns in Calunga are based on Bantu-derived words for 'man' (*camano*, likely from Kimbundu) and 'woman' (*ocai*, likely from Kimbundu or Umbundu) and use Portuguese locatives for distinction (i.e., *cá* 'here,' *aí* 'there'), though locative elements are not always used during discourse. Since context is necessary to clarify pronominal ambiguities, subject and object pronouns, which are sometimes realized as BPV pronouns, are generally required as part of the verb phrase. The basic subject and object pronouns are listed in table 6.3.

Table 6.3. Calunga subject and object pronouns

	Singular	**Plural**
First person	(o) camano-cá 'I, me' (masc.) (o) camano-(o)fú / (o) umbundu-cá 'I, me' (black) (a/o) ocai(a/o) 'I me' (fem.)	os camano-cá 'we, us' (masc.) as/os ocai(a/o) 'we, us' (fem.) nóis 'we, us' (masc. or fem.) (from BPV)
Second person	(o) camano-(aí) 'you' (masc.) (a/o) ocai(a/o) 'you' (fem.) (vo)cê 'you' (masc. or fem.) (from BPV)	os camano-(aí) 'you' as/os ocai(a/o) 'you' (fem.) (vo)cês 'you' (masc. or fem.) (from BPV)
Third person	(o) camano 'he, him' (a/o) ocai(a/o) 'she, her'	os camano 'they, them' as/os ocai(a/o) 'they, them' (fem.)

Calunga has a reduced verbal paradigm, which results in it being non-pro-drop for the most part: subject pronouns are generally realized, object pronouns as well. Syntactically realized object pronouns are often governed by a variant of a Portuguese preposition with a DET: *para (pro, pra, pa), por (pu), em (na, no)*. Note the following examples:

33. *o imbundo-cá ia aprumá(r) calunga cum ocaio*
   'I (lit., black man-here) was going to talk with the girl'

34. *ocai aprumô pu sêngo*
'the woman went to the rural estate/forest'

35. *nóis quinhamô pa ota cumbaca pa queimá(r) uns ingomo*
'we went to another city to sell some cattle'

Of the twenty-seven verbs collected in the Calunga lexicon (see chapter 5), many of which are derived from Bantu languages, all are first-conjugation *-ar* verbs. All infinitives are phonetically realized without the word-final /-r/ (but, when asked, Calunga speakers will write the verbs with the final *-ar*). Calunga verbs are conjugated as regular, third-person singular *-ar* inflections from Portuguese. In regular discourse, however, many Portuguese verbs, both regular and irregular, are utilized: *tá/tava* (from *estar* 'to be'), *é/foi/era* (from *ser* 'to be'), *tem/teve/tinha* (from *ter* 'to have'), *quer/quis/queria* (from *querer* 'to want')—all conjugated in the third-person singular. As noted above, Calunga employs mostly obligatory subject pronouns with the verb. Note the conjugation paradigms of the verb *quinhamá(r)* 'to walk, go, travel' in tables 6.4–6.9.[2]

Table 6.4. Calunga present tense

(o) camano-cá quinhama 'I walk'	os camano-cá quinhama 'we walk'
(o) camano-(aí) quinhama 'you walk'	os camano-(aí) quinhama 'you (pl.) walk'
(o) camano quinhama 'he walks'	os camano quinhama 'they walk'

Table 6.5. Calunga present tense, progressive aspect
tá (from Portuguese *[es]tá* 'is, are') and stem + *-anu* (from Portuguese *-ando*)

(o) camano-cá tá quinhamanu 'I am walking'	os camano-cá tá quinhamanu 'we are walking'
(o) camano-(aí) tá quinhamanu 'you are walking'	os camano-(aí) tá quinhamanu 'you (pl.) are walking'
(o) camano tá quinhamanu 'he is walking'	os camano tá quinhamanu 'they are walking'

Table 6.6. Calunga past tense, perfect aspect

stem + *-ô* (from Portuguese third-person *-ou*)

(o) camano-cá quinhamô 'I walked'	*os camano-cá quinhamô* 'we walked'
(o) camano-(aí) quinhamô 'you walked'	*os camano-(aí) quinhamô* 'you (pl.) walked'
(o) camano quinhamô 'he walked'	*os camano quinhamô* 'they walked'

Table 6.7. Calunga past tense, imperfect aspect

stem + *-ava* (from Portuguese third-person *-ava*)

(o) camano-cá quinhamava 'I walked'	*os camano-cá quinhamava* 'we walked'
(o) camano-(aí) quinhamava 'you walked'	*os camano-(aí) quinhamava* 'you (pl.) walked'
(o) camano quinhamava 'he walked'	*os camano quinhamava* 'they walked'

Table 6.8. Calunga past tense, progressive aspect

tava (from Portuguese *estava* 'was/were') and stem + *-anu*

(o) camano-cá tava quinhamanu 'I was walking'	*os camano-cá tava quinhamanu* 'we were walking'
(o) camano-(aí) tava quinhamanu 'you were walking'	*os camano-(aí) tava quinhamanu* 'you (pl.) were walking'
(o) camano tava quinhamanu 'he was walking'	*os camano tava quinhamanu* 'they were walking'

Table 6.9. Calunga future tense

vai (from Portuguese *ir* 'to go') + infinitive

(o) camano-cá vai quinhamá 'I will walk'	*os camano-cá vai quinhamá* 'we will walk'
(o) camano-(aí) vai quinhamá 'you will walk'	*os camano-(aí) vai quinhamá* 'you (pl.) will walk'
(o) camano vai quinhamá 'he will walk'	*os camano vai quinhamá* 'they will walk'

Calunga speakers often cite the verb *aprumá(r)* 'to do, make' (along with its negative counterpart *desaprumá[r]* 'to undo') as a key verb in regular discourse. Informant José Astrogildo (personal interview, 2003), for instance, noted that "a calunga tem só um verbo e um 'desverbo,' que é *'aprumá(r)'*" (Calunga has only a verb and an "unverb," which is "*aprumá[r]*"). Even though this statement is not accurate in that Calunga does employ over twenty verbs (see the lexical analysis in chapter 5), Astrogildo provides some insight into a Calunga speaker's perception of the reduced morphosyntax. On the other hand, Astrogildo is correct in that *aprumá(r)* (and *desaprumá[r]*) is a multiuse verb that generates a number of verb phrases in Calunga. The verb itself is of Portuguese origin, meaning 'to lift, to set straight or vertical,' and it has grammaticalized into a multipurpose verb that can be used to convey a variety of verbal phrases and meanings:

36. *vamu aprumá pa dentu du injó*
    'let's go inside the house'

37. *camanu num tá apumanu a nanga mai não*
    'he is not getting his pants anymore'

38. *camanu deve tê aprumadu marafa nu cumba passada*
    'he must have drunk yesterday'

39. *camanu gosta de aprumá uíque na mucota?*
    'do you like to drink?'

40. *aí num é lugar de aprumá ocaio*
    'that is not a place to meet women'

41. *quando mexia cus ingomo, aprumava injó*
    'when I used to work with cattle, I was able to find shelter'

42. *o camano é aprumado do zipaque*
    'the man is rich'

Calunga utilizes preverbal markers to realize different categories of tense and aspect. These markers are derived from Portuguese, typically the adverb *já* 'already' or verbal forms of *ter* 'to have':

43. *ei já calungô com ocai com a nanga daquele jeito*
    'he already spoke with the woman with pants like that'

44. *o camanu já apruma nessas cumbaca há quantos cumba?*
    'how long have you been in the region?'

45. *camanu deve tê aprumadu marafa nu cumba passada*
    'he must have drunk yesterday'

Calunga syntax, with few exceptions, follows a subject-verb-object (SVO) template, though some passive constructions are also employed. There is redundancy in subject and object pronouns and frequent use of double negation. Questions, like declarative sentences, are typically SVO, although "tag questions" may sometimes occur (see example 60, p. 186). Observe the following examples:

46. *ocê é ocaio santo?*
    'are you a single woman?'

47. *os camanu é de qual omenha?*
    'where are you (pl.) from?'
    (lit., 'the men is from which water?')

48. *camanu gosta de aprumá uíque na mucota?*
    'do you like to drink (alcohol)?'

Negation (NEG) in Calunga, as in BPV, can be realized in any number of ways, including preverbal and postverbal negation:

49. *ocai não calunga* (NEG + VP)
    'she does not speak Calunga'

50. *ocai calunga não* (VP + NEG)
    'she does not speak Calunga'

51. *ocai não calunga não* (NEG + VP + NEG)
    'she does not speak Calunga'

52. *camanu num tá apumanu a nanga mai não* (NEG + VP + NEG)
    'he is not putting on (his) [nice] pants (no)'

53. *ei foi aprumá malumbí não* (VP + NEG)
    'he did not go fishing'

Calunga employs Portuguese prepositions *para, por,* and *em* and their corresponding phonetic variations (*p[r]a, pu, no[s], na[s]*) with NPs. These prepositional phrases often carry thematic roles of direction or goal as well as generate direct and indirect object phrases:

54. *camanu gosta de aprumá uíque na mucota?*
    'do you like to drink?'
    (lit., 'man likes to arrange sweet in mouth?')

55. *aprumô no sengo*
    '[she] went to the rural estate/forest'

56. *aprumô no injó*
    '[she] went home'

57. *a ocaio tá aprumano mirante é no camanim*
    'the girl is looking at the boy'

Dependent clauses are triggered with the Portuguese complementizer *que* (*qui*):

58. *aqueis imbuninhu qui os camanu pegava e levava pa omenha*
    'the black boys that white men grabbed and took to the water'

59. *quantas cumba que ele tem?*
   'how old is he?'

Calunga verb phrases have no morphological distinction for mood; all verb phrases are realized solely in the indicative mood. Even subjunctive "trigger verbs," such as *querer* (to want), do not trigger subjunctive forms in the dependent clause:

60. *o camanu e a ocai tá querenu que os camanu-cá calunga sobre?*
   'you are wanting us to speak (Calunga) about?'

Morphosyntactic Analysis

Looking first at the nominal, Calunga, like Portuguese, employs a system of singular-plural, masculine-feminine nouns. Unlike Portuguese, however, Calunga gender and number are marked generally by a DET (*o[s]*, *a[s]*, *oto[s]*, *ota[s]*, etc.). In SBP, for example, adjectives must agree with the head NP in gender and number: *a casa branca* > *as casas brancas*. Such agreement is mostly absent, or not necessary, in Calunga—a characteristic of BPV as well in regard to nominal agreement (i.e., bare plurals). Note the comparisons between Calunga and BPV in tables 6.10 and 6.11:

Table 6.10. Noun phrase comparison, Calunga and BPV

Calunga		BPV	
o camano 'the man'	*os camano* 'the men'	*o home* 'the man'	*os home* 'the men'
(a/o) ocai(a/o) 'the woman'	*as/os ocai(a/o)* 'the women'	*a muié (mulher)* 'the woman'	*as muié (mulher)* 'the women'
ot(r)a cumba 'another year'	*ot(r)as cumba* 'other years'	*ot(r)o ano* 'another year'	*ot(r)os ano* 'other years'

Table 6.11. Noun phrase comparison with adjectives, Calunga and BPV

Calunga		BPV	
o injó indaro 'the red house'	*os injó indaro* 'the red houses'	*o livro branco* 'the white book'	*os livro branco* 'the white books'
o injó aprumado 'the expensive house'	*os injó aprumado* 'the expensive houses'	*a casa branca* 'the white house'	*as casa branca* 'the white houses'
a duana indaro 'the red shirt'	*as duana indaro* 'the red shirts'	*a camisa branca* 'the white shirt'	*as camisa branca* 'the white shirts'
a duana aprumada 'the expensive shirt'	*as duana aprumada* 'the expensive shirts'	*a camisa cara* 'the expensive shirt'	*as camisa cara* 'the expensive shirts'

Calunga pronominal forms of subject and object pronouns are rather peculiar when compared with their BPV counterparts: that is, Calunga pronoun patterns cannot be traced to BPV. Note, for example, first-person singular pronouns in Calunga: *camano-ca* 'I, me,' *camano-(o)fú* or *umbundu-cá* 'I, me' (lit., 'black man-here,' if a male, black speaker wishes to emphasize his ethnicity). BPV instead has all its pronominal forms based on Portuguese (table 6.12).

Table 6.12. Subject pronoun comparison, Calunga and BPV

Calunga		BPV	
(o) camano-cá 'I' (default, masc.)	*os camano-cá* 'we' (masc.)	*eu* 'I'	*nós (nóis)* 'we'
(o) camano-(o)fú 'I' (black masc.)	*as/os ocai(a/o)* 'we' (fem.)		
(o) umbundo-cá 'I' (black masc.)			
(a/o) ocai(a/o) 'I' (fem.)			

Calunga		BPV	
(o) camano-aí 'you' (masc.) (a/o) ocai(a/o) 'you' (fem.)	os camano-aí 'you' (pl. masc.) as/os ocai(a/o) 'you' (pl. fem.)	você ocê 'you' cê	vocês ocês 'you' (pl.) cês
(o) camano 'he' (a/o) ocai(a/o) 'she'	os camano 'they' as/os ocai(a/o) 'they' (fem.)	ele (ei) 'he' ela 'she' a gente 'we'	eles (eis) 'they' (masc.) elas (esa) 'they' (fem.)

As table 6.12 shows, BPV, nor the Portuguese nominal system for that matter, does not have a notion of ethnicity or gender as Calunga does with first-person and second-person forms. In addition, a white speaker of Calunga cannot say *camano-(o)fú* or *umbundu-cá*, while a black speaker of Calunga can employ *camano-cá*. Another peculiarity is that a female speaker cannot express her ethnicity in Calunga, while men can. Also of interest is that *eu* is the only subject pronoun that tends to be dropped in BPV morphosyntactic constructions since it maintains specific verbal inflections in some verbal forms (i.e., present and preterit). Calunga, for its part, does not typically permit pro-drop, though it may occur sporadically in the first-person singular, on par with BPV morphosyntax.

In terms of verbal morphology, Calunga is largely on par with the local BPV. However, one striking characteristic of Calunga is that verbal paradigms are all regular, first-conjugation *-ar* verbs with third-person conjugations realized solely in the indicative mood, unless a Portuguese verb (which may be irregular) is employed. Such reduced, systematized patterns are typical in pidgin and creole languages, including varieties of Atlantic creoles (Holm 2004:81), which possibly correlate to the utilization of third-person forms in Calunga. Moreover, creole verbs seem to have been derived from imperative forms rather than infinitives (Holm 2004:81), which may partially explain such systematic patterns. Observe tables 6.13–6.17:

Table 6.13. Calunga and BPV present indicative

Calunga quinhamá(r) 'to go, walk'		BPV andar 'to go, walk'	
(o) camano-cá quinhama	os camano-cá quinhama	(eu) ando	nós anda/andamo(s)
(o) camano-aí quinhama	os camano-aí quinhama	(vo)cê anda	(vo)cês anda
(o) camano quinhama	os camano quinhama	ele anda	eles anda

Table 6.14. BPV and SBP present indicative

BPV andar 'to go, walk'		SBP andar 'to go, walk'	
(eu) ando	nós anda/andamo(s)	(eu) ando	(nós) andamos
(vo)cê anda	(vo)cês anda	você anda	vocês andam
ele anda	eles anda	ele anda	eles andam

Table 6.15. Calunga and BPV indicative, perfect aspect (verbal forms only)

Calunga quinhamá(r) 'to go, walk'		BPV andar 'to go, walk'	
quinhamô	quinhamô	andei	andô/andamo(s)
quinhamô	quinhamô	andô	andô/andaram/andaro
quinhamô	quinhamô	andô	andô/andaram/andaro

Table 6.16. Calunga and BPV indicative, perfect aspect (verbal forms only)

Calunga curiá(r) 'to eat'		BPV comê(r) 'to eat'	
curiô	curiô	comi	comeu/comemo(s)
curiô	curiô	comeu	comeu/comeram/comero
curiô	curiô	comeu	comeu/comeram/comero

Table 6.17. Calunga and BPV indicative, imperfect aspect (verbal forms only)

Calunga quinhamá(r) 'to go, travel'		BPV andar 'to go'	
quinhamava	quinhamava	andava	andava/andávamo(s)
quinhamava	quinhamava	andava	andava
quinhamava	quinhamava	andava	andava

Similar to BPV, Calunga syntax follows systematic SVO patterns for the most part. There are, however, some interesting syntactic features to note. First, double negation (e.g., *num vai sê não*: BPV from Patrocínio, Minas Gerais [Ferreira and Ferreira 1993:16]) may represent evidence of a relation to a Portuguese-based pidgin or creole, though this is debatable (Lipski 2005:258–60). Schwegler (1998:221), for instance, argues that BPV double negation could have a possible genetic relationship to other Afro-Hispanic creoles, including Colombian Palenquero and Angolan Portuguese vernacular, which also employ similar double negative patterns. Second, the peculiar syntactic use of prepositions is another parallel of interest: mainly *por, para,* and *em* (and their corresponding variants with a DET: *pro, pra, no[s], na[s]*). In Calunga and BPV these are realized especially with the thematic role of goal:

61. *camano apruma no injó* (Calunga)
    'the man/he goes to the house'

62. *o home vai na casa* (BPV)
'the man goes to the house'

63. *camano apruma pro injó* (Calunga)
'the man/he goes to the house'

64. *o home vai pra casa* (BPV)
'the man goes to the house'

In both Calunga and BPV object pronouns are realized with prepositions:

65. *camano-cá apruma marafo pra camano-aí* (Calunga)
'I give you cachaça'

66. *eu dou cachaça pra você* (BPV)
'I give you cachaça'

In terms of clauses, both Calunga and BPV are virtually identical in their realization of independent and dependent clauses. With both, few verbal inflections are realized, including the absence of subjunctive mood. Observe, for example, the following BPV data from Patrocínio:

67. *É pra isso qui nóis tá qui*
'That is why we are here'
(Ferreira and Ferreira 1993:50)

68. *Nóis cumeu uns trem! . . . Um'as coisa qui nóis trôxe lá de casa*
'We ate something! . . . Some things that we brought from home'
(Ferreira and Ferreira 1993:13)

Theoretical Discussion

In considering appropriate theoretical models for Calunga, "anti-creole" is one possibility (see chapter 3). Even though the terminology is perhaps unusual, or perhaps imprecise as Petter (1999) argues, the definitions provided by Couto (1992a, 1997, 2002) fit well with Calunga due to its using of BPV for its phonology and morphosyntax. As Couto (1997:106) notes, when there is something of African linguistic influence in these Afro-Brazilian speech communities, it is typically lexical items, not grammar. The exception to his claim, however, is Calunga's peculiar pronominal system (e.g., *camano-cá, umbundo-cá, ocai,* etc.), unless one makes the argument that these, too, are Africanized lexical items.

Thomason (2001:204) explains that language contact and language change are unpredictable matters, which is especially true for mixed languages. In that light the mixed (or intertwined) language model is also appropriate to consider for Calunga (see chapter 3). That is, Calunga features a strong lexical component and uses the dominant grammar of the immediate surroundings, and the speakers have a sense that the speech pertains to a specific ethnic group: "a língua dos escravo" or "a língua dos preto (velho)." If we assume that BPV is purely a dialect of Portuguese resulting from internal linguistic change, following the thinking of Naro and Scherre (2007), then the anti-creole or mixed language models appear to work well with Calunga.

However, a question that is worth raising is whether or not there is African influence in the grammar of Calunga *and* in the local BPV that influenced Calunga? If yes, then the reduced morphosyntax, lack of agreement rules, and so forth would not be solely internal linguistic change but instead would have originated from some form of influence from speakers of African languages. These linguistic changes could possibly have stemmed from native African languages, from some type of pidgin or creole, or simply from language-learning errors, thus resulting in a "partially restructured grammar" (Holm 1987, 1992, 2004). Guy (1989:237), for example, writes that "we should note the existence all over Brazil of rural dialects that are . . . creole-like. . . . There is the 'caipira' dialect in the southeast described . . . as having a total lack of agreement rules, a radical reduction in the verbal paradigms, and so on." In addition, Castro (1980:17–18, italics hers, my translation) contends that there was a process of "double interaction": "a process of 'Portuguesement' of the Africanisms and of Africanization of Portuguese, with the emergence of a new speech that we will call *rural dialect.*" Following the thinking of these scholars, it would be reasonable to hypothesize that Calunga has more African influence in its grammar that can be detected on the surface, which is something that seems particularly evident in Calunga's pronominal system of Bantu-Portuguese hybrid forms. In short, if there indeed was an "Africanization of Portuguese" or a "partially restructured grammar" in the phonology and morphosyntax of BPV, then the theoretical model in question would have to factor in African linguistic influence that has percolated into both the lexicon *and* the grammar of the regional Portuguese and, vice versa, into the various falares africanos of Brazil such as Calunga.

To what extent were African languages an influence in Brazil? This is, of course, a difficult question. In examining Calunga, for example, it is clear that Bantu languages such as Kimbundu, Umbundu, and Kikongo (the latter probably to a lesser extent) were an important factor: lexically, there is no question. But did these languages contribute any influence to the morphosyntax of Calunga, or more generally to BPV? Obviously such a question is very difficult to answer with certainty, but it is worth raising nonetheless. Observe, for instance, some examples of descriptive data on Kimbundu as documented by Chatelain (1888–1889/1964:32–33):

Kimbundu infinitives

-*banga* 'to do'

-*beta* 'to beat'

-*kuambata* 'to guide'

-*kuenda* 'to walk'

-*longa* 'to teach'

-*xinga* 'to insult'

-*zeka* 'to sleep'

-*zola* 'to love'

69. *Eme ngolo-banga*
    I INFL-do[3]
    'I am doing'

70. *Eie uolo-banga*
    you (sg.) INFL-do
    'you (sg.) are doing'

71. *Muene uolo-banga*
    he INFL-do
    'he is doing'

72. *Etu tuolo-banga*
    we INFL-do
    'we are doing'

73. *Enu nuolo-banga*
    you (pl.) INFL-do
    'you (pl.) are doing'

74. *Ene olo-banga*
    they INFL-do
    'they are doing'

75. *o mumbundu uolo-kuambata o mundele*
    the black man INFL-guides the white man
    'the black man guides the white man'

In the above examples Kimbundu shows preverbal inflections attached to the verbal stem for forming paradigms; the verbal stem does not change. Calunga, although different, features a single conjugated verbal form throughout, somewhat similar to the infinitival form in Kimbundu. But whether or not Calunga and BVP have any such influence from Bantu verbal morphology—or possibly influence via pidginization/creolization—is an open question and probably will remain unknown. Of course, other factors, such as errors from acquiring Portuguese as a foreign language, could likely be part of the morphosyntax of both Calunga and BVP. The workings of internal grammatical change are very possibly involved as well. But pinpointing certain aspects of grammar to one or another specific African language or pidgin/creole is typically a problematic endeavor.

Questions and problems noted, observe a comparison of conjugations in table 6.18:

Table 6.18. Conjugation of the verb 'to do' in the present indicative in Kimbundu, Calunga, BPV, and SBP

Kimbundu -banga 'to do'		Calunga aprumá(r) 'to do'		BPV fazê(r) 'to do'		SBP 'fazer 'to do'	
eme ngi-banga	etu tu-banga	camano-cá apruma	os camano-cá apruma	eu faço	nós faz/ fazemo(s)	eu faço	nós fazemos
eie u-banga	enu nu-banga	camano-aí apruma	os camano-aí apruma	(vo)cê faz	(vo)cês faz	você faz	vocês fazem
muene u-banga	ene a-banga	camano apruma	os camano apruma	ele faz	eles faz	ele faz	eles fazem

From the table it can be observed that both Kimbundu and Calunga show one verbal form and overt subject pronouns. One key difference to note, however, is the Kimbundu preverbal inflections, which have no corresponding equivalent in Calunga or in the varieties of Brazilian Portuguese. On the other side of the table, BPV has two to three verbal conjugations with mostly obligatory subject pronouns. SBP has four verbal conjugations and is moderately pro-drop (usually in first-person forms). Of course, neither solid hypotheses nor conclusions can be drawn from such comparisons, but the comparative data do offer a panorama of verbal paradigms and an area of morphosyntax where "Africanization" or "partial restructuring" may or may not have occurred.

Comparative Grammatical Analysis of Afro-Brazilian Varieties

In terms of grammar, Calunga is virtually on par with other forms of Afro-Brazilian speech from Minas Gerais and São Paulo, particularly in the morphosyntax. Some documented speech communities that are good candidates for comparison are Cafundó (São Paulo state), Bom Despacho (Minas Gerais), and Catumba (Minas Gerais).

Cupópia, spoken in the Cafundó community, employs few verbs—some fifteen—and has a reduced verbal system on par with BPV morphology. Vogt and Fry (1996:127) note, "O que imediatamente sobressai quando se ouve o pessoal do Cafundó falando 'africano' é que as estruturas gramaticais que sistematizam o uso do vocabulário, dando-lhe uma certa consistência de emprego, são estruturas tomadas emprestadas do português." (What immediately stands out when one hears the people of Cafundó speaking "African" is that its grammatical structures systematize the use of the vocabulary, giving it a certain consistency of usage, which are structures borrowed from Portuguese.) All "Africanized" verbs are first-conjugation (-*ar*) verbs with corresponding regular inflections. Also noteworthy is the use of the verbs *estar* and *ir*, which form a variety of periphrastic phrases similar to forms used in Calunga. Further prepositions, particularly *de* and *em*, are frequently employed to generate phrases. Note the following examples of Cupópia (Vogt and Fry 1996:128):

76. *vimbundo está cupopiando no injó do tata*
    [black man is speaking in the house of the father]
    '[the] black man is speaking in the house of [his] father'
    (possible Calunga translation: *camano-ofú tá calungando no injó do otaca)*

77. *o nhamanhara cuendou para coçumbar a cupópia*
    [the man walked to hear the speech]
    'the man went to hear the conversation'
    (possible Calunga translation: *o camano quinhamô pra aprumá[r] escutante na calunga*)

78. *o cafombe cuendou da ambara para cunuaravero com nhapecava*
    [the white man walked to the city to drink milk with coffee]
    'the white man came to the city to drink coffee with milk'
    (possible Calunga translation: *O camano mavero quinhamô a cumbaca pra aprumá[r] mavero com gatuvira*)

One key difference to note is that, unlike Calunga, subject pronouns in Cupópia are derived from BPV (see tables 6.3 and 6.12 for Calunga and BPV pronominal forms). That said, Calunga may sporadically employ BPV subject pronouns (see example 59 under "Morphosyntax"). Lastly, even though the morphosyntax is quite similar, the African-derived lexicon is somewhat different from Calunga (see the lexical analysis in chapter 5 and Vogt and Fry [1996] for a lexical comparison of Cupópia to Calunga).

Another Afro-Brazilian speech that is also similar to Calunga in terms of grammar is Língua do Negro da Costa from Bom Despacho, Minas Gerais. Like Cupópia, Língua do Negro da Costa uses subject pronouns from BPV (*eu, ocê, ele, nóis,* etc.) (Queiroz 1998:83). In addition, all verbs are first-conjugation (*-ar*) verbs; however, Língua do Negro da Costa has two verbal conjugations (first- and third-person singular) in its respective tenses and aspects: *eu curimbo* 'I work,' *ele curimba* 'he works.' As can be noted from table 6.19, Calunga's verbal paradigms are practically on par with this Afro-Mineiro speech, with the exception of first-person forms and BPV pronouns:

Table 6.19. Verbal paradigms of Língua do Negro da Costa

tipurá *'to see, look, understand'* (present)	tipurá *'to see, look, understand'* (preterit)
eu tipuro 'I see'	*eu tipurei* 'I saw'
ocê, cê tipura 'you see'	*ocê, cê tipurô* 'you saw'
ele, ela tipura 'he, she sees'	*ele, ela tipurô* 'he, she saw'
nóis, a gente tipura 'we see'	*nóis, a gente tipurô* 'we saw'
ocês, cês tipura 'you (pl.) see'	*ocês, cês tipurô* 'you (pl.) saw'
eles, elas tipura 'they see'	*eles, elas tipurô* 'they saw'

Source: Adapted from Queiroz (1998:83).

Note the following sentences as documented by Queiroz (1998:95):

79. *os camonim chega no conjolo do cuete*
    [the boys arrive in the house of the man]
    'the boys arrive in the man's house'
    (possible Calunga translation: *os camanim apruma no injó do camano*)

80. *eu to curimbano já avura*
   [I am working already too much]
   'I am working too much already'
   (possible Calunga translation: *camano-cá tá curimano já demais*)

Lastly, the Afro-Mineiro speech community of Catumba documented by Dornas Filho also has similar grammatical characteristics. Dornas Filho (1943:73, my translation) offers the following observations of the "Kimbundu" spoken in Catumba: "[I]t does not possess the attributes and inflections that are present in more evolved languages such as Portuguese. Therefore, the Kimbundu that is found in Minas [Gerais] resorts always to Portuguese in the cases where the dialect does not possess the resources to form expressions." Dornas Filho (73) also provides a few examples to consider:

81. *João oméra uavuro quiapossóca undaca de quimbundo*
   [João has very well language of black]
   'João speaks very well the language of the blacks'
   (possible Calunga translation: *João apruma uma calunga ôa*)

82. *ocuêto vindêro cachia no curima*
   [man white arrives in the service/work]
   'the white man arrives at work'
   (possible Calunga translation: camano mavero apruma na *curima*)

Even though Dornas Filho provides no comprehensive grammatical analysis to better compare and contrast with Calunga, from his examples it seems evident that much of the same BPV morphosyntax template that has been discussed above is employed in this Afro-Mineiro speech community.

In sum, Calunga's phonetics/phonology and morphosyntax are largely on par with BPV, resulting in this Afro-Brazilian speech being primarily a lexical phenomenon. However, besides the African influence in the lexical aspect, which is a category unto itself, some possible African—or pidgin/(semi-)creole—grammatical influences that can be observed both in Calunga and generally in other varieties of Afro-Brazilian speech are:

- Mostly CV syllables in the phonology
- Peculiar pronominal forms (Calunga only)
- Bare plurals
- Lack of gender/number agreement
- Simplified verbal morphology
- Simplified syntactic structures (mostly SVO, no subjunctive mood)
- Double negation in the syntax

With the exception of the pronominal forms, BPV seems to be a clear determining factor in most of the grammatical characteristics listed above for Calunga. On the other hand, Calunga does present grammatical patterns that are equivalent to the characteristics that are argued to be the results of "Africanization" or "partial restructuring." Moreover, what is particularly interesting is the relative consistency of the morphosyntax across the varieties of Afro-Brazilian speech listed herein. Given the lack of historical data regarding African languages in Brazil, however, it is difficult to formulate hypotheses or draw any solid conclusions from this relative consistency.

As previously discussed, the linguistic evolution of Calunga is virtually unknown, and the "Africanization" or semi-creolization of BPV is a highly debated and controversial topic. It is nevertheless interesting to consider whether BPV and varieties of Afro-Brazilian speech evolved together or separately and if there is African linguistic influence beyond the lexicon in both. To fully address and answer such questions requires a more comprehensive knowledge of African languages in Brazil, the evolution of BPV, and Afro-Brazilian speech varieties. Simply put, more data are needed to understand the connections among these varieties, or the lack thereof.

Even though the odds are bleak that some unprecedented evidence will be uncovered regarding the history of African languages in Brazil, it is nonetheless a worthwhile endeavor to continue to seek answers to Bonvini and Petter's question: what do we really know about the languages spoken by the slaves in Brazil?

Appendix

This appendix includes excerpts of transcribed recorded interviews in Calunga with linear English translations. All informants in these interviews consented to recording; all recordings took place in Patrocínio, Minas Gerais. The transcribed interviews were translated by the author and Daniela Bassani Moraes, a native of southern Minas Gerais. All Calunga transcriptions follow an informal Brazilian spelling pattern in order to better represent the speech patterns of the informants: for example, *camanu* < *camano* 'man,' *apumanu* < *aprumando* 'making,' and so forth. The translations were made into American English.

Calunga Interview 1
August 1, 2003
Patrocínio, Minas Gerais

Participants:
B: Belarmindo, born 1926
JB: José de Barros, born 1935
JC: João Crispim, born 1933
TB: Tadeu de Barros, born 1960
DB: Daniela Bassani (researcher)
SB: Steven Byrd (researcher)

Calunga	*English*
JC: Na cumbaca grande. Aí, de lá nóis quinhamô pa ota cumbaca pa queimá uns ingomo. Foi quemano, foi quemano. Posô lá no oto ingomo, injó de cuzeca, lá tinha oto ocaio tamém.	JC: In the big city. From there, we went to another city to sell cattle. We were selling, selling [the cattle]. We lodged there at another ranch, an inn, there were women there too.
B: Aprumada?	B: Pretty?

Calunga	English
JC: Aprumada tamém.	JC: Pretty too.
JB: ... nóis tinha tudo que era bão. Era peteca, era tudo ... tudo era bão.	JB: ... we had everything that was real good. We had *peteca* [badminton-type game], we had ... everything good.
B: Lá o povo ... ô camano, fala uma calunga aí pra mim?	B: There the people ... oh man, can you speak some Calunga for me?
JB: Ha, ha ... uma calunga pra mim?!	JB: Ha, ha ... speak Calunga for me?!
JC: Não, o imbundo cá ia aprumá calunga cum ocaio, se ele é ... quantas cumba que ele tem ... Ah, camano tem pocas cumba ...	JC: No, I was going to speak Calunga with the woman, if she is ... how old is he ... Ah, oh man he is young ...
B: Se ia sucaná cu camano ... cê tem que aprumá a calunga é cu camanim, camano tá ...	B: If she was going to marry the man ... you have to speak Calunga with the boy, he is ...
JB: Camanim ... tá aprumano a calunga.	JB: The boy ... is speaking Calunga.
B: Ocaio não, ocaio é do camano cá.	B: The woman no, the woman is with the man here.
JC: Agora, a ocaio tá cu mirante aprumado ... no cemá né? As quinhama, né? Mas a ocaio tá aprumano mirante é no camanim! Num sabemo se é sucanado ô não.	JC: Now, the woman has pretty eyes, hair, right? Legs, right? But the woman is looking at [interested in] the boy! We do not know if she is married or not.
DB: Nós num somos casados não.	DB: We are not married.
TB: É. Ele falô ... cê intendeu, né?	TB: Yes. He said ... you understood, right?

Calunga	English
DB: Entendi, eu tô entendeno já.	DB: I understood, I am understanding now.
JB: É. Ela tá entendeno.	JB: Yes. She is understanding.
JC: Isso que eu falei aqui agora cê entendeu?	JC: That which I said here did you understood?
DB: Entendi. Tudo.	DB: I understood. Everything.
B: Ela tá intendeno. Viu ô camano!	B: She is understanding. Did you see friend!
JC: Tão num pode calungá bestera . . . calungá mafora.	JC: So we cannot talk nonsense, speak about immoral things.
B: Dá ôa na calunga. Ceis num é casadu não, né?	B: Stop speaking Calunga. You are not married, right?
DB: Não, a gente namora.	DB: No, we are dating.
JB: Intão ocê é ocaio santo?	JB: Then you are single [girl]?
DB: É, ocaio santo.	DB: Yes, single.
JB: Camano tá . . . camano tá aprumano curima noto *imbú*, ó!	JB: The man is . . . the man is working in another *imbú* [unknown word], oh!
B: Ah é? É ele continua, num tá apumano cuzeca mai não . . .	B: Oh yes? Yes, he continues, he is not resting anymore?
JB: Ah não?! Só apruma cuzeca agora . . .	JB: Ah no?! He just rests now ['he is retired'] . . .
B: Não, ele só apruma a cuzeca . . .	B: No, he just rests . . .
JC: É.	JC: Yes.
B: Hum . . . é só lá nu injó de curiá?	B: Hum . . . just there in the restaurant?

Calunga	English
JB: É . . . tá curimano só lá noto injó.	JB: Yes . . . he is working just there in another house.
B: Ocaio tamém?	B: And the woman too?
JB: É . . . ocaio tamém.	JB: And . . . the woman too.
B: Mai num é sucanado, né?	B: But she is not married, right?
JC: Não, vai sucaná. É o pedaço?	JC: No, she is going to marry. It is your son?
B: É, é pedaço.	B: Yes, he is my son.
JC: Pois é, mais os ocaio apruma a cuzeca aqui nu injó?	JC: Yes, but the women sleep here in the house?
JB: É nu injó.	JB: Yes, in the house.
JC: Mai pa curimá é aqui o nu oto injó?	JC: But to work, it is here or in another house?
JB: É noto injó. No enjó de curiá.	JB: It is in the other house, in the restaurant.
TB: O camanim pedaço quinhama no urungo.	TB: The son drives.
JB: E a ocaio quinhama tamém.	JB: And the woman [drives] too.
JC: A curima noto injó é, é . . . menos zipaque, né?	JC: To work in another house is . . . less pay, right?
TB: É.	TB: Yes.
JB: E, lá é injó de curiá.	JB: Yes, there is the restaurant.
TB: A curima lá é aprumada!	TB: The work there is good!
JC: Puis é.	JC: That's right.

Calunga	English
B: E . . . que dia que é, qual é cumba que o camano qué quinhamá? Pa cumbaca?	B: And . . . what day is it, which day do you want to go? To the city?
JB: Inda num sabe não.	JB: Still don't know.
B: E o camano pedaço . . .	B: And the son . . .
TB: O camanim vai quinhamá pota cumbaca, o camanim lá ó.	TB: The boy is going to go to another city, the boy, to look there.
B: Ocaizim tamém?	B: And the girl too?
TB: É, a ocaizim também, no urungo.	TB: Yes, the girl too, in the car.
B: O urungo é do camano ô . . .	B: The car is the man's . . .
TB: É do camano, do camano pedaço.	TB: It is the man's, the son's.
B: Tão eis tem urungo . . .	B: So they have a car . . .
TB: Tem.	TB: They have.
B: Eis quinhama no urungo deis. E né ôa o urungo deis não?	B: They go in their car. And their car is not bad, right?
TB: Não, é aprumado! O camano é aprumado do zipaque.	TB: No, it's good! The man has money.
JC: É! Ha, ha, ha . . .	JC: Yes! Ha, ha, ha . . .
DB: E, se tem urungo, né? É aprumado do zipaque.	DB: Yes, [the man] has money, right? [He] has some money.
B: Ea tá boa no negócio já. Num tá?	B: She is good at this business [of Calunga] already. Isn't she?

Calunga	English
JC: Tá aprendeno tudo, né? O zipaque é coisa boa, num é?	JC: She is learning everything, right? Money is a good thing, right?
B: Num sei, mais quem tem urungo, normalmente tem zipaque. Pissá tomá cuidado que o zipaque é inimigo do dono, né?	B: I don't know, but who has a car, normally has money. You need to be careful because money is the enemy of the owner, right?
DB: É.	DB: Yes.
B: É. Hoje tá difícil, né?	B: Yes. Today is difficult, isn't it?
DB: É. Hoje tá.	DB: Yes. Today is.
B: Mai camano cá quinhamô muito cum ingomo, né?	B: But I worked a lot walking with cattle, right?
B: Umbundu tamém. O camanu du injó tamém.	B: The black man too. The friend of this house too.
JB: Aprumava u curiá.	JB: He used to eat [with us].
B: Cê aprumava tamém.	B: You used to eat [with us] too.
TB: Tamém. E aprumava u curiá.	TB: Me too. I used to eat [with you] too.
JB: Aprumava u curiá.	JB: He used to eat [with us].
B: É.	B: Yes.
B: U cumpadi Gerardo . . . tamém. Aprumô cumigu muitas veis! Muito memo! Ocê aprumô tamém?	B: Our friend Geraldo . . . also. He ate with me many times! Many times! You too?
JB: Mai o camanu aí tamém quinhamô juntu.	JB: But you also traveled together.

Calunga	English
B: Puis é! Ele quinhamô muito cumigu tamém. Ele o Zé, o Negu, o Joaquim . . . tudu.	B: Of course! He traveled with me too. And José, Black, Joaquim . . . all of them.
DB: Quantus dias cês ficavam fora?	DB: How many days were you traveling?
JB: Iche! 60, 90 dia.	JB: Wow! 60, 90 days.
DB: Ah, era muito, né?	DB: Ah, it was a lot, right?
B: Que? As viage nossa? Ah, era um meis, dois meis, treis meis . . . depende do lugar que ia, né?	B: What? Our trips? Ah, it was a month, two months, three months . . . it depended on the place we were going.
JB: Nóis viaja mais pu istadu de São Paulu.	JB: We traveled mostly to the state of São Paulo.
DB: Ah, é?	DB: Oh, yes?
SB: E . . . vocês calungavam o tempo todo?	SB: E . . . you spoke Calunga all the time?
TB: Ah . . . calungava muitu. Quandu chegava uma pessoa nóis ia . . . "Ah camanu tá aprumado nu enjó, tá quereno apruma u curiá, qué aprumá a cuzeca."	TB: Oh . . . we spoke Calunga a lot. When someone would arrive we would begin . . . "Oh the man has a nice house, [we] are wanting to eat, to sleep."
JB: Gatuvira cê sabe quê que é, né?	JB: *Gatuvira*, you know what that is, right?
DB: Gatuvera . . . café.	DB: *Gatuvira* . . . coffee.
B: E *mirante*?	B: And *mirante*?
DB: Olhu.	DB: Eye.
B: E pontu de puenti.	B: And *ponto de poente*?

Calunga	English
DB: Não. Issu eu num sei que qui é.	DB: No, I don't know what that is.
TB: E ingrimo?	TB: And *ingrimo*?
DB: Ingrimu . . .	DB: *Ingrimo* . . .
JB: Ingrimu, ingrimu é os denti.	JB: *Ingrimo* are teeth.
DB: Ah é! Ingrimu é denti.	DB: Oh yes! *Ingrimo* is tooth.
B: E mucota?	B: And *mucota*?
DB: Boca.	DB: Mouth.
TB: E pontu de poenti é o nariz.	TB: And *ponto de poente* is the nose.
DB: Ah, é? A genti ficô sem sabê! Tá vendo? Como qui é?	DB: Oh yes? We don't know! You see? How is it?
B: Pontu puenti.	B: *Ponto de poente*.
DB: Pontu puenti.	DB: *Ponto de poente*.
TB: E escutanti?	TB: And *escutante*?
DB: Ovidu.	DB: Ear.
TB: É . . . ea tá aprendenu.	TB: Yes . . . she is learning.
B: E cemá? Aprumadu, disaprumadu . . .	B: And *cemá* ['hair']? *Aprumado, desaprumado* ['pretty, ugly'] . . .
DB: Quê que é cemá?	DB: What is *cemá*?
TB: É cabelu. E munzá?	TB: It is hair. And *munzá* ['hand']?
DB: Num sei.	DB: I don't know.
TB: E a mão. E embuá?	TB: It is the hand. And *embuá* ['dog']?

Calunga	*English*
DB: Tamém num sei.	DB: Again I don't know.
B: Cê apruma maveru de ingomo na mucota?	B: Do you drink *maveru de ingomo* ['milk']?
DB: Não, maveru de ingomu não.	DB: No, milk no.
JB: É leite de vaca.	JB: It is cow's milk.
DB: É, eu tomo.	DB: Yes, I drink [it].
B: Mavero é o leite, farinha e mapuim e ingomu é a vaca.	B: *Mavero* is milk, flour is *mapuim*, and *ingomu* is cow.
TB: Camanu cá, camanu cá, quinhamô muitu cumigu. Cu camanu cá não. E imberela, cê sabe o quê que é?	TB: This man, this man, traveled a lot with me. And *imberela*, do you know what that is?
DB: Imberela . . . carne.	DB: *Imberela* . . . meat.
B: E imberela de ingomu?	B: And *imberela de ingomu*?
DB: Carne de vaca.	DB: Cow's meat.
TB: E imberela de [. . .]	TB: And *imberela de* [*inaudible*]
JB: É porco.	JB: It is pork.
B: E imberela de sanjo?	B: And *imberela de sanjo*?
DB: É frango.	DB: It is chicken.
TB: Ea tá boa na calunga já!	TB: She is good at Calunga now!
B: Massa de viango?	B: *Massa de viango*?
DB: Massa de viango é . . . quejo?	DB: *Massa de viango* is cheese?
B: Rapadura!	B: *Rapadura* [a raw, hard, brown sugar candy]!

Calunga	*English*
DB: Ah, é . . . viango é . . .	DB: Oh, it is . . . *viango* is . . .
TB: Quejo é massa de mavero.	TB: Cheese is *massa de mavero*.
DB: Ah é, tá certo.	DB: Oh it is, certain.
B: Cê apruma omenha de viango na mucota?	B: Do you drink *omenha de viango*?
SB: Num sei.	SB: I don't know.
DB: Não.	DB: No.
B: Num pruma não, né? Cê tamém não? Camanu aqui apruma.	B: You don't drink, right? You don't either? I drink.
TB: Não, aprumu não!	TB: No, I don't drink!
JB: O camanu aprumava.	JB: You used to drink [it].
TB: Mai num aprumu mai não.	TB: But I don't drink [it] anymore.
B: Mai aprumava muito, camanu cá tamém aprumava.	B: But he used to drink a lot, I used to drink [it] too.
DB: Agora num apruma mais, né? É pinga, né? Ele num apruma não.	DB: Now you don't drink [it] anymore, right? Cachaça, right? He doesn't drink [it] now.
SB: E aí, teve mulheres que calungavam?	SB: Yes, but were there women that spoke Calunga?
B: Hein?	B: What?
SB: Mulheres?	SB: Women?
TB: Mulher é ocaio.	TB: Woman is *ocaio*.
SB: É, mais as mulheres calungavam?	SB: Yes, but were there women that spoke Calunga?

Calunga	English
B: Tamém, tamém.	B: Also, also.
TB: Tem também. Tem umas que calunga. Tem ocaio faceiro, tem ocaio sucanado, ocaio mucafu.	TB: There are also. There are some that speak Calunga. There are distinguished women, there are married women, black women.
JB: Mai ei tá perguntano se tem ocaio que calunga.	JB: But he is asking if there are women that speak Calunga.
B: Tem, tem ocaio que calunga tamém. Tem sim, mai num é muitas não.	B: There are, there women that speak Calunga. There are yes, but there are not many.
JB: É pocas.	JB: They are few.
B: A minha, quase que arguma coisa ela apruma.	B: My [woman], almost can speak some.
TB: É pocas muié que sabi.	TB: There are few that know [it].
SB: Por que?	SB: Why?
JB: Porque num viajava, né? Na época eas num viajava, né?	JB: Because they didn't travel, right? At the time, they didn't travel.
TB: Isso tamém era muita brincadera que o povu inventava, né? Intão as muié ficava em casa, né?	TB: There was also a lot of jokes that the people invented, right? So the women stayed at home.
DB: Num tinha muita mulher tropera, né? Era difícil de tê mulher tropera, né?	DB: There were no women cowboys, right? It was difficult to have women cowboys, right?

Calunga	English
JB: E marangola? Cê sabe quê que é?	JB: And *marangola* ['horse, donkey']? Do you know what that is?
DB: Não.	DB: No.
B: Camanu cá aprumava na marangola.	B: I used to ride horses.
DB: Ah é, cavalo.	DB: Oh yes, horse.
B: Cavalo, burro. E embuá, cê sabe quê que é?	B: Horse, donkey. And *embuá* ['dog'], do you know what that is?
DB: Já vi mais eu num lembru.	DB: I saw but I don't remember.
B: Cachorru.	B: Dog.
DB: Ah é, cachorru. E tem o gatu qui é . . .	DB: Oh yes, dog. And cat is . . .
B: Papa ratu.	B: *Papa rato.*

Calunga Interview 2
June 25, 2004
Patrocínio, Minas Gerais

Participants:
MF: Marlenísio Ferreira, born 1955
C: Carlos, born 1947
AF: Ângela Ferreira, born 1960
TB: Tadeu de Barros, born 1960

Calunga	*English*
MF: Calunga cá. O ocai aprumô nus casuá, aprumô nus casuá, das cumbaca.	MF: Speak here. The woman left for the streets, she left for the streets of the city.
AF: Não a mas a ocai apruma pus casuá da cumbaca mai p'que ea foi buscá zipaque, né?	AF: No, but the woman left for the streets of the city because she went to get money, right?
C: Ah, foi buscá zipaque . . .	C: Ah, she went to look for money . . .
AF: Foi buscá zipaque.	AF: She went to look for money.
C: Pa aprumá noto injó!	C: So to go to another house!
AF: Pa aprumá noto injó, entendeu?	AF: So to go to another house, you understand?
C: Esse zipaque nu pruma nesse injó de cá.	C: That money is not gotten in this house here.
AF: Não. Sabe? O camanu aí ficô disaprumadu du zipaque calunga ôa.	AF: No. You know? That man there got poor, speaking nonsense.
MF: Isso!	MF: That's right!
C: É oto injó mais aprumado.	C: It's another house that is more beautiful.

Calunga	*English*
MF: Isso!	MF: That's right!
AF: Isso.	AF: That's right.
MF: . . . mas aqui, a ocai cumeça aprumá os cumba, cumeça aprumá os cumba, cumeça calungá ôa.	MF: . . . but here, this woman is beginning to get old, she starts to speak nonsense.
C: Não, não.	C: No, no.
MF: E fica aprumanu calunga ôa.	MF: And keeps speaking nonsense.
C: Num tá calunga ôa não, tá bem aprumada a calunga.	C: She is not speaking nonsense, she is speaking very well.
MF: A ocai, o camanu cá . . .	MF: That woman, I . . .
AF: Eu vô fa . . . a ocai bem aprumada . . . eu aprumo, né?	AF: I am going to sp[eak] . . . the woman is real pretty . . . yes, I get excited, right?
C: Ocai morrudu, né?	C: Strong woman, right?
MF: Morrudu.	MF: Strong.
C: Ai ó, tá veno, assim apruma muito, assim apruma.	C: Look there, she is looking, so she gets excited, so she gets excited.
AF: Pra ocai que apruma o indaro, pra ocai que apruma um . . . sabe? Pra í pru injó de letra. Hoje no cumba ofu.	AF: So that a woman that lights the fire ['gets ahead in life'], so that a women that . . . you know? So she goes to school. Today at night.
MF: No cumba ofu.	MF: At night.
C: É.	C: Yes.
MF: Aí ocai, a ocai sucanada cu camanu cá, né? Apruma os cumba cum calunga desaprumada, né? E o camanu cá num cupia.	MF: There a woman, a woman married with me, right? She gets old speaking nonsense, right? And I don't understand.

Calunga	*English*
AF: Hummm!	AF: Hummm!
C: Ah mai o camano pedaço da ocai era broto da calunga tamém!	C: Ah, but the woman's son spoke Calunga also!
MF: Sim!	MF: Yes!
AF: Ah era, era!	AF: He did, he did!
C: Eu lembo, nóis brincava muito. Ei calungava muito comigo, às veis eu num sabia, falava "o camano pô, o camanu cá ta viajanu nessa aí."	C: And I remember, we used to play a lot. He used to speak Calunga a lot with me, at times I didn't know, I used to say "oh man, I don't understand that."
AF: É! Porque o camanu sucanadu aí é aprumadu de calunga, né?	AF: Yes! Because the married man there speaks Calunga well.
C: É.	C: Yes.
AF: Mai a hora que cê apruma num zipaque . . .	AF: But when you ask for money . . .
C: Calunga ôa. É ôa, num pode calungá zipaque não?	C: Nonsense. It's bad, you can't talk about money, no?
AF: Calunga ôa. Eu falo "apruma um zipaque pa mim compá imberela, no injó di imberela." Ei fala "não, emberela de camanu desaprumado du zipaque é imberela de sengo."	AF: Nonsense. I say, "Give me some money so I can buy meat, at the butcher." He says, "No, meat for a poor man is forest meat [from hunting]."
C: De sengo? Nossa!	C: From the forest? Gosh!
AF: E é imberela mucafa ainda.	AF: It's even old meat.
C: É! Uai, porque que é imberela mucafa? Uai, uai! Uai, ai não uai! Imberela mucafa não, uai! É aprumá nu indaro, fica muitas cumba pa aprumá, uai, que isso, uai!	C: Yes! *Uai* [regional expression], why is it old meat? Uai, uai! Uai, there no uai! Old meat, no, uai! It has to be cooked, it takes a long time to get good, uai, what's that, uai!

Calunga	*English*
AF: Diz que é melhor, né?	AF: You say it is better, right?
MF: Ô mas o camanu cá num cupia essa calunga de zipaque, aprumá zipaque.	MF: Oh, but I don't understand that talk about money, to get money.
AF: "Ó aprumá zipaque" a calunga é oa!	AF: "To get money" and the Calunga [talk] is bad!
C: É fala de zipaque que o camanu viaja, ai ó! Ei tá ôa de zipaque, ó!	C: It's just to talk about money that the man doesn't pay attention there, look! He is bad with money, look!
AF: Aprumá calunga de ocai de pocas cum[ba] . . . sabe? De, de, de pocas cumba, ocaizim de pocas cumba. Assim ó, de mataca aprumado, assim sabe? Aí os mirante que tá . . . , sabe? Apruma que é uma beleza!	AF: To speak Calunga about a young woman, do you know? Young, young girls. So look, nice butt, you know? His eyes are . . . , you know? They work beautifully!
C: Ha, ha, ha, mira longe!	C: Ha, ha, ha, look far [away]!
AF: Mira longe!	AF: Look far [away]!
C: Muitas cumba pra frente!	C: Very many years ahead!
AF: Muito, muito pra fente!	AF: Very, very ahead!
C: Tá certo, aí eu sei, aí eu sei. Mai num pode calungá de zipaque cu camanu?	C: That's right, I know, I know. But you can't speak (Calunga) about money with him?
AF: Não. É ôa!	AF: No. It's bad!
MF: Camanu cá num cupia calunga . . .	MF: I don't understand Calunga . . .
C: Camanu cá . . . cumé que fala "quando nóis istudava juntu," cumé que fala na calunga?	C: I . . . how do you say "when we used to study together," how do you say that in Calunga?

Calunga	English
MF: É no "injó de letra," "dandarazim."	MF: It's "in school," "kid."
AF: Injó de letra.	AF: In school.
C: É dandarazim calungava cu camanu cá "não camanu, assim num dá," queria que fosse assim muito certim, nunca fui, né? Uai! Si fui expulso do Colégio Santo Antônio. Uai, expulso! Do Colégio Santo Antônio, então quer dizer que num foi boa a . . .	C: And the kid used to say to me, "No man, that doesn't work," he wanted me to be very correct, I never was, right? Uai! If I was expelled from the Colégio Santo Antônio. Uai, expelled! From Colégio Santo Antônio, then that means that it wasn't good . . .
AF: É eu sei, a calunga é ôa desde dandará mes[mo]! Ha, ha, ha . . .	AF: And I know, that Calunga [speech] is bad since he was a kid! Ha, ha, ha . . .
C: Aí pegô, né? Mas o camanu cá era aprumadu!	C: That was harsh, right? But I was good!
AF: É!?	AF: Yes!?
C: Era aprumadu lá!	C: I was good there!
MF: É!	MF: Yes!
AF: É!? Muito santim pa ocaia sucanada!	AF: Yes!? A lot of saints for a married woman!
MF: Ah!	MF: Ah!
C: Não mai nu injó de letra, eu e o camanu, muito certinho, né?	C: No, but at school, me and him, very correct, right?
MF: Muito bem!	MF: Very good!

Calunga Interview 3
June 26, 2004
Patrocínio, Minas Gerais

Participants:
VO: Vicente Otaviano, born 1938
EA: Eurípedes Alves, born 1940
Mãe de EA: Mother of Eurípedes Alves

Calunga	*English*
EA: Pode. Pode ir. O camanu cá, o camanu cá tava aprumadu lá nu injó onde o camanu apruma cuzeque, na onde o camanu lá apruma marafu pus camanu. Aí u camanim quinhamô lá naqueli injó, aí o camanu calungô com o camanu: "Quê que cê qué aqui camanu? Qué aprumá marafu?"	EA: You can, you can go [speak]. I, I was there in the house where you sleep, where you drink cachaça. There the man went to that house, there the man spoke with the man: "What do you want here, man? Do you want to drink cachaça?"
(cont.): "Queru."	(cont.): "I do."
(cont.): Tem um camanu aí que nóis já quinhamô cos ingomu, ele foi cuzecu aqui per . . . du . . . du . . . onde se apruma marafa, Vicente Otavianu.	(cont.): There is a man there that we already went walking with the cattle, he went to sleep here close by . . . by . . . where you drink wine, Vicente Otaviano.
(cont.): "E aí, quem é aqueli camanu?"	(cont.): "And there, who is that man?"
VO: É aquei camanu imbundu que gosta de aprumá ua marafa na cupia, né?	VO: It is that black man that likes to drink cachaça, right?
EA: Ah . . . esse camanu apruma marafa na cupia até hoje, uai?	EA: Ah . . . that man drinks cachaça until today, uai?
VO: Apruma.	VO: He drinks.

Calunga	English
EA: Ah . . . mai esse camanu, nóis quinhamô cum ingome, aquei camanu era aprumadu nu berrante. Cadê o berrante? Eta mundu, se nóis tivesse um berrante pa nóis tocá.	EA: Ah . . . but that man, we went walking with the cattle, that man was good at the gaudy [cattle horn]. Where is the gaudy? If we only had a gaudy for us to play.
VO: Pois é!	VO: That's right!
EA: Camanu, eu lembru, nóis tava quinhamanu cus ingome, o camanim cá, ocê trabaiava na guia da boiada, eu lembu duma passage, camanu, cê calungô:	EA: Man, I remember, we used to walk with the cattle, me, you used to work on the cattle routes, I remember a passage, man, you said:
(cont.): "O boi, da Vera." Nóis tava quinhamanu cus ingome lá, das ota cumbaca que tem. Cê era solteru camanu, cê vê o tan de anu qui tem issu.	(cont.): "Oh ox, of Vera." We were walking with the cattle there, from other cities. You were single, you see how long ago it was.
VO: Tem muitus cumba.	VO: It was a long time ago.
EA: Muintus cumba, camanu! Aí camanim, agora vortanu a falá lá donde cê tá aprumanu cuzeca, eu fui aprumá ua marafa na cupia, camanu, lá naquei . . .	EA: Many years, man! There, boy, now returning to speak about where you were sleeping, I went to drink cachaça, man, there in that . . .
VO: Nu injozim . . .	VO: In the little house . . .
EA: Nu injozim de marafa.	EA: In the little bar.
VO: Nu injó de marafa per du enjó du camanu cá.	VO: In the bar by my house.
EA: Camanu.	EA: Man.
VO: Calunga!	VO: Speak!
EA: Camanu, tava aprumanu marafu. Marafu não, omenha de viago, camanu.	EA: Man, I was drinking cachaça. Cachaça, no, cachaça [another type of cachaça, or liquor], man.

Calunga	*English*
VO: Omenha de viangu!	VO: Cachaça!
EA: Porque marafa é de . . . Centru Ispírita né, camanu?	EA: Because *marafa* ['cachaça'] is from the . . . Spiritual Center, right, man?
VO: É, é sim.	VO: It is, it is, yes.
EA: Nóis tava aprumanu omenha de viango, aí chegô um camanu imbundu, e calungô cu camanu maioral du injó: Pruma marafu aí! Aí o camanu, prumô marafa pra ele, o camanu . . .	EA: We were drinking cachaça, there arrived a black man and spoke with the owner of the house: Put a cachaça there! There the man grabbed a cachaça for him, the man . . .
VO: Prumô na mucota.	VO: He drank.
EA: Prumô na mucota.	EA: He drank.
VO: E aí?	VO: And then?
EA: E aí cumeçô a calungá vapora.	EA: And then he began to speak about crazy things.
VO: Calungá vapora.	VO: Speaking about crazy things.
EA: E cumeçô a calungá vapora. O camanu cá aprumô nu injó pra aprumá . . . os uíque.	EA: And he began to speak crazy things. I went home to drink . . .
VO: Uíque.	VO: A "sweet" drink.
EA: Mais o camanu qui tava aprumanu omenha di viangu na mucota, cumeçô a ficá vapora.	EA: But the man that was drinking cachaça began to get crazy.
VO: Calungá vapora.	VO: To speak crazy things.
EA: Na calunga, e o camanu, que foi aprumá . . . "leiti de ingome."	EA: In Calunga, and the man went to drink "milk" of the cow.

Calunga	English
VO: "Omenha de ingome," omenha de ingome!	VO: *Omenha de ingome* ['milk'], omenha de ingome!
EA: É o omenha de engome, camanu?	EA: Is it *omenha de engome*, man?
VO: "Omenha de engome!"	VO: *Omenha de engome!*
EA: "Omenha de engome!"	EA: *Omenha de engome!*
VO: O camanu tá . . .	VO: The man is . . .
Mãe de EA: É a marafa na cupia.	Mother of EA: It is the cachaça in [his] head.
EA: Aí foi calunganu, foi calunganu, foi calunganu, aí o camanu que foi aprumá a omenha de ingome, calungô:	EA: There he went on talking, went on talking, went on talking, there the man that drank milk spoke:
(cont.): "Ô camanu, cê tá aprumanu omenha de viangu na mucota e . . . tá calunganu vapora." Ele, u camanu qui tava aprumanu omenha de viangu calungô:	(cont.): "Oh man, you are drinking cachaça and speaking crazy things." He, the man that was drinking cachaça, said:
(cont.): "Que! Calunganu calunga vapora! Eu vô ti aprumá o faim." Foi aprumô o faim nu camanu, o camanu aprumô nele o mocó de indaru.	(cont.): "What! Speaking, speaking things without making sense! I am going to stab you [with a knife]." He went and attacked the man, the man grabbed a firearm [a gun].
VO: Ah . . . o mocó de indaru!	VO: Ah . . . a firearm!
EA: E aprumô nele o mocó de indaru. E o camanu aprumô na Ingraterra, aprumô quimbimbi.	EA: And he shot him. And the man fell to the floor and died.
VO: Aprumô quimbimbi.	VO: He died.

Calunga	English
EA: E o camanu qui foi aprumá... a omenha de maveru, quinhamô e saiu fora da calunga. O camanu maioral du injó calungô cus caiumba:	EA: And the man that went to drink... drink milk, left the conversation. The owner of the house spoke with the "soldiers" [the police]:
(cont.): "Opa, aprumô o quimbimbi aqui nu meu injó de marafu e os caiumba aprumô. É o camanu cor de imbundu que levô o mocó de indaru, qui aprumô o mocó de indaru, qui tava aprumanu marafa e foi cu camanu aprumá o maveru. O camanu maveru aprumô o mocó de indaru nu camanu imbundu, ... caiu fora."	(cont.): "Oh, someone died here in my bar and the soldiers got interested. It is the black man that took the firearm, that was drinking cachaça and went with the man to drink milk. The white man shot the black man, ... he left.
VO: Aí os caiumba...	VO: There the soldiers....
EA: Os caiumba... saiu procuranu o camanu.	EA: The soldiers left to look for the man.
Mãe de EA: Caiu nu sengu.	Mother of EA: He went to the forest.
VO: Nu sengu.	VO: To the forest.
EA: E o camanu aprumô fora da cumbaca, aprumô fora da cumbaca e... não deu pa pegá o camanu.	EA: And the man went outside of the city, left the city and they couldn't catch him.
VO: O camanu quinhamô.	VO: The man got away.
EA: O camanu quinhamô! Ah mas e o camanu qui aprumô o quimbimbi? O camanu qui aprumô o quimbimbi, tava com o marafu na cupia, a omenha de viangu na cupia e calunganu vapora. E aprumô nu camanu qui ia aprumá a omenha de de de de de...	EA: The man got away! Ah, but the man that died? The man that died was drunk, he was drinking and speaking crazy things. And he grabbed the man that was going to grab *omenha* ['water'] of of of of...

Calunga	English
VO: De viangu. Omenha de viangu!	VO: *De viango* ['cachaça']. *Omenha de viango!*
EA: Ah sô! Omenha de viangu não, camanu! Omenha de ingome! O camanu que ia aprumá a omenha de engome que aprumô o mocó de indaru nu camanu qui ia aprumá cu ele nu faim.	EA: Ah senor! *Omenha de viango* ['cachaça'], no, man! *Omenha de ingome* ['milk']! The man that was going to grab the milk that shot the man that was going to hurt him with a knife.
VO: Ah . . .	VO: Ah . . .
EA: E aí camanu, e aprumô o mocó e aprumô o faim.	EA: And there the man, and he took out a firearm and took out a knife.

Calunga Interview 4
June 27, 2005
Patrocínio, Minas Gerais

Participants:
JB: "Barraca" (João Batista), born 1954
JRS: Jorge de Souza, born 1964
JLS: Joel de Souza, born 1962
JL: Joaquim Luís, born 1928
GL: Glauce de Souza
TB: Tadeu de Barros, born 1960
SB: Steven Byrd (researcher)
DB: Daniela Bassani (researcher)

Calunga	*English*
JB: E aí camanu ofú, vamu aprumá pa dentu du injó, uai.	JB: And there black man, let's go in the house, uai.
JRS: Camanu num tá apumanu a nanga mai, não.	JRS: He is not putting on [nice] pants anymore.
JL: Eu falei que era pa aprumá uma nanga, sô!	JL: I said that it was to wear [nice] pants, sir!
JRS: O camanu!	JRS: Oh, man!
JB: Uai! Ei já calungô ca ocai ca nanga daquei jeito, agora . . . vamu lá Chiquito, que ocê é mai veio.	JB: Uai! He has already spoken with the woman in that way, now . . . let's go, Chiquito, you are older.
DB: Num precisa trocá de calça não, né?	DB: You do not need to change your pants, ok?
JRS: Bora lá Chiquito!	JRS: Let's go, Chiquito!
JB: Vá, vai lá Chiquito que o senhor é mai veio eu num vô te matá.	JB: Go, go there Chiquito, that you are older I am not going to get in your way.

Calunga	English
JL: Nãã, eu vô . . . o que ceis calungá, eu vô dá ôa na calunga do ceis!	JL: No, I am going . . . what you speak, I am going to do bad in your Calunga [talk]!
JL: Entra pra dentro, sô!	JL: Come inside, sir!
TB: Tá bão!	TB: OK!
JB: O camanu e a ocai tá querenu qui os camanu cá calunga sobri?	JB: The man and the woman are wanting that we speak [Calunga] about?
DB: Qualqué coisa que ceis quisé calungá.	DB: Whatever you want to talk [in Calunga] about.
JB: Os camanu é de qual omenha?	JB: You [both] are from which *omenha* ['water, region']?
DB: Eu? Omenha é o quê memo?	DB: Me? *Omenha* is what?
JB: De qual água que ceis é?	JB: From which *water* are you [both] from?
DB: Uai num sei, eu num intendu issu não!	DB: Uai, I don't know, I don't understand that!
TB: Qual cidade?	TB: Which city?
DB: Qual água?	DB: Which water?
JB: Qual cidade, qual cumbaca que ceis é?	JB: Which city, from which *cumbaca* ['city'] are you [both] from?
DB: Ah! Eu sô de . . . daqui de Minas, eu sô de Arceburgo.	DB: Ah! I am from . . . from here, from Minas, I am from Arceburgo.
JB: E o camanu?	JB: And the man?
DB: Ele é de . . .	DB: He is from . . .

Calunga	*English*
SB: Inglaterra.	SB: Land [not understanding].
JB: Ó!	JB: Oh!
SB: Inglaterra qué dizê fora, né?	SB: *Inglaterra* means 'away,' doesn't it?
DB: Ei é d'otas inglaterra.	DB: He is from other *lands* ['foreign lands'].
SB: Otras inglaterra.	SB: Other *lands*.
JB: E . . . o camanu gosta de aprumá saravá o cumé que é?	JB: And . . . you like to dance or what?
SB: Saravá? Quê que é saravá? Saravá é . . . ah! esqueci saravá.	SB: *Saravá* ['dance']? What is *saravá*? *Saravá* is . . . ah! I forgot *saravá*.
JB: Camanu gosta de aprumá uíque na mucota?	JB: You like to drink [alcohol]?
SB: Ah! Gosto, gosto de cerveja.	SB: Ah! I like, I like beer.
JB: Omenha de vinhango não, né?	JB: Not Cachaça, right?
SB: É . . . um poquinho.	SB: Yes . . . a little bit.
JB: E marafa?	JB: And wine?
SB: Ah . . . eu gosto, de vez em quando, um pouquinho só, né.	SB: Ah . . . I like, sometimes, only a little bit.
JB: O camanu gosta de ocai ou não?	JB: Do you like the woman or not?
SB: Gosto.	SB: I like her.
JB: O camanu é sucanado?	JB: Are you married?
SB: Hum?	SB: Hum?

Calunga	*English*
JB: Ocai tamém não, né?	JB: The woman isn't neither, right?
DB: Não.	DB: No.
JB: O camanu já apruma nessas cumbaca há quantus cumba?	JB: How long have you been in the region?
SB: Eu tô com trinta.	SB: I am thirty. [Not understanding question]
DB: Não quatro *escumba*.	DB: No, four years. [Not understanding question]
SB: Juntos?	SB: Together? [Not understanding question]
JB: Quantos cumba que o camanu apruma nessas cumbaca aqui?	JB: How many years have you been in this region here?
SB: Quatro? É, quatro cumba.	SB: Four? Yes, four years. [Not understanding question]
JB: E o camanu tá . . . quereno calungá pes . . .	JB: And you are . . . wanting to speak [Calunga] about?
JL: Mai cum . . . , né?	JL: But with . . . , right?
DB: Oi?	DB: What?
JL: Morrudu, né?	JL: *Morrudu* ['strong, great'], right?
DB: Qué isso? Num sei.	DB: What is that? I don't know.
JB: Agora cê tem que expricá pra ela.	JB: Now you have to explain for her.
JB: É . . .	JB: It is . . .
JRS: O mucafo tá calunganu . . .	JRS: The old black man is speaking [Calunga] . . .

Calunga	*English*
JB: Tá . . . calunganu mei . . . otas calunga, calunga de umbundu.	JB: He is . . . speaking Calunga with some other Calunga words, Calunga words of blacks [an unknown Calunga].
DB: Você calunga tamém?	DB: Do you speak Calunga too?
GL: Não, não. Entendo alguma coisa só mas num calungu não.	GL: No, no. I understand some things but I don't speak Calunga, no.
JB: O camanu vai aprumá curima aqui nu . . . nu . . . nas otas cumbaca?	JB: Are you going to work here in . . . in . . . in these parts?
SB: Aprumá curima . . . cumbaca . . .	SB: *Aprumá curima* ['to do work'] . . . *cumbaca* ['city'] . . . [*not understanding*]
TB: Trabalhá aqui na região?	TB: Work here in the region?
DB: Não, nós num vamu.	DB: No, we are not going to.
SB: Ah, Serra do Salitre.	SB: Ah, Serra do Salitre. [not understanding]
JL: Vai aprumá calunga nas cumbaca e saravá lá nas cumbaca da omenha grande.	JL: You are going to speak Calunga in the region and dance there in the big city.
DB: Quê que é saravá?	DB: What is *saravá* ['dance']?
JRS: Mai o mucafo é . . . !	JRS: But the old black man is . . . !
JL: Num sabe quê que é saravá não?	JL: He doesn't know what *saravá* is, right?
DB: Na calunga não.	DB: In Calunga, no.
JL: É í . . .	JL: It's 'to go' . . .

Calunga	*English*
DB: Oi?	DB: What?
JL: É í lá pra cidade, í lá . . .	JL: It's there in the city, to go there . . .
DB: Ah tá!	DB: Ah, ok!
JRS: O camanu aprumô ua marafa na mucota ali.	JRS: You drank cachaça there.
JB: O camanu aprumô ua marafa, num tá querenu calungá.	JB: The man [JRS] drank cachaça, he is not wanting to speak [Calunga].
JRS: Não é que . . .	JRS: No, it's that . . .
JB: Por que que esse camanu tá sem calungá?	JB: Why is that man not speaking [Calunga]?
JRS: Camanu tá . . . ofu tá . . . tá . . .	JRS: Man is . . . the black man is . . . is . . .
JB: Tá ôa de calunga lá.	JB: His Calunga is bad.
JL: Não! Pode aprumá na calunga. Num tem nada a vê, uai.	JL: No! He can speak Calunga. It has nothing to do with it, uai.
DB: A lá chegô!	DB: There, he arrived!
JL: Num é só cum ocai que cê vai aprumá não. Cê vai aprumá cu imbundu, cu [. . .]	JL: It's not just with the woman that you are going to speak. You are going to speak with the black man, with [. . .]
JB: Cu imbundu.	JB: With the black man.
JLS: Pó aprumá gatuvira na mucota?	JLS: Can I drink coffee?
JL: Heim? E vai aprumá . . .	JL: What? And he is going to do . . .

Calunga Interview 5
June 28, 2004
Patrocínio, Minas Gerais

Participants:
R: Ramiro Paulino, born 1930
O: Oswaldo Diniz, born 1949
J: José de Barros, born 1935

Calunga	*English*
O: Camanu cá, ummm.	O: Me, ummm.
R: E o imbundu, o imbundu.	R: And the black man ['I'], the black man ['I'].
O: Foi atrás do imbundu e traz.	O: Went after the black man [me] and brought [me].
R: E o imbundu quinhamô, nu urungu aqui . . .	R: And the black man ['I'] came, in the car here . . .
O: Tava aprumanu cuzeca.	O: You were sleeping.
R: Tava aprumanu cuzeca e . . .	R: I was sleeping and . . .
O: A cuzeca tava ôa e . . . disaprumô du injó . . . cu mirante ôa.	O: You slept bad and you left the house . . . with tired eyes.
R: O mirante aprumô e o mirante tava disaprumandu mais aprumô o mirante.	R: I opened my eyes which were tired but now they are all right.
J: Num aprumô uma omenha na cupia, não?	J: You did not put water on your head, no?
O: Oh oche! O camanu cá, o camanu cá chamô o camanu pra aprumá um gatuvira ei diz que num, já tinha aprumadu.	O: Oh, gosh! I, I called the man to drink coffee and he said no, that he had already drank [some].

Calunga	English
J: Hmmm já tinha aprumadu, né?	J: Hmmm, he had already drank some, right?
R: Então, aí, o imbundu cá aprumô nu urunguim pa vim aprumá calunga, sabe?	R: So, there, I got in the little car to come and speak Calunga, you know?
O: Nota cumbaca?	O: In another city?
R: Nessa cumbaca. Agora, o imbundu cá já tá acustumadu a quinhamá potas cumbaca, transportanu ingomo, sabe? Isso eu tinha, já tem uns trinta, quarenta ano qui eu cumpanho.	R: In this city. Now, I am already used to going to other cities, taking cattle, you know? That I have done, it has been some thirty, forty years that I accompany [the cattle].
O: O camanu cá chegô na casa du imbundu . . . o imbuá queria aprumá o zingrin nu . . .	O: I arrived at the black man's home [your home] . . . the dog wanted to put the tooth in [bite me] . . .
J: É!	J: Yes!
O: Quis, é!	O: He wanted to, yes!
J: Nossa!	J: Wow!
R: Ei lá, no injó du imbundu cá, tem um punhadu de . . .	R: He there, in my house, has a lot of . . .
J: Imbuá?	J: Dogs?
R: De imbuazim mas eis é custoso, sabe? E agora, os camanu apruma na batedera do injó du imbundu cá, ele tem que tá de oio senão eis poi aprumá o zingrim na quinhama dus camanu, né? E . . . a gente fica assim, coisa, quilibranu.	R: Puppies, but they are difficult, you know? And now, the men knock on the door of my house, I have to keep an eye on them because if not they can bite the legs of the men, right? And . . . we get like, something, dealing with it.

Calunga	English
O: E esse camanu cá aprumava a marafa.	O: And I used to drink cachaça.
J: É? Fica ôa.	J: Yes? It is bad.
R: E prumava bem aprumadu, né?	R: And I used to drink a lot, right?
J: Marafa na cupia.	J: Drunk.
R: Hoje, o imbundu tá ôa de tudu, tá ôa, mais ou meno. Ei pruma aquelis marafinha, esses marafinha, que num pode aprumá a marafa, sabe? Porque . . . o relógio do imbundu cá, é quatorze, sabe? Assim mei quatorze, sabe? Tá quereno dá ôa, já deu ôa já uma veizi, mais prumô.	R: Today, I am unhealthy of everything, I am unhealthy, more or less. I drink those little cachaças, those little cachaças, but I can't drink cachaça, you know? Because . . . my clock is fourteen ['bad'], you know? Like about fourteen, you know? It is asking for a problem, I already had a problem once, but I recovered.
O: Se não, . . . ele ia aprumá e ia pu embuete, né?	O: If not, . . . it would go to the wood ['coffin,' you would die], right?
R: Pois é. E eu sempre tô [. . .]	R: That's it. And I always am [. . .]
J: É uai!	J: It is, uai!
R: Pa vê se escapa. Nos cumba que vem vino mais pa tras, a gente já tá mais desaprumado assim de . . .	R: To see if I escape. The years that keep coming, we get worse like that of . . .
J: O camanu tem imbunim?	J: Do you have [black] children?
O: Ah, tem uai!	O: Ah, I have, uai!
J: Quantos imbunim?	J: How many [black] children?
R: Sô . . . o imbundu cá é . . . aprumô dez imbunim.	R: Sir . . . I have ten [black] children.
J: Dez!?	J: Ten!?

Calunga	*English*
R: Dez imbunim, o imbundu cá é aprumadu cum dez imbunim.	R: Ten [black] children, I have ten children.
J: E ocai inda tá aprumada?	J: And your wife is well?
R: Ocai du imbundu cá?	R: My wife?
J: É.	J: Yes.
R: A ocai de camanu cá já ficô quatorze.	R: My wife became fourteen already.[1]
J: Já ficô catorze!? Nossa!!	J: She already became fourteen!? Wow!!
R: Já quatorze, tá cum quinze anu que . . . tô desaprumadu.	R: She [is] already fourteen, it has been fifteen years since . . . I am worse.
O: Tá aprumadu em otas cumbaca.	O: You are going to other cities.
R: Tá aprumada em otas cumba, sabe?	R: She was pretty in other times, you know?
J: Ah sei.	J: Ah, I know.
R: Em otos cumba. Agora, imbundu cá, tá ôa, tá quinhamanu . . . pa vê se pruma alguma ocai e coisa. As ocai tá aprumada em riba du imbundu mas o imbundu, né? Tá ôa.	R: In other times. Now, I am unhealthy, I am going to see if I can get another woman and such. The women are interested in me but I, right? I am unhealthy.
J: O imbundu tem injó?	J: Do you have a house?
R: Tem injó, o injó lá.	R: I have a house, a house there.
O: O camanu tá caçanu ocai aprumada de zipaque.	O: You are hunting [looking for] a rich woman.
J: De zipaque!	J: With money!

Calunga	English
R: Maisi os ocai tá querenu aprumá nu imbundu cá, aprumá assim qué. O imbundu cá tem injó, é pu bem aprumandu.	R: But the women are wanting to stay with me, to stay so they want. I have a house and it is nice.
J: E o zipaque?	J: And the money?
R: O zipaque, ele é ôa! Maisi qué disaprumá o imbundu cá! Qué disaprumá o imbundu cá! E o imbundu cá, sem injó num tem jeitu de . . .	R: The money, it is little! But it causes problems! It causes problems! And I, without a house, there is no way to . . .
J: Sucaná.	J: To marry.
R: De prumá, né?	R: To arrange, right?
O: O camanu-cá . . .	O: I . . .
J: Ummm . . .	J: Ummm . . .
O: O camanu-cá ele . . . o camanu cá arrumô ocai que tem urungu.	O: I . . . I arranged a woman that has a car.
R: É! Ha ha ha . . .	R: Yes! Ha ha ha . . .
J: Tem urungu?!	J: She has a car?!
R: Ha ha ha . . . é issaí.	R: Ha ha ha . . . that's it there.
J: Mai tem que sucaná memo, uai!	J: But you have to marry, uai!
O: É uai!	O: Yes, uai!
R: É . . . eu . . . vão levanu, né? O imbundu cá quinhama assim cu as ocai . . . mai só mes calunga com eles, a calunga assim . . .	R: Yes . . . I . . . we are going on, right? I go out with women . . . but I just talk to them, just talk . . .
O: O camanu cá já apumô muito em riba de ingomo potas cumbaca.	O: I have driven many cattle to other cities.

Calunga	English
J: Tamém? Ah! Intão foi que nem eu!	J: Also? Ah! So you were like me!
R: Ah muitas cumbaca, tem quarenta, quarenta e cinco anu, eu aprumava . . .	R: Ah, many cities, it has been forty, forty-five years, [that] I used to do . . .
O: Injó de ingomu.	O: Cattle's house.
J: Quandu mexia cus ingomu, aprumava injó . . .	J: When I used to work with cattle, I used to get a house . . .
O: Marangola.	O: Horse.
R: Marangora. Eu quemava o aio . . .	R: Horse. I used to cook . . .
O: Tipoque.	O: Beans.
R: É, eu quemava o aio, o tipoque pa pus camanu, sabe? Dez camanu . . .	R: Yes, I used to cook, beans for the men, you know? Ten men . . .
O: Aprumá na mucota.	O: To eat.
R: Dez camanu quinhamanu . . . quinhamanu cus ingomu, né? Cumigu. E nóis, eu sempe quemava o aiu; todus, todus cumba. Todu dia, né? Du cumba, eu quemava o aiu direitinho pra eles, né? Dois cargueru, né? Porque . . . de quinhamá cu macenete nosso, né? Eu quemava o aiu, arriava, disarriava, tudu diretu.	R: Ten men travelling . . . travelling with the cattle, right? With me. And we, I used to cook every, every day. Every day, right? One year, I used to cook every day for them, right? Two cargos, right? Because . . . to travel with our *macenete*, right? I used to cook, I used to prepare, to dismantle [the cargo], all right.
O: Cumbaca dali . . .	O: City there . . .

Calunga	English
R: Pus ingomu num soprá, pus ingomu num soprá os urungu. É . . . o imbundu-cá quinhamô muito!	R: So that the cattle would not blow [die], for the cattle not to blow [to die on] the cargos. Yes . . . I traveled a lot!
J: O camanu doido pa sucaná cu ocai!	J: The man is crazy to marry [a woman]!
O: Não mai o camanu que eu tabaiava no urungu du injó tem muito zipaque.	O: No, but the man that I used to work for in the mechanic shop has a lot of money.
R: É u camanu é aprumadu du zipaque! É dotas cumbaca, né? Aprumá o . . .	R: Yes, the man has a lot of money! He is from somewhere else, right?
J: Intão é pur isso que qué sucaná, uai!	J: So it for that that he want to marry, uai!
O: É, iche, é!	O: It is, *iche*, it is!
R: Eu aprumava em muitas cumbaca!	R: I used to go to many cities!
O: Cumbaca de longe.	O: Faraway cities.

Calunga Interview 6
June 29, 2004
Patrocínio, Minas Gerais

Participants:
JI: João Ilarindo, born 1925
JEM: José Eustáquio Mendes, born 1945
MDF: Marcely Damião Fernandes, born 1954
TB: Tadeu de Barros, born 1960

Calunga	*English*
JI: Qualqué assuntu?	JI: Any topic?
TB: Quarqué assuntu qui cês falá.	TB: Any topic that you [want] to talk about.
MDF: O João, a abertura é sua.	MDF: João, you start.
JEM: É, João ocê qui é o chefe, o mais véio . . .	JEM: Yes, João, you are the boss, the oldest . . .
JI: Ieu num sei, uai.	JI: I don't know, uai.
JEM: Cê qui é o camanu maioral. O camanu du sengo, o camanu du sengu tá de . . . mirante.	JEM: You that are the boss. The man from the forest, the man from the forest is . . . watching.
JI: Ei foi caçá . . . ei foi pescar.	JI: He went hunting . . . he went to fish.
JEM: Remante, remanu . . .	JEM: Boat, rowing . . .
JI: Mai ei foi aprumá nu sengo ei foi aprumá malumbí não, ei foi aprumá o curima.	JI: But he went to the forest, he did not go to fish, he went to get some food.
JEM: Pois é, aprumá o curiá cus camanu . . .	JEM: Yes, to get some food with the men . . .
JI: Cus camanu maiorá lá, né?	JI: With the bosses there, right?

Calunga	*English*
JEM: É.	JEM: Yes.
JI: Pegá malumbí, né? E ele diz quei quimbimbô, né?	JI: To fish, right? And he says he died, right?
JEM: É. Levaru imbuá?	JEM: Yes. Did they take the dogs?
JEM: O colega.	JEM: Hey, friend.
TB: Ô Marcely!	TB: Hey, Marcely!
MDF: Hum.	MDF: Hum.
JEM: Levaru imbuá? Pu sengu.	JEM: Did they take the dogs? To the forest.
MDF: É. Levaru.	MDF: Yes. They took [them].
JEM: Levô?! Ha ha ha . . .	JEM: He took?! Ha ha ha . . .
MDF: A omenha de viangu, era . . . é forte.	MDF: The cachaça was . . . it is strong.
JEM: Pois é, isso que eu . . .	JEM: Yes it is, that that I . . .
JI: Tudu marafu.	JI: All cachaça.
MDF: Omenha de viangu, uai.	MDF: Cachaça, uai.
JEM: Pois é, esquentô uma marafa na cupia lá.	JEM: Yes, he got warmed up with cachaça there.
MDF: Omenha de viangu.	MDF: Cachaça.
JI: Nooosa!	JI: Wow!
JEM: Tá doido.	JEM: You're crazy.
JI: Mas ficava . . . o cumba, quandu dava ôa, tava dismorumbinu a mema . . . o memo cumba?	JI: But he was . . . the year, when he was doing bad, he was "fishing" the same . . . the same day?[2]

Calunga	*English*
MDF: Os camanu maioral?	MDF: The bosses?
JI: É . . . aprumava café na mucota e . . . pegava o molumbí de omenha e aprumava os cumba só pra apruma . . .	JI: Yes . . . he drank coffee and . . . fished and spent the days only to . . .
JEM: Embe . . . emberela . . . ?	JEM: Meat . . . meat [beef]?
MDF: Só pa aprumá na mucota.	MDF: Just to eat.

Abbreviations

The following abbreviations are used in the glossary in chapter 5, in table 5.1, and in examples in chapter 6.

Lexical sources

CA: Falares africanos na Bahia (Castro 2001:131–358)

DF: Undaca de Quimbundo (Dornas Filho 1943:74–81)

MF: Dialeto crioulo sanjoanense (Machado Filho 1943/1985:121–41)

Q: Língua do Negro da Costa (Queiroz 1998:108–38)

VF: Cupópia (Vogt and Fry 1996:281–341)

Etymological sources

A: Alves (1951)

B: Bentley (1887/1967, 1895/1967)

C: Cunha (2001)

CA: Castro (2001)

J: Johnston (1919)

L: Lopes (2003)

LA: Laman (1964)

M: Maia (1994)

N: Nascentes (1988)

VF: Vogt and Fry (1996)

Sociolects in which Africanized terms are encountered (Castro 2001: chap. 4).

BA: "Bahia"; Bahian Portuguese

BR: "Brasil"; Brazilian Portuguese, or standard Brazilian Portuguese

LP: "Linguagem Popular"; Brazilian Portuguese vernacular

LS: "Língua-de-Santo"; speech from Afro-Brazilian religions of Bahia

PS: "Povo-de-Santo"; a particular Afro-Brazilian religious sect of Bahia

Notes

CHAPTER ONE

1. The population figure is from the 2007 census. See www.patrocinio.mg.gov.br for official government statistics and other information relating to the municipality of Patrocínio, Minas Gerais.
2. Additional Calunga interviews and corresponding translations can be found in the appendix.

CHAPTER TWO

1. Luís de Camões, often referred to as the Shakespeare of Portugal by literary scholars, has immortalized Vasco da Gama's India voyage in his epic poem *Os Lusíadas* (*The Lusiads*), published in 1572.
2. Portugal's twentieth-century military engagement in Angola was referred to as "Os cus de Judas" by celebrated Portuguese novelist and Angolan war veteran António Lobo Antunes (1979/2004). His novel by that title was translated into English as *South of Nowhere* and *The Land South of Nowhere* but in Portuguese literally means 'the assholes of Judas.'
3. This is only a sample of the indigenous Brazilian peoples that Abreu describes. See his *Chapters of Brazil's Colonial History, 1500–1800*, for the complete list.
4. For a comprehensive overview of the origins of slavery and the slave system in the Americas, see Klein (1986), chapter 1.
5. In contrast, the 1790 census of the United States reported that 20 percent of the population was of African origin (Olsen 2003:59).
6. Contemporary statistics regarding the percentage of Afro-Brazilians are in dispute. For instance, Boadi-Siaw (2007:164) writes that 44 percent of the total population of Brazil is of African descent, while Leal (2001:291) contends that Afro-Brazilians represent 53 percent of Brazil's total population.
7. Other than Brazil, significant maroon slave communities have existed in Mexico, Colombia, Ecuador, Suriname, Cuba, and Jamaica (Price 1999).

8. For further discussion of African and Afro-Brazilian resistance and rebellion and the proliferation of quilombos in Brazil, see Leal (2001) and Reis (2001).

CHAPTER THREE

1. See Lipski (2005) for a comprehensive list and analyses of Afro-Iberian texts from the Iberian Peninsula and Latin America. The appendices provide excerpts of Afro-Portuguese and Afro-Brazilian literature.
2. See Holm (1989:272–77) for further discussion, bibliography, and examples of Upper Guinea Portuguese creoles.
3. Holm (2004:51) argues that "there are abundant phonological, syntactic, and lexical features linking São Tomé Creole Portuguese and [Brazilian Portuguese vernacular, BPV]." See the discussion on the origins of BPV later in this chapter.
4. See Holm (1989:277–84) and Hagemeijer (2009) for further discussion, bibliography, and examples of Gulf of Guinea Portuguese creoles.
5. See Maurer (1995) and Lorenzino (1998a) for further discussion, bibliography, and examples of Angolar Creole Portuguese.
6. Mello (1997:211–12) notes that Língua Geral is still spoken along the Rio Negro in the Amazon region.
7. It is worth noting that evidence of Portuguese is found in various creole languages of the Caribbean: Papiamentu, Saramaccan, and the French-based creole of Guyana. This evidence suggests that Portuguese may have been spoken on the early coastal plantations of Brazil and then moved north into the Caribbean region in some unclear manner. See Holm (1989:312–16, 2004:51–54) for further discussion.
8. According to Azevedo (2005:196), some forty languages are spoken in contemporary Angola, mostly Bantu. "Fluency in Portuguese is limited," he notes, "and most speakers speak a variety of European Portuguese influenced by native languages." Umbundu is the most spoken language in the country (at 29.8 percent of the population), more so than Portuguese (26.3 percent). As for Kimbundu (15.4 percent), Azevedo states that it "seems to be in a process of replacement by Angolan Popular Portuguese." Although Azevedo provides no comparative statistical data, he notes that approximately 1.5 million people speak Kikongo in Angola.
9. This text is similar in nature to an earlier publication: José de Anchieta's *Arte de grammatica da lingoa mais usada na costa do Brasil*, published in 1595, which was written for Portuguese Jesuits to learn Língua Geral (Leite and Callou 2002:64).

10. My 2002 visit to the small village of Quartel de Indaiá, near São João da Chapada, showed the presence of Bantu architecture and traditional sugarcane cultivation. Unfortunately, informants were unwilling to share their Afro-Brazilian language (which they called Língua Antiga [ancient language]) and vissungos with me.

Observe the following excerpt of a vissungo documented by Nascimento (2003:108) that includes the term *Calunga* (she does not provide a Portuguese translation):

Vissungo I

> Ô cundero di ê num tem tempo
> Oi vero o copo nuá tem tempo
> Aiê!
> Ô caí conde . . . ê . . . ê . . . ê
> Ô calunga me toma bebê
> Ô calunga me toma sambá . . . á
> Êi . . .
> Pê . . . rê . . . rê . . . rê
> O mico cumbaro num tem tempo
> Ô pu cumbaro num tem tempo
> Ô . . . ê . . . ê . . . êi
> Cumbarauê . . . ê . . . ê . . . ê . . . êi
> Cumbará . . .
> Cumbarauê . . . êi . . . ê

11. I did not encounter the reported Bantu-based language during my visits to Chapada do Norte in 2002 and 2007, but people of the community attest to its presence in very remote Afro-Brazilian villages of the region that are accessible only by very precarious roads or on foot. However, Afro-Brazilian traditions, such as congados, are practiced there.
12. Other than BPV, Holm (2004) also regards African American English, Afrikaans, nonstandard Caribbean Spanish, and the vernacular of Réunion French as "partially restructured vernaculars."
13. Lipski (1998:55–56) also demonstrates grammatical parallels of double negation (e.g., *não sei não*) and inverted questions (e.g., *você faz isso porquê?*), which are typical in Angolan Portuguese vernacular (spoken by both African and European descendants) and in Bantu languages such as Kikongo and Kimbundu. These are common structures in BPV as well.

14. Guy (1981:309) questions, "From the social historical standpoint, our question probably would not be 'Was Portuguese creolized in Brazil?' but rather, 'How could it possibly have avoided creolization?'"
15. In addition to syncretic languages, Dimmendaal (2011:248–52) reviews modern urban youth languages in Africa, labeled as "antilanguages," which "function as sociolects or social registers expressing conscious social and linguistic opposition" (248). He adds, "In all these register-like languages, conscious language engineering appears to be involved, i.e. speakers are controlling the language. These speech varieties contain special vocabulary, and phonological features that are emblematic of non-conformity to social norms in a community" (249).
16. This is not an exhaustive list of Afro-Hispanic grammatical aspects, but it includes examples of some peculiar morphosyntactic samples that are similar to the descriptive Calunga data documented herein.
17. The Chota Valley of Ecuador is another particularly interesting case. According to Schwegler (1996:282), the *choteño* dialect may have some possible connections to Palenquero and, by extension, to an Afro-Portuguese pidgin/creole. For example, like Palenquero, the choteño dialect has a pronoun of Portuguese origin (*ele*) and invariant and bare plurals. Schwegler writes, "Traídos del Valle del Chota en los siglos XVI–XVII por padres jesuitas, los negros de este valle andino deben de haber llegado al Ecuador principalmente por dos rutas que se originaron en Cartagena. No hay en el Valle del Chota un habla criolla similar al palenquero, pero el registro familiar del español local exhibe algunos rasgos que apuntan hacia un posible origen pidgin/criollo del dialecto chotaño." (282; Brought to the Chota Valley in the sixteenth and seventeenth centuries by Jesuit priests, the blacks of this Andean valley must have arrived in Ecuador principally by two routes that originated in Cartagena. In the Chota Valley there is no creole speech similar to Palenquero, but the popular registrar of the local Spanish exhibits some traits that point to a possible pidgin/creole origin of the Chota dialect.)
18. Regarding this system of pluralization, Schwegler (1998:262) notes that the same type of grammatical characteristic is present in the Spanish of Chota, Ecuador, which could represent a possible link between Chota and Palenquero. Moreover, it should also be noted that such a system of pluralization is also employed in BPV, as well as in Calunga.
19. Regarding this syntactic stucture, Schwegler writes, "[T]ales construcciones de negación predicativa, muy comunes en ciertas partes del Caribe (p. ej., República Dominicana) y asimismo en Brasil y Angola (cf. *não falo inglês não*) . . . favorecen la idea de que, de hecho, el antiguo afroespañol caribeño se asemejaba al palenquero moderno. La distribución geolingüística de este tipo de postnegación, concentrada

sin excepción en áreas con una notable presencia étnica negra, así como consideraciones de orden sociohistórico sugieren que el rasgo bajo inspección verosímilmente pertenecía al antiguo pidgin afroportugués, y que el mismo fenómeno probablemente había sido calcado sobre estructuras paralelas de una o varias lenguas subsaháricas. (1998:263, italics his; Such construction of predicate negation, very common in certain parts of the Caribbean [e.g., the Dominican Republic] and in Brazil and Angola [cf. *não falo inglês não* 'I don't speak English no'] . . . favors the idea that, in fact, an older Caribbean Afro-Spanish was similar to modern Palenquero. The geolinguistic distribution of this type of post-negation, concentrated without exception in areas with a notable presence of black ethnicity, and with sociohistorical considerations, suggests that the characteristic under inspection truly pertained to an older Afro-Portuguese pidgin and that the same phenomenon probably had been calqued from parallel structures of one or various sub-Saharan languages.)

20. English translation:

> the dead person, the dead person is yours [= it is your child]
> your face is the same [= the face of the dead person is the same as that of the dead person's mother]

> María, good-bye;
> the dead person, the dead person is yours;
> good-bye, mother, why did you have your child?
> the dead person, the dead person is yours;
> your face is the same [of that of the mother];
> María; it is yours [= the dead person is your child]
> the dead person, the dead person is yours.

21. According to Herman Bauman, *Schöpfung und Urzeit des Menschen im Mythus der afrikanischen Völker* (as cited in Schwegler 1996:288–89), in the Bantu-speaking zone of Africa *kalunga* means 'supreme being, god of the underworld, underworld,' in addition to its use as an aquatic term ('sea, river, lake,' etc.). The root of the word is derived from *lunga* or *longa* 'river.'

22. English translation:

> Tigrillo: Let's talk between Juan de Dios and Tigrillo, and in the heart, let's have a drink, but right now I am going to tell you something, because he went angry to the lottery, I said to

you Juan de Dios that the devil is touching us, we went to Bocadita, you yourself went there, left the net in the water, knowing that you had . . .

Juan de Dios: You are crazy, I did not go to play the lottery with . . .

CHAPTER FOUR

1. Interestingly, the Spanish philosopher José Ortega y Gasset (1957:231) cites examples of masculine and feminine languages used in ancient and modern history. One contemporary example he cites is Swahili, which possesses a "feminine idiom that no man can understand and that is the only language employed in the strictly female mysteries."
2. Libby (2007:420) further notes that the population of freed slaves of African origin in Minas Gerais was significant during the colonial era, much more so than the population of freed slaves found in the Caribbean during the same time period.
3. See the municipality of Patrocínio's website, www.patrocinio.mg.gov.br, for government documents, statistics, photos, and other information. Also, it must be noted that during the field research for this study only the most basic information on the history of the region was available from Patrocínio's city hall. There was no public archive, and the town's public library was very rudimentary.
4. About thirty kilometers to the south of Patrocínio, in the Boqueirão region, a long stone wall can be found that was built in the late eighteenth or early nineteenth century. This wall was built by slave labor to divide Portuguese fazendas (Tadeu de Barros, personal interview, 2005). See figure 4.2.
5. According to legend the name Patrocínio comes from a wealthy landowner who had a sick daughter. He made a promise to Brazil's patron saint, Nossa Senhora da Aparecida, that he would build a chapel in the village if she would grant his daughter "protection" from her illness. The daughter regained her health, and the chapel was built in the name of the patron saint of protection (i.e., Nossa Senhora do Patrocínio).
6. See Palmares Fundação Cultural, "Os Kalungas: Descobrindo as próprias riquezas," news release, September 27, 2006, www.palmares.gov.br/?p=1727, for more information regarding the Goiás Kalunga communities.

CHAPTER FIVE

1. See Batinga (1994) and Vogt and Fry (1996) for documentation of other Calunga lexical items.
2. Spelling patterns for African languages vary among the cited sources. Some use peculiar orthographic symbols to describe the phonetic patterns of the African languages in question. I have adopted in a general manner the orthographic patterns employed by Alves (1951), Castro (2001), Maia (1994), and Vogt and Fry (1996).
3. Verbs in Calunga are regular, first conjugation (-*ar*). Word-final /r/ is typically not realized phonetically in verbal infinitives in Calunga, hence the parenthetic (-*r*). Irregular verbs used in Calunga are all from Portuguese (i.e., *ter*, *ser*, *estar*, *ir*, etc.). See also Vogt and Fry (1996:278–341) for other documented Calunga verbs.
4. Observe, for example, a few words from the Mina-Jeje language collected by Peixoto (1731/1945) that are derived from Fon (Castro 2002:60): *asim* 'water' (cf. Calunga *omenha* 'water'), *zo* 'fire, light' (cf. Calunga *indaro* 'fire'), *suno* 'man' (cf. Calunga *camano* 'man'), *hinhono* 'woman' (cf. Calunga *ocai* 'woman').
5. While caution must apply in examining such statistics, it is worth recalling that Castro's study of Bahian Portuguese—excluding the liturgical language of Candomblés—indicates that 77.3 percent of African lexical items originate from Bantu languages (Castro 1981:4). Hence, 82 percent of words in this sample being of Bantu origin might be a plausible statistic to consider, though, again, reservations should apply.

CHAPTER SIX

1. The example *negro* > *nego* may be analyzed as a separate lexical item all together (i.e., *meu nego* 'my buddy,' derived from *meu negro; sapato negro* 'black shoe,' *?*sapato nego*).
2. These tables employ only the subject pronoun forms of *camano*. See table 6.3 for a complete list of possible subject pronouns that may constitute the verb phrase.
3. "INFL-" refers to a verbal inflection.

APPENDIX

1. It is not clear here if the wife passed away fourteen years ago or if he has been married for fourteen years.
2. It is not clear here if the speaker is simply referring to fishing or is commenting on his friend's poor fishing skills.

References

Abreu, João Capistrano de. (1907/1997). *Chapters of Brazil's colonial history, 1500–1800*. Arthur Brakel (Trans.). With a preface by Fernando A. Novais and an introduction by Stuart Schwartz. Oxford: Oxford University Press.

Ajayi, Tayo Julius. (2002). *Empréstimo e variação interlingüística: O iorubá em contato com o português no Brasil*. Unpublished PhD dissertation, Universidade Federal de Minas Gerais.

Alkmim, Tania, and Margarida Petter. (2008). Palavras da África no Brasil de ontem e de hoje. In José Luiz Fiorin and Margarida Petter (Eds.), *África no Brasil: A formação da língua portuguesa* (pp. 145–78). São Paulo: Editora Contexto.

Alpha Bah, M. (1998). Legitimate trade, diplomacy, and the slave trade. In Mario Azevedo (Ed.), *Africana studies: A survey of Africa and the African diaspora* (2nd ed., pp. 69–88). Durham, NC: Carolina Academic Press.

Althoff, Daniel. (1994). Afro-mestizo speech from Costa Chica, Guerrero: From Cuaji to Cuijla. *Language Problems and Language Planning, 18*, 242–56.

Alvarez, Alexandra, and Enrique Obediente. (1998). Sociolingüística del español del Caribe: 'Virtualidad' de las lenguas semicriollas. In Matthias Perl and Armin Schwegler (Eds.), with Gerardo Lorenzino, *América negra: Panorámica actual de los estudios lingüísticos sobre variedades hispanas, portuguesas y criollas* (pp. 40–61). Frankfurt/Madrid: Vervuert/Iberoamericana.

Alves, P. Albino. (1951). *Dicionário etimolólogico bundo-português* (2 vols.). Lisbon: Tipografia Silvas.

Amaral, Amadeu. (1920/1976). *O dialeto caipira* (3rd ed.). São Paulo: Hucitec.

Andrade Filho, Sílvio Vieira de. (2009). *Um estudo sociolingüístico das comunidades negras do Cafundó, do antigo Caxambu e de seus arredores* (2nd ed.). Sorocaba, Brazil: Edição do Autor.

Antunes, António Lobo. (1979/2004). *Os cus de Judas* (25th ed.). Lisbon: Dom Quixote.

Azevedo, Mario. (1998). African studies and the state of the art. In Mario Azevedo (Ed.), *Africana studies: A survey of Africa and the African diaspora* (2nd ed., pp. 5–29). Durham, NC: Carolina Academic Press.

Azevedo, Milton M. (1989). Vernacular features in educated speech in Brazilian Portuguese. *Hispania, 72*, 862–72.

Azevedo, Milton M. (2005). *Portuguese: A linguistic introduction.* Cambridge: Cambridge University Press.

Bakker, Peter. (2002). Some future challenges for pidgin and creole studies. In Glenn Gilbert (Ed.), *Pidgin and creole linguistics in the twenty-first century* (pp. 69–92). New York: Peter Lang.

Bakker, Peter, and Maarten Mous (Eds.). (1994). *Mixed languages: 15 case studies in language intertwining.* Amsterdam: Institute for Functional Research into Language and Language Use (IFOTT).

Bakker, Peter, and Pieter Muysken. (1995). Mixed languages and language intertwining. In Jacques Arends, Pieter Muysken, and Norval Smith (Eds.), *Pidgins and creoles: An introduction* (pp. 41–52). Amsterdam: John Benjamins.

Barbosa, Waldemar de Almeida. (1964). Quilombo Grande. *Revista de História e Arte, 6,* 24–28.

Barbosa, Waldemar de Almeida. (1970). O negro em Minas Gerais. *Revista do instituto histórico e geográfico de Minas Gerais, 14,* 309–18.

Bastide, Roger. (1979). The other quilombos. In Richard Price (Ed.), *Maroon societies: Rebel slave communities in the Americas* (pp. 191–201). Baltimore, MD: Johns Hopkins University Press.

Batibo, Herman M. (2005). *Language decline and death in Africa: Causes, consequences and challenges.* Clevedon, UK: Multilingual Matters.

Batinga, Gastão. (1994). *Aspectos de presença do negro no triângulo mineiro/alto paranaíba: Kalunga.* Uberlândia, Brazil: Editora Indústria e Comércio.

Baxter, Alan N. (1992). A contribuição das comunidades afro-brasileiras isoladas para o debate sobre a crioulização prévia: Um exemplo do estado da Bahia. In Ernesto D'Andrade and Alain Kihm (Eds.), *Actas do colóquio sobre crioulos de base lexical portuguesa* (pp. 7–36). Lisbon: Colibri.

Baxter, Alan N. (1998). Morfossintaxe. In Matthias Perl and Armin Schwegler (Eds.), with Gerardo Lorenzino, *América negra: Panorámica actual de los estudios lingüísticos sobre variedades hispanas, portuguesas y criollas* (pp. 97–134). Frankfurt/Madrid: Vervuert/Iberoamericana.

Baxter, Alan N., and Dante Lucchesi. (1993). Processos de descrioulização no sistema verbal de um dialeto rural brasileiro. *Papia, 2,* 59–71.

Bentley, W. Holman. (1887/1967). *Dictionary and grammar of the Kongo language.* Ridgewood, NJ: Gregg Press.

Bentley, W. Holman. (1895/1967). *Appendix to the dictionary and grammar of the Kongo language.* Ridgewood, NJ: Gregg Press.

Bickerton, Derek. (2008). *Bastard tongues: A trailblazing linguist finds clues to our common humanity in the world's lowliest languages.* New York: Hill and Wang.

Birmingham, David. (1966). *Trade and conflict in Angola: The Mbundu and their neighbours under the influence of the Portuguese, 1483–1790.* Oxford: Clarendon Press.

Birmingham, David. (1993). *A concise history of Portugal.* Cambridge: Cambridge University Press.

Birmingham, David. (2000). *Trade and empire in the Atlantic, 1400–1600.* London: Routledge.

Boadi-Siaw, Samuel. (2007). The African presence in Brazil—A legacy of the transatlantic slave trade. In James Kwesi Anquandah (Ed.), *The transatlantic slave trade: Landmarks, legacies, expectations* (pp. 164–77). Accra, Ghana: Sub-Saharan Publishers.

Bonvini, Emilio. (2000). La langue des "pretos velhos" ("vieux noirs") au Brésil: Un créole à base portugaise d'origine africaine? *Bulletin de la Société de Linguistique de Paris, 95,* 389–416.

Bonvini, Emilio. (2008a). Línguas africanas e português falado no Brasil. In José Luiz Fiorin and Margarida Petter (Eds.), *África no Brasil: A formação da língua portuguesa* (pp. 15–62). São Paulo: Editora Contexto.

Bonvini, Emilio. (2008b). Os vocábulos de origem africana na constituição do português falado no Brasil. In José Luiz Fiorin and Margarida Petter (Eds.), *África no Brasil: A formação da língua portuguesa* (pp. 101–44). São Paulo: Editora Contexto.

Bonvini, Emilio, and Margarida Maria Taddoni Petter. (1998). Portugais du Brésil et langues africaines. *Langages, 130,* 68–83.

Bosi, Alfredo. (1980). *História concisa da literatura brasileira* (2nd ed.). São Paulo: Editora Cultrix.

Botelho, Tarcísio R. (2007). Introdução. In Maria Efigênia Lage de Resende and Luiz Carlos Villalta (Eds.), *História de Minas Gerais: As Minas setecentistas* (Vol. 1, pp. 403–6). Belo Horizonte, Brazil: Autêntica Editora/Companhia do Tempo.

Bueno, Eduardo. (2003). *Brasil: Uma história* (2nd ed.). São Paulo: Ática.

Burkholder, Mark A., and Lyman L. Johnson. (2001). *Colonial Latin America* (4th ed.). New York: Oxford University Press.

Byrd, Steven. (2006). Calunga: An Afro-Brazilian speech of Minas Gerais. *Papia: Revista Brasileira de Estudos Crioulos e Similares, no. 16,* 62–80.

Byrd, Steven. (2007). Calunga: Uma fala afro-brasileira de Minas Gerais, sua gramática e história. *Revista Internacional de Lingüística Iberoamericana (RILI) V, 1(9),* 203–22.

Byrd, Steven. (2010a). The lexicon of Calunga—An Afro-Brazilian speech of Minas Gerais. *Journal of Hispanic and Lusophone Linguistics, 3(1),* 41–76.

Byrd, Steven. (2010b). *The lexicon of Calunga and a lexical comparison with other forms of Afro-Brazilian speech from Minas Gerais, São Paulo, and Bahia.* (Research Paper Series No. 52.) Albuquerque: Latin American and

Iberian Institute, University of New Mexico. Available online at http://hdl.handle.net/1928/11569.

Byrd, Steven, and Daniela Bassani Moraes. (2007). Calunga and calungadores: An Afro-Brazilian speech community of Minas Gerais. *Afro-Hispanic Review, 26(2)*, 27–45.

Cabeza de Vaca, Álvar Núñez. (1542/2003). *The narrative of Cabeza de Vaca.* Rolena Adorno and Patrick Charles Pautz (Eds. and Trans.). Lincoln: University of Nebraska Press.

Cacciatore, Olga Gudolle. (1988). *Dicionário de cultos afro-brasileiros* (3rd ed.). Rio de Janeiro: Forense-Universitária.

Cadernos do arquivo. (1988). *Escravidão em Minas Gerais.* Belo Horizonte, Brazil: Arquivo Público Mineiro.

Carneiro, Edison (Ed.). (2005). *Antologia do negro brasileiro.* Rio de Janeiro: Agir.

Castro, Yeda Pessoa de. (1967). A sobrevivência das línguas africanas no Brasil: Sua influência na linguagem popular da Bahia. *Afro-Ásia, 4–5*, 25–34.

Castro, Yeda Pessoa de. (1980). *Os falares africanos na interação social do Brasil colônia.* Salvador, Brazil: Publicação da Universidade Federal da Bahia (Centro de Estudos Baianos).

Castro, Yeda Pessoa de. (1981). A presença cultural negro-africana no Brasil: Mito e realidade. *Centro de Estudos Afro-Orientais: Ensaios e Pesquisas, 10*, 1–12.

Castro, Yeda Pessoa de. (1983). Das línguas africanas ao português brasileiro. *Afro-Ásia, 14*, 81–106.

Castro, Yeda Pessoa de. (1995). Dimensão dos aportes africanos no Brasil. *Afro-Ásia, 16*, 24–35.

Castro, Yeda Pessoa de. (1997). Línguas africanas como objeto de estudo e ensino no Brasil. *Lusorama, 34*, 52–60.

Castro, Yeda Pessoa de. (2001). *Falares africanos na Bahia: Um vocabulário afro-brasileiro.* Rio de Janeiro: Academia Brasileira de Letras.

Castro, Yeda Pessoa de. (2002). *A língua mina-jeje no Brasil: Um falar africano em Ouro Preto do século XVIII.* Belo Horizonte, Brazil: Fundação João Pinheiro/Secretaria de Estado da Cultura.

Catz, Rebecca. (1995–1996). Who really discovered Brazil? *Portuguese Studies Review, 4(2)*, 77–84.

Chaplin, Joyce E. (2009). The Atlantic Ocean and its contemporary meanings, 1492–1808. In Jack P. Greene and Philip D. Morgan (Eds.), *Atlantic history: A critical appraisal* (pp. 35–51). New York: Oxford University Press.

Chatelain, Héli. (1888–89/1964). *Grammatica elementar do Kimbundu ou lingua de Angola.* Ridgewood, NJ: Gregg Press.

Chomsky, Noam. (1993). *Year 501: The conquest continues*. Boston: South End Press.
Coelho, F. Adolfo. (1880/1967). Os dialectos românicos ou neolatinos na África, Ásia e América. *Boletim da Sociedade de Geografia de Lisboa, series 2, no. 3*, 129–96. Reprinted in Jorge Morais-Barbosa (Ed.), *Estudos linguísticos crioulos* (pp. 1–108). Lisbon: Academia Internacional de Cultura Portuguesa.
Coelho, F. Adolfo. (1882/1967). Os dialectos românicos ou neolatinos na África, Ásia e América: Notas complementares. *Boletim da Sociedade de Geografia de Lisboa, series 3, no. 8*, 451–78. Reprinted in Jorge Morais-Barbosa (Ed.), *Estudos linguísticos crioulos* (pp. 109–52). Lisbon: Academia Internacional de Cultura Portuguesa.
Coelho, F. Adolfo. (1886/1967). Os dialectos românicos ou neolatinos na África, Ásia e América: Novas notas suplementares. *Boletim da Sociedade de Geografia de Lisboa, series 6, no. 12*, 705–55. Reprinted in Jorge Morais-Barbosa (Ed.), *Estudos linguísticos crioulos* (pp. 153–234). Lisbon: Academia Internacional de Cultura Portuguesa.
Costa, Carlos Pereira da. (1937). Vocabulário pernambucano. *Revista do Instituto Arqueológico, Histórico e Geográfico Pernambucano, Recife, 34*, 159–62
Couto, Hildo Honório do. (1992a). Anti-crioulo. *Papia, 2(1)*, 71–82.
Couto, Hildo Honório do. (1992b). Lançados, grumetes e a origem do crioulo português no noreste africano. In Ernesto D'Andrade and Alain Kihm (Eds.), *Actas do colóquio sobre crioulos de base lexical portuguesa* (pp. 109–22). Lisbon: Colibri.
Couto, Hildo Honório do. (1997). Os estudos crioulos no Brasil. In Eberhard Gärtner (Ed.), *Pesquisas lingüísticas em Portugal e no Brasil* (pp. 99–112). Madrid/Frankfurt: Iberoamericana/Vervuert.
Couto, Hildo Honório do. (2002). *Anticrioulo: Manifestação lingüística de resistência cultural*. Brasília: Thesaurus Editora.
Cuba, María del Carmen. (1996). *El castellano hablado en Chincha*. Lima: Universidad Mayor de San Marcos, Escuela de Posgrado.
Cunha, Antônio Geraldo da. (2001). *Dicionário etimológico Nova Fronteira da língua portuguesa* (2nd ed.). Rio de Janeiro: Nova Fronteira.
Curtin, Philip D. (1969). *The Atlantic slave trade: A census*. Madison: University of Wisconsin Press.
Davidson, Basil. (1973). *In the eye of the storm: Angola's people*. Garden City, NY: Anchor Books.
Davidson, Basil. (1993). *African civilization revisited: From antiquity to modern times* (3rd ed.). Trenton, NJ: Africa World Press.
Davidson, Basil. (1998). *West Africa before the colonial era: A history to 1850*. London: Longman.

Dimmendaal, Gerrit J. (2011). *Historical linguistics and the comparative study of African languages.* Amsterdam: John Benjamins.

Dodson, Howard. (2001). The transatlantic slave trade and the making of the modern world. In Sheila S. Walker (Ed.), *African roots/American cultures: Africa in the creation of the Americas* (pp. 118–22). Lanham, MD: Rowman and Littlefield.

Dornas Filho, João. (1943). *A influência social do negro brasileiro.* Curitiba, Brazil: Editora Guaíra Limitada.

Duffy, James. (1962). *Portugal in Africa.* London: Penguin.

Elia, Sílvio. (1940/1979). *A unidade lingüística do Brasil.* Rio de Janeiro: Padrão.

Elia, Sílvio. (1965). A difusão das línguas europeias e a formação das variedades ultramarinas, em particular dos crioulos (aplicação especial ao português do Brasil). In *V Colóquio Internacional de Estudos Luso-Brasileiros (Coimbra 1963): Actas* (Vol. 3, pp. 217–73). Coimbra, Portugal: Universidade de Coimbra.

Enciclopédia Luso-Brasileira de cultura. (1963). (Vol. 4). Lisbon: Editorial Verbo.

Estado de Minas. (1983, April 24). O caminho empoeirado do difícil desenvolvimento do norte de Minas. Belo Horizonte, Brazil.

Estudos afro-brasileiros. (1939). (2 vols.). Rio de Janeiro: Ariel.

Falola, Toyin. (2002). *Key events in African history: A reference guide.* Westport, CT: Greenwood Press.

Ferraz, Luiz. (1975). African influences on Principense creole. In Marius F. Valkhoff (Ed.), *Miscelânea Luso-Africana: Colectânea de estudos coligidos* (pp. 153–64). Lisbon: Junta de investigações científicas do ultramar.

Ferreira, Ângela Maria de Arvelos, and Marlenísio Ferreira. (1993). *Cisquim—O menino bóia-fria.* Patrocínio, Brazil: Gráfica Pimenta e Souta.

Ferreira, Carlota. (1985). Remanescentes de um falar crioulo brasileiro. *Revista Lusitana, 5,* 21–34.

Flory, Thomas. (1979). Fugitive slaves and free society: The case of Brazil. *Journal of Negro History, 64,* 116–30.

Fraginals, Manuel Moreno. (1984). Cultural contributions and deculturation. Leonor Blum (Trans.). In Manuel Moreno Fraginals (Ed.), *Africa in Latin America: Essays on history, culture, and socialization* (pp. 5–22). New York/Paris: Holmes and Meier/UNESCO.

Freyre, Gilberto. (1956). *The masters and the slaves (Casa Grande e senzala): A study in the development of Brazilian civilization.* Samuel Putnam (Trans.). New York: Alfred A. Knopf.

Freyre, Gilberto. (1971). *New world in the tropics: The culture of modern Brazil.* New York: Alfred A. Knopf.

Friedemann, Nina S. de, and Carlos Patiño Rosselli. (1983). *Lengua y sociedad en el Palenque de San Basilio*. Santafé de Bogotá, Colombia: Instituto Caro y Cuervo.

Fuentes Guerra, Jesús, and Armin Schwegler. (2005). *Lengua y ritos del Palo Monte Mayombe: Dioses cubanos y sus fuentes africanas*. Madrid/Frankfurt: Iberoamericana/Vervuert.

Gilbert, Glenn (Ed.). (2002). *Pidgin and creole linguistics in the twenty-first century*. New York: Peter Lang.

Gomes, Núbia Pereira de Magalhães, and Edimilson de Almeida Pereira. (2000). *Negras raízes mineiras: Os Arturos* (2nd ed.). Belo Horizonte, Brazil: Mazza Edições.

Grande enciclopédia portuguesa e brasileira. (1936–1960). (Vol. 5). Lisbon: Editorial Enciclopédia Limitada.

Green, Katherine. (1997). *Non-standard Dominican Spanish: Evidence of partial restructuring*. Unpublished PhD dissertation, City University of New York.

Greenberg, Joseph H. (1966). *The languages of Africa*. The Hague: Mouton.

Guimarães, Carlos Magno. (1983). *Uma negação da ordem: Quilombos em Minas Gerais no século XVIII*. Unpublished master's thesis, Universidade Federal de Minas Gerais.

Guimarães, Carlos Magno. (1999). *Quilombos: Classes, estado e cotidiano (Minas Gerais—Século XVIII)*. Unpublished PhD dissertation, Universidade de São Paulo.

Guimarães, Carlos Magno. (2007). Escravidão e quilombos nas Minas Gerais do século XVIII. In Maria Efigênia Lage de Resende and Luiz Carlos Villalta (Eds.), *História de Minas Gerais: As Minas setecentistas* (Vol. 1, pp. 439–54). Belo Horizonte, Brazil: Autêntica Editora/Companhia do Tempo.

Guy, Gregory R. (1981). *Linguistic variation in Brazilian Portuguese*. Unpublished PhD dissertation, University of Pennsylvania.

Guy, Gregory R. (1989). On the nature and origins of popular Brazilian Portuguese. In *Estudios sobre español de América y lingüística afroamericana* (pp. 227–45). Santafé de Bogotá, Colombia: Instituto Caro y Cuervo.

Hagemeijer, Tjerk. (2009). As línguas de S. Tomé e Príncipe. *Revista de Crioulos de Base Lexical Portuguesa e Espanhola, 1(1)*, 1–27.

História do Brasil (1997). (2nd ed.). São Paulo: Folha de São Paulo (Publifolha).

Holm, John. (1987). Creole influence on Popular Brazilian Portuguese. In Glenn Gilbert (Ed.), *Pidgin and creole languages* (pp. 406–29). Honolulu: University of Hawaii Press.

Holm, John. (1988). *Pidgins and creoles: Vol. 1. Theory and structure*. Cambridge: Cambridge University Press.

Holm, John. (1989). *Pidgins and creoles: Vol. 2: Reference survey.* Cambridge: Cambridge University Press.
Holm, John. (1992). Popular Brazilian Portuguese: A semi-creole. In Ernesto D'Andrade and Alain Kihm (Eds.), *Actas do colóquio sobre crioulos de base lexical portuguesa* (pp. 37–66). Lisbon: Colibri.
Holm, John. (2004). *Languages in contact: The partial restructuring of vernaculars.* Cambridge: Cambridge University Press.
Hufferd, James. (2005). *Cruzeiro do sul: A history of Brazil's half millennium* (Vol. 1). Bloomington, IN: AuthorHouse.
Isichei, Elizabeth. (1997). *A history of African societies to 1870.* New York: Cambridge University Press.
Johnston, Sir Harry H. (1919). *A comparative study of the Bantu and Semi-Bantu languages.* Oxford: Oxford University Press.
Keen, Benjamin. (1996). *A history of Latin America* (5th ed.). Boston: Houghton Mifflin.
Klein, Herbert S. (1986). *African slavery in Latin America and the Caribbean.* New York: Oxford University Press.
Klein, Herbert S. (2002). As origens dos escravos brasileiros. In Sérgio D.J. Pena (Ed.), *Homo brasilis: Aspectos genéticos, lingüísticos, históricos e socioantropológicos da formação do povo brasileiro* (pp. 93–112). Riberão Preto, Brazil: FUNPEC-RP.
Kihm, Alain. (1994). *Kriyol syntax: The Portuguese-based creole language of Guinea-Bissau.* Amsterdam: John Benjamins.
Laman, K. E. (1964). *Dictionnaire Kikongo-Français.* Ridgewood, NJ: Gregg Press.
Landers, Jane G. (2006). Introduction. In Jane G. Landers and Barry M. Robinson (Eds.), *Slaves, subjects, and subversives: Blacks in Colonial Latin America* (pp. 1–8). Albuquerque: University of New Mexico Press.
Laytano, Dante de. (1936). *Os africanismos no dialeto gaúcho* (2nd ed.). Porto Alegre, Brazil: Oficina Livraria do Globo.
Leal, Gilberto R. N. (2001). Fárígá/Ìfaradà: Black resistance and achievement in Brazil. In Sheila S. Walker (Ed.), *African roots/American cultures: Africa in the creation of the Americas* (pp. 291–300). Lanham, MD: Rowman and Littlefield.
Leite, Yonne, and Dinah Callou. (2002). *Como falam os brasileiros.* Rio de Janeiro: Jorge Zahar Editor.
Libby, Douglas Cole. (2007). As populações escravas das Minas setecentistas: Um balanço preliminar. In Maria Efigênia Lage de Resende and Luiz Carlos Villalta (Eds.), *História de Minas Gerais: As Minas setecentistas* (Vol. 1, pp. 407–38). Belo Horizonte, Brazil: Autêntica Editora/Companhia do Tempo.
Lipski, John M. (1987). The Chota Valley: Afro-Hispanic language in highland Ecuador. *Latin American Research Review, 22,* 155–70.

Lipski, John M. (1989). *The speech of the Negros Congos of Panama*. Amsterdam: John Benjamins.
Lipski, John M. (1994a). El español afroperuano: Eslabón entre África y América. *Anuario de Lingüística Hispánica, 10,* 179–216.
Lipski, John M. (1994b). *Latin American Spanish*. New York: Longman.
Lipski, John M. (1997). El lenguaje de los *negros congos* de Panamá y el *lumbalú* palenquero de Colombia: Función sociolingüística de criptolectos afrohispánicos. *América Negra, 14,* 147–65.
Lipski, John M. (1998). Latin American Spanish: Creolization and the African connection. *Publication of the Afro-Latin/American Research Association (PALARA), 2,* 54–78.
Lipski, John M. (2004). El español de América y los contactos bilingües recientes: Apuntes microdialectológicos. *Revista Internacional de Lingüística Iberoamericana (RILI), 2(4),* 89–103.
Lipski, John M. (2005). *A history of Afro-Hispanic language: Five centuries, five continents*. Cambridge: Cambridge University Press.
Lipski, John M. (2008a). *Afro-Bolivian Spanish*. Madrid/Frankfurt: Iberoamericana/Vervuert.
Lipski, John M. (2008b). Angola e Brasil: Vínculos lingüísticos afro-lusitanos. *Veredas (Porto Alegre, Brazil), 9,* 83–98.
Lipski, John M. (2009a). El habla de los afroparaguayos: Un nuevo renglón de la identidad étnica. *Lexis, 33(1),* 91–124.
Lipski, John M. (2009b). Tracing the origins of Panamanian *Congo* speech: The pathways of regional variation. *Diachronica, 26(3),* 380–407.
Lopes, Nei. (2003). *Novo dicionário banto do Brasil*. Rio de Janeiro: Pallas.
Lorenzino, Gerardo A. (1998a). *The Angolar Creole Portuguese of São Tomé: Its grammar and sociolinguistic history*. Munich: Lincom Europa.
Lorenzino, Gerardo. (1998b). El español caribeño: Antecedentes sociohistóricos y lingüísticos. In Matthias Perl and Armin Schwegler (Eds.), with Gerardo Lorenzino, *América negra: Panorámica actual de los estudios lingüísticos sobre variedades hispanas, portuguesas y criollas* (pp. 26–39). Frankfurt/Madrid: Vervuert/Iberoamericana.
Lovejoy, Paul E. (2006). The context of enslavement in West Africa. In Jane G. Landers and Barry M. Robinson (Eds.), *Slaves, subjects, and subversives: Blacks in Colonial Latin America* (pp. 9–38). Albuquerque: University of New Mexico Press.
Macedo Soares, A. J. de. (1880). Estudos lexicographicos do dialecto brasileiro sobre algumas palavras africanas introduzidas no portuguez que se fala no Brasil. *Revista Brasileira (Rio de Janeiro), 4,* 243–71.
Machado Filho, Aires da Mata. (1943/1985). *O negro e o garimpo em Minas Gerais*. Belo Horizonte/São Paulo: Editora Itatiaia/Editora da Universidade de São Paulo.

Maia, António da Silva. (1994). *Dicionário complementar: Português-Kimbundu-Kikongo (Línguas nativas do centro e norte de Angola)* (2nd ed.). Lisbon: Cooperação Portuguesa.

Marroquim, Mário. (1934). *A língua do nordeste.* São Paulo: Nacional.

Maurer, Philippe. (1995). *L'angolar, un créole afro-portugais parlé à São Tomé.* Hamburg, Germany: Helmut Buske.

Maurer, Philippe. (1998). El papiamentu de Curazao. In Matthias Perl and Armin Schwegler (Eds.), with Gerardo Lorenzino, *América negra: Panorámica actual de los estudios lingüísticos sobre variedades hispanas, portuguesas y criollas* (pp. 139–217). Frankfurt/Madrid: Vervuert/Iberoamericana.

Maurer, Philippe. (2009). *Principense (Lung'Ie). Grammar, texts, and vocabulary of the Afro-Portuguese creole of the island of Príncipe, Gulf of Guinea.* London: Battlebridge.

Mattoso Câmara, Joaquim, Jr. (1972). *The Portuguese language.* Anthony J. Naro (Trans.). Chicago: University of Chicago Press.

McWhorter, John H. (2000). *The missing Spanish creoles: Recovering the birth of plantation contact languages.* Berkeley: University of California Press.

Megenney, William W. (1978). *A Bahian heritage: An ethnolinguistic study of African influences on Bahian Portuguese.* Chapel Hill: University of North Carolina Press.

Megenney, William W. (1984). Traces of Portuguese in three Caribbean creoles: Evidence in support of the monogenetic theory. *Hispanic Linguistics, 1(2),* 177–89.

Megenney, William W. (1986). *El palenquero: Un lenguaje post-criollo colombiano.* Santafé de Bogotá, Colombia: Instituto Caro y Cuervo.

Megenney, William W. (1990). *África en Santo Domingo: La herencia lingüística.* Santo Domingo, Dominican Republic: Museo del Hombre Dominicano.

Megenney, William W. (1998). A relevância das línguas africanas no português do Brasil. In Matthias Perl and Armin Schwegler (Eds.), with Gerardo Lorenzino, *América negra: Panorámica actual de los estudios lingüísticos sobre variedades hispanas, portuguesas y criollas* (pp. 75–92). Frankfurt/Madrid: Vervuert/Iberoamericana.

Megenney, William W. (1999). *Aspectos del lenguaje afronegroide en Venezuela.* Madrid/Frankfurt: Iberoamericana/Vervuert.

Megenney, William W. (2001). A penetração de influências africanas no Brasil. *Lusorama, 47–48,* 94–105.

Megenney, William W. (2002). (H)ouve um linguajar crioulo panbrasileiro? *Hispania, 85(3),* 587–96.

Mellafe, Rolando. (1975). *Negro slavery in Latin America.* J. W. S. Judge (Trans.). Berkeley: University of California Press.

Mello, Heliana R. de. (1997). *The genesis and development of Brazilian Vernacular Portuguese.* Unpublished PhD dissertation, City University of New York.

Mello, Heliana R. de. (1998). Introdução. In Matthias Perl and Armin Schwegler (Eds.), with Gerardo Lorenzino, *América negra: Panorámica actual de los estudios lingüísticos sobre variedades hispanas, portuguesas y criollas* (pp. 72–74). Frankfurt/Madrid: Vervuert/Iberoamericana.

Mello, Heliana R. de, Alan N. Baxter, John Holm, and William Megenney. (1998). O português vernáculo do Brasil. In Matthias Perl and Armin Schwegler (Eds.), with Gerardo Lorenzino, *América negra: Panorámica actual de los estudios lingüísticos sobre variedades hispanas, portuguesas y criollas* (pp. 71–137). Frankfurt/Madrid: Vervuert/Iberoamericana.

Melo, Gladstone Chaves de. (1946/1971). *A língua do Brasil* (2nd ed.). Rio de Janeiro: Fundação Getúlio Vargas.

Mendonça, Renato. (1933). *A influência africana no português do Brasil.* Rio de Janeiro: Civilização Brasileira.

Miranda, V. Chermont de. (1905/1936). Glossário paraense ou coleção de vocábulos peculiares à Amazônia e especialmente à ilha de Marajó. *Revista do Instituto Arqueológico, Histórico e Geográfico Pernambucano (Recife), 34,* 59–162.

Moñino, Yves, and Armin Schwegler (Eds.). (2002). *Palenque, Cartagena y Afro-Caribe: Historia y lengua.* Tübingen, Germany: Niemeyer.

Morais-Barbosa, Jorge. (1975). Cape Verde, Guinea-Bissau and São Tomé and Príncipe: The linguistic situation. In Marius F. Valkhoff (Ed.), *Miscelânea Luso-Africana: Colectânea de estudos coligidos* (pp. 133–51). Lisbon: Junta de Investigações Científicas do Ultramar.

Morgan, Philip D. (2009). Africa and the Atlantic, c. 1450 to c. 1820. In Jack P. Greene and Philip D. Morgan (Eds.), *Atlantic history: A critical appraisal* (pp. 223–48). New York: Oxford University Press.

Moura, Clóvis. (1987). *Quilmobos: Resistência ao escravismo.* São Paulo: Editora Ática.

Munteanu, Dan. (1996). *El papiamento, lengua criolla hispánica.* Madrid: Gredos.

Naro, Anthony Julius, and Maria Marta Pereira Scherre. (2007). *Origens do português brasileiro.* São Paulo: Parábola Editorial.

Nascentes, Antenor. (1922). *O linguajar carioca.* Rio de Janeiro: Organização Simões.

Nascentes, Antenor. (1988). *Dicionário da língua portuguesa da academia brasileira de letras.* Rio de Janeiro: Bloch Editores.

Nascimento, Lúcia Valéria do. (2003). *A África no Serro-Frio: Vissungos—uma prática social em extinção.* Unpublished master's thesis, Universidade Federal de Minas Gerais.

Nina Rodrigues, Raimundo. (1932/1977). *Os africanos no Brasil*. São Paulo: Editora Nacional.

Oliveira, Anésio José de, and Eliany Assis. (2008). *Contos e encantos mineiros*. Curitiba, Brazil: Base Editora.

Olsen, Steve. (2003). *Mapping human history: Genes, race, and our common origins*. Boston: Mariner Books.

Ortega y Gasset, José. (1957). *Man and people*. Willard R. Trask (Trans.). New York: W. W. Norton.

Ortiz López, Luis. (1998). *Huellas etno-sociolingüísticas bozales y afrocubanas*. Madrid/Frankfurt: Iberoamericana/Vervuert.

Peixoto, Antônio da Costa. (1731/1945, July). Linguagem dos escravos de Minas Gerais. *Documentos do arquivo português que importam ao Brasil (Lisbon)*, 8, 10–11.

Pereira, Edimilson de Almeida, and Núbia Pereira de Magalhães Gomes. (2003). *Ouro Preto da palavra: Narrativas de preceito do congado em Minas Gerais*. Belo Horizonte, Brazil: Editora PUC Minas.

Perl, Matthias. (1998). Introducción. In Matthias Perl and Armin Schwegler (Eds.), with Gerardo Lorenzino, *América negra: Panorámica actual de los estudios lingüísticos sobre variedades hispanas, portuguesas y criollas* (pp. 1–24). Frankfurt/Madrid: Vervuert/Iberoamericana.

Petter, Margarida Maria Taddoni. (1999). A linguagem do Cafundó: crioulo ou anticrioulo? In Klaus Zimmermann (Ed.), *Lenguas criollas de base lexical española y portuguesa* (pp. 101–17). Madrid/Frankfurt: Iberoamericana/Vervuert.

Phillips, Carla Rahn. (2009). Europe and the Atlantic. In Jack P. Greene and Philip D. Morgan (Eds.), *Atlantic history: A critical appraisal* (pp. 249–75). New York: Oxford University Press.

Price, Richard. (1999). Reinventando a história dos quilombos: Rasuras e confabulações. *Afro-Ásia*, 23, 239–65.

Queiroz, Sônia Maria de Melo. (1984). *A língua do Negro da Costa: Um remanescente africano em Bom Despacho (MG)*. Unpublished master's thesis, Universidade Federal de Minas Gerais.

Queiroz, Sônia Maria de Melo. (1998). *Pé preto no barro branco: A língua dos negros da Tabatinga*. Belo Horizonte, Brazil: Editora UFMG.

Raimundo, Jacques. (1933). *O elemento afro-negro na língua portuguesa*. Rio de Janeiro: Editora Renascença.

Ramos, Arthur. (1979). *As culturas negras no novo mundo* (3rd ed.). São Paulo/Brasília: Editora Nacional/INL.

Reader, John. (1999). *Africa: A biography of the continent*. New York: Vintage.

Reinecke, John E. (1975). *A bibliography of pidgin and creole languages*. Honolulu: University Press of Hawaii.

Reis, João José. (2001). *Quilombos* and rebellions in Brazil. In Sheila S. Walker (Ed.), *African roots/American cultures: Africa in the creation of the Americas* (pp. 301–13). Lanham, MD: Rowman and Littlefield.

Resende, Maria Efigênia Lage de. (2007a). Introdução. In Maria Efigênia Lage de Resende and Luiz Carlos Villalta (Eds.), *História de Minas Gerais: As Minas setecentistas* (Vol. 1, pp. 19–23). Belo Horizonte, Brazil: Autêntica Editora/Companhia do Tempo.

Resende, Maria Efigênia Lage de. (2007b). Itinerários e interditos na territorialização das Geraes. In Maria Efigênia Lage de Resende and Luiz Carlos Villalta (Eds.), *História de Minas Gerais: As Minas setecentistas* (Vol. 1, pp. 25–53). Belo Horizonte, Brazil: Autêntica Editora/Companhia do Tempo.

Révah, Isreal. (1963). La question des substrats et superstrats dans le domaine linguistique brésilien: Les parles populaires brésilien doivent-ils être considerés comme des parles "créoles" ou "semi-créoles"? *Romania, 84*, 433–50.

Ribeiro, João. (1897/1906). *Diccionário grammatical* (3rd ed.). Rio de Janeiro: Livraria Francisco Alves.

Rodrigues, Ayron D. (1996). As línguas gerais sul-americanas. *Papia, 4*, 6–18.

Rohter, Larry. (2001, January 23). Former slave havens in Brazil gaining rights. *New York Times*, section A, p. 1.

Romano de Sant'anna, Affonso. (2010, July 18). Nós e a África depois da Copa. *Estado de Minas*, Cultura, p. 8.

Rosa, João Guimarães. (2001). *Grande sertão: Veredas* (19th ed.). Rio de Janeiro: Nova Fronteira.

Rougé, Jean-Louis. (2008). A inexistência de crioulo no Brasil. In José Luiz Fiorin and Margarida Petter (Eds.), *África no Brasil: A formação da língua portuguesa* (pp. 63–73). São Paulo: Editora Contexto.

Russell-Wood, A. J. R. (1998). *The Portuguese Empire: 1415–1808*. Baltimore: Johns Hopkins University Press.

Russell-Wood, A. J. R. (2009). The Portuguese Atlantic, 1415–1808. In Jack P. Greene and Philip D. Morgan (Eds.), *Atlantic history: A critical appraisal* (pp. 81–109). New York: Oxford University Press.

Ryder, A. F. C. (1969). Portuguese and Dutch in West Africa before 1800. In J. F. Ade Ajayi and Ian Espie (Eds.), *A thousand years of West African history* (Rev. ed., pp. 217–36). Ibadan, Nigeria: Ibadan University Press.

Sampaio, Antônio Borges. (1904). Sertão da farinha pôdre: Actual triângulo mineiro. *Revista de Uberaba*, 9–18.

Sandoval, Padre Alonso de. (1627/1987). *De instaurada Aethiopum salute. Un tratado sobre la esclavitud*. Enriqueta Vila Villar (Trans. and Intro.). Madrid: Alianza Editorial.

Santos, Ricardo Ventura, and Marcos Chor Maio. (2002). Injetando sangue no mito da democracia racial? Genética, relações raciais e política no Brasil contemporâneo. In Sérgio D. J. Pena (Ed.), *Homo brasilis: Aspectos genéticos, lingüísticos, históricos e socioantropológicos da formação do povo brasileiro* (pp. 175–92). Riberão Preto, Brazil: FUNPEC-RP.

Schneider, John T. (1991). *Dictionary of African borrowings in Brazilian Portuguese*. Hamburg, Germany: Helmut Buske.

Schwartz, Stuart B. (1997). A house built on sand: Capistrano de Abreu and the history of Brazil. In João Capistrano de Abreu, *Chapters of Brazil's colonial history, 1500–1800*. Arthur Brakel (Trans.) (pp. xvii–xxxiv). Oxford: Oxford University Press.

Schwegler, Armin. (1991). El español del Chocó. *América Negra, 2*, 85–119.

Schwegler, Armin. (1996). *"Chi ma ⁿkongo": Lengua y rito ancestrales en El Palenque de San Basilio (Colombia)* (2 vols.). Madrid/Frankfurt: Iberoamericana/Vervuert.

Schwegler, Armin. (1998). El palenquero. In Matthias Perl and Armin Schwegler (Eds.), with Gerardo Lorenzino, *América negra: Panorámica actual de los estudios lingüísticos sobre variedades hispanas, portuguesas y criollas* (pp. 218–91). Frankfurt/Madrid: Vervuert/Iberoamericana.

Schwegler, Armin. (2010). Pidgin and Creole studies: Their interface with Hispanic and Lusophone linguistics. *Studies in Hispanic and Lusophone Linguistics, 3(2)*, 431–81.

Sebba, Mark. (1997). *Contact languages: Pidgins and creoles*. New York: St. Martin's Press.

Segal, Ronald. (1962). Editorial foreword. In James Duffy, *Portugal in Africa* (pp. 9–17). London: Penguin.

Senna, Nelson de. (1938). *Africanos no Brazil (Estudos sobre os negros africanos e influências afro-negras sobre a linguagem e costumes do povo brasileiro)*. Belo Horizonte, Brazil: Oficinas Gráficas Queiroz.

Silva Neto, Serafim da. (1950/1986). *Introdução ao estudo da língua portuguesa no Brasil* (5th ed.). Rio de Janeiro: Presença.

Smith, Adam. (1776/1976). *An inquiry into the nature and causes of the wealth of nations* (Ed. Edwin Cannan) (2 vols. in 1). Chicago: University of Chicago Press.

Tarallo, Fernando. (1993). Sobre a alegada origem crioula do português brasileiro: Mudanças sintáticas aleatórias. In Ian Roberts and Mary Kato (Eds.), *Português brasileiro: Uma viagem diacrônica* (pp. 35–68). Campinas, Brazil: Editora da UNICAMP.

Teixeira, José A. (1938). O falar mineiro. Separata da *Revista do arquivo municipal de São Paulo*.

Teixeira, José A. (1944). *Estudos de dialetologia portuguesa. Linguagem de Goiás*. São Paulo: Editora Anchieta.

Thomas, Hugh. (2004). *Rivers of gold: The rise of the Spanish Empire.* London: Phoenix.
Thomason, Sarah G. (1995). Language mixture: Ordinary processes, extraordinary results. In Carmen Silva-Corvalán (Ed.), *Spanish in four continents: Studies in language contact and bilingualism* (pp. 15–33). Washington, D.C.: Georgetown University Press.
Thomason, Sarah G. (2001). *Language contact: An introduction.* Washington, D.C.: Georgetown University Press.
Thornton, John K. (1998). *Africa and Africans in the making of the Atlantic world, 1400–1800* (2nd ed.). Cambridge: Cambridge University Press.
Thornton, John K. (2006). Central Africa in the era of the slave trade. In Jane G. Landers and Barry M. Robinson (Eds.), *Slaves, subjects, and subversives: Blacks in Colonial Latin America* (pp. 83–110). Albuquerque: University of New Mexico Press.
Triana y Antorveza, Humberto. (1997). *Léxico documentado para la historia del negro en América (siglos XV–XIX): Vol. 1, Estudio preliminar.* Santafé de Bogotá, Colombia: Instituto Caro y Cuervo.
Vasconcellos, J. Leite de. (1883, October 21). Dialecto portuguez do Brazil. *Revista de estudos livres (Porto, Portugal)*, 459–73.
Vasconcellos, J. Leite de. (1901). *Esquisse d'une dialectologie portugaise.* Paris: Aillaud.
Venâncio, Renato Pinto. (2007). Antes de Minas: Fronteiras coloniais e populações indígenas. In Maria Efigênia Lage de Resende and Luiz Carlos Villalta (Eds.), *História de Minas Gerais: As Minas Setecentistas* (Vol. 1, pp. 87–102). Belo Horizonte, Brazil: Autêntica Editora/Companhia do Tempo.
Vogt, Carlos, and Peter Fry. (1996). *Cafundó: A África no Brasil: Linguagem e sociedade.* São Paulo: Companhia das Letras.
Wald, Benji. (1990). Swahili and the Bantu languages. In Bernard Comrie (Ed.), *The world's major languages* (pp. 991–1014). New York: Oxford University Press.
Warner-Lewis, Maureen. (2003). *Central Africa in the Caribbean: Transcending time, transforming cultures.* Kingstown, Jamaica: University of the West Indies Press.
Weber de Kurlat, Frida. (1963). Sobre el negro como tipo cómico en el teatro español del siglo XVI. *Romance philology, 17,* 380–91.
Zinn, Howard. (1999). *A people's history of the United States: 1492–present.* New York: HarperCollins.

Index

Page numbers in italics indicate illustrations.

abolition of slavery, 36, 43, 47, 64; ignored by landowners, 50
acculturation, 49, 59, 65
adufe, 124
affricate sounds, 169
afochê, 124
Afonso IV (king of Portugal), 20
Africa: cultural influence of, 84; diaspora, 84, 89; ethnic groups, 118; etymology dictionaries of, 73; and language patterns, 166; three regions providing slaves to Brazil, 61
African languages, *53*, 166; alterations due to slaves' acquisition of Portuguese, 65; grammatical and semantic changes to lexical items of, 146; and linguistic influence, 89; maintenance of some form of, 119; need for more data, 198; and patterns, 166
Africanos no Brasil (de Senna), 71
Afro-Brazilian languages and culture, studies on, 64–69
Afro-Brazilian speech, 148; and language patterns, 166; and Portuguese slave trade, 8; and speech communities in Minas Gerais, São Paulo, and Bahia, *149–64*
Afro-Brazilian village, *68*
Afro-Hispanic language: compared to Afro-Portuguese creoles, *97–98*; grammatical peculiarities in, 88; in Latin America, 83–100; and pidgin, 95
Afro-Mineiro communities, 80, 120, 196–97
Afro-Paraguayans, 87
Afro-Portuguese creoles, *97–98*
Afro-Portuguese pidgin, 87, 88, 90; evolved into a creole, 91
Afro-Yungueños, 87
aiêto, 124
A influência africana no português do Brasil (Raimundo), 70
Akan (language), 13, 46, *55*, 62, 63, 112; contributions to Spanish American dialect, 85
Alagoas, 64
Alcáçovas-Toledo (1479), Treaty of, 20, 29
Algarve, 38
Ambrósio quilombo, *117*
Ambundu people, 25, 62
amera, 124
amparo, 124
amparo de conena, 124
amparo de cupia, 124
amparo de curiá(r), 124
amparo de cuzeca, 124
amparo de omenha, 124
Andalus, al- (region), 16, 17
Angola, 8, 45, 46, 63; 1.5 million Kikongo speakers in, 242n8; adoption of European culture, 29; central, 61; colonization by Bantu groups, 25; forty languages spoken in, 242n8; as major source of slaves, 46; Portuguese expansion

into, 24; and shipment of slaves, 41, 62; white rule in, 28. *See also* Luanda
Angolares: and "secret language," 59
angora, 124
anti-creoles, 79–81, 117, 118, 190, 191; defined, 10; as imprecise term, 79; similarity to cryptolects, 79
Anzicos, 27
"aportuguesamento," 72, 142, 147, 148. *See also* "Portuguesement"
aprumado, 125
aprumá(r), 125
aprumá(r) banzo, 125
aprumá(r) curiá, 125
aprumá(r) cuzeca, 125
aprumá(r) mirante, 125
aprumá(r) mucota, 125
aprumá(r) omenha, 125
aprumá(r) omenha do ganzipe, 125
Aragón: as Christian dominion, 16
arangá, 125
Araxá, 112
Arguim Island, 39; fort established on, 22
ariranha, 125
Arte da língua de Angola (Dias), 62
Aspectos de presença do negro no triângulo mineiro/alto paranaíba: Kalunga (Batinga), 6
assungá(r), 125
Astrogildo, José, 124, 166, 182
atindundu, 125
atuá, 125
Azevedo, Milton, 78
Azores, 19, 53; and wheat exportation, 21

bacuri, 125
bacuri de calunga, 125
bacuri de cumba, 125
Bahia (language), 34, 35, 36, 62, 64, 72, 142, 146, 148, *149–64*
Bahia (state), 48, 67, 110; independence movement in, 36

Bahian Heritage: An Ethnolinguistic Study of African Influences on Bahian Portuguese, A (Megenney), 65
Bahian Portuguese, 62, 65, 142, 247n5; five sociolinguistic levels of, 72
Bakongo, 40
Bakri, Abu Ubayd al-, 17
bambi, 125
bandeirantes, 34, 59, 111, 112, 113; defined, 10; motives for exploration, 110
banga, 125
Bantu (language), 25, *53*, *55*, 56, 65, 147, 148; and adjectives, 178; and Africanisms, 140; as "congo-angola," 62; consonantal changes in, 174, 175; defined, 11; derivation of lexical items from, 120; and double negation, 77; and etymologies, 8; and evolution of Calunga, 118; folkloric terms traced to, 71; glides, 174; greatest language influence in Brazil, 62, 65; lexical items derived from, 120, 146; and "linguistic fossils," 165; number of, 11; and prenasal stops, 170, 173; in *quilombos*, 64, 118; verbs derived from, 180
Bantu slaves: cultural elements of, 48; sent to Minas Gerais, 112
banzo, 125
Barbosa, Ruy, 50
Barros, Tadeu de, 50, 106
Bassani Moraes, Daniela: dialogue with Joaquim Luís, 6–8, 104, 167
Belém, 45
Benguela, 19, 33, 41, 45, 46, 62, 112, 131, 155, 164
berrida, 126, 143
Bight of Benin, 23, 40, 61
Bight of Biafra, 40
Black Death, 37
black mammy, 47

Black Spanish: none spoken in Latin America today, 85
Bleek, Wilhelm, 11
Bom Despacho, 67, 80, 120, 195, 196
Book of the Routes and Realms, The (al-Bakri), 17
bozal Spanish, 76, 84, 85, 86, 87, 90, 95, 96, *97*, *98*, 99; and post-*bozal* speech communities, 86
BPV. *See* Brazilian Portuguese vernacular
Brandão, Ambrósio Fernandes, 32
Brazil, 63, 94; African influence on, 51, 147; African languages in, 61–64; Africans forcibly transported to, 3; Africans re-create native culture in, 47; Afro-Brazilian speech communities in, 5; decline in African languages spoken in, 64; effects of end of slavery, 50; independence from Portugal, 36; largest importer of slaves and slavery, 4; as largest single recipient of slaves, 44, 83; linguistic landscape of, 9; percent of population of African descent, 241n6; Portuguese colonial plantations in, 84; Portuguese credited with discovery of, 30; and sugar boom, 84; teaching of African and Afro-Brazilian history in public schools, 51; territorial expansion of, 34; three African regions providing slaves to, 61
Brazilian Portuguese, 4, 61; African contribution to, 9; African influence in, 69–83, 142; as a dialect of Portuguese, 78; publications on regional dialects of, 70
Brazilian Portuguese vernacular (BPV), 12, 104, 167; BPV and SBP present indicative, *188*; characteristics of rural, with parallels in creole, 74; defined, 11; grammatical parallels with São Tomé and Príncipe Portuguese, 76; originated from a semi-creole, 74; possible African influence on linguistic characteristics, 87; possible linguistic connection with Angolan Portuguese vernacular, 76; as semi-creole derivative, 73; verbal conjugations, 194
brazilwood, 31, *31*, 32
bungulá(r), 126
buraca, 126
buraco, 126
buraco de nanga, 126

Cabeza de Vaca, Álvar Núñez, 84
Cabinda, 41
Cabo São Vicente, 21
Cabral, Pedro Álvares, 23; erects a *padrão* on Brazilian shore, 30
Cabrera, Denga, 108
Cabrera, Senhor, 106, 108, 109; quoted, 103
caceba, 126
cacimbo, 126
cacunda, 126
caçutu, 126
cafamo, 126
cafangá(r), 126
cafifa, 126
cafofo, 126
cafuim, 126
Cafundó, 4, 68, 80, 121, *149–64*, 195
Cafundó: A África no Brasil (Vogt and Fry), 6
caipira: defined, 11
Caipira Portuguese, 6, 8, 166; defined, 12
caiumba, 126
caixinha de semá (cemá), 126
Caló, 82
Calunga, 16, 25, 64, 120, 126–27, 176; adjectives and adjectival gender agreement, 177–78; as Afro-Brazilian speech, 4; compared with

BPV, 185, *185*, 186, *186*, 187, *187*, 188, 189, *189*; as Brazilian linguistic puzzle, 9; communicating in secrecy, 6; consonantal changes, 174–75; consonantal phonemes, 173; consonants, *167–68*; conversations, 106; as cryptolect, 6; dependent clauses, 184–85; double negation in, 189; as ethnolinguistic speech community, 6; evolution of, 52–100; and evolution of *quilombos* of Minas Gerais, 116; as *falar africano* (Afro-Brazilian speech), 6; future tense, *181*; glossary, 123–39; grammar, 166–99; as hybrid pidgin speech, 118; initial contact between Portuguese and African languages, 52–61; lack of female speakers of, 6; lexicon, 123, 168, 180, 192; linguistic description of, 10; as masculine language, 108; and men, 109; as microdialect, 9; noun phrases, 176, 185, *185*, 186, *186*; origins of, 5, 10, 15; past tense, *181*; peculiarities in, 186; phonemes and allophones, 168–70; phonetics and phonology, 167–76; phonetic transcriptions of, 10; Portuguese influence, 139–40; and Portuguese language, 10; possession, 177; and prenasal stops, 173–74; prepositions, 184; present tense, *180*; preverbal markers, 183–84; as remnant of slave population of Triângulo Mineiro, 8; reserved for select topics, 141; and similarity to Cafundó, 148; singular nouns, 176–77; subject and object pronouns, 179, *179*; subject-verb-object template, 183; as symbol of African identity, 115; syntax, 183, 189; tentative analysis of, 124; as type of Bantu-Portuguese hybrid language, 8; and used by slaves, 6; verbs and verb phrases, 142, *180–81*, 185, *194*; vowels, *167*, 174. See also Afro-Brazilian speech
calungá(r), 127
calungadores, 4, 6; defined, 12
calungas, 48
Calunga speech community, 9, 10, 121; evasiveness of members of, 104; gender specific, 107; and women, 107–8
camanim, 127
camano, 127
camano cafamo, 127
camano de outras inglaterra, 127
camano desaprumado, 127
camano maioral, 127
camano ôa, 127
camano ofú, 127
camboque, 127
Camões, Luís de, 241n1
Campos, Inácio Oliveira de, 113
Cananéia, 30
Canary Islands, 20
Cancioneiro geral (de Resende), 55
candando, 127
candango, 127–28
Candomblé, 4, 13, 51, 62, 64, 72, 93
candunga, 128
cangundo, 128
cannibalism, 30, 111
Cão, Diogo, 23, 24, 25
Cape Bojador, 21–22
Cape of Good Hope, 19, 23
Cape Verde, 22, 53, 57–59, 60, 76, 78, 87, 96
captaincies, creation of, 32
caputo, 128
Caraíbas, 30
Carijós (Guaranis), 30
Cariris, 31
Cartagena, 90, 91, 95
casa grande, 47; defined, 12
Castilla: as Christian dominion, 16
Castro Alves, Antônio, 50
Cataguá, 50, 112
Catalonia: as Christian dominion, 16

Catholic Church, 28
Catopé, 14
Catumba, 66, 118, 121, 195, 197
cauba, 128
cavanza, 128
cazumbi, 128
cemá, 128, 138
cená, 138
Ceuta, Morocco, 21
cheba, 128
chia, 128
chicongo, 128
chipoque, 128, 138
chipoquê, 128, 138
choteño dialect, 244n17
Christian crusade, 20
Christian Iberians, 17
ciamá, 138
Columbus, Christopher: interrogated by João II, 29; and slaves, 41
common vocabulary, 141
comparative grammatical analysis of Afro-Brazilian varieties, 194–98
conena, 128
congado, 68, 243n11; defined, 12
Congo (nation), 8, 12, 45; colonization by Bantu groups, 25; corruption of leaders in, 26; material exploitations in, 27; Portuguese expansion into, 24; and shipment of slaves, 41; war with Jagas and Anzicos, 27
Congo speech, 99
copiá(r), 129
Costa Peixoto, Antônio da, 63
coteque, 128
Count of Valadares, 113
cowboy terms, 142
creoles, 8, 22, 56–74, 75, 78, 85, 90; Cape Verdean, 59; defined, 12; different, 57; European-based, 56, 57; Portuguese-based, 40, 53, 57, 58; stable, 87; verbs derived from imperative forms, 187, *187–89*; word origin, 53

creolization, 4, 57, 61, 65, 69, 79, 81, 82, 86, 193
Cresques Atlas, 17
Cruz, Viriato da: quoted, 15
cryptolects, 4, 64, 68, 106, 121, 141; defined, 12
Cuba, 42, 43, 76, 86, 88, 89, 94; and sugar boom, 84
cubá(r), 128
cuciá(r), 133
cueto, 128
cultural shift, 65
cumba, 128
cumbaca, 128
cumba de indaro, 128
cumba imbuno, 128
cumba ofú, 128
cumbata, 128
cupia, 129
cupiá, 129
cupiá(r), 129
Cupópia, 4, 64, 68, 121, 195; speech spoken in São Paulo, 6; subject pronouns derived from BPV in, 196
curiá, 129
curima, 129
curimá(r), 129
curirá(r), 129
curitá(r), 129
curriola, 129
cutá, 129
cuzeca, 129
cuzecá(r), 129

dandara, 129
dandará, 129
dandará ofú, 129
dandará santo, 129
dandarazim, 129
Day of Kings celebration, 14
deba (drum), 17
decreolization, 4, 61, 66, 69, 79, 80, 121; defined, 12
degredados: sent to Angola, 28
desaprumá(r), 129

desaprumado, 129
Diálogos das Grandezas do Brasil
   (Brandão), 32
Diamantina, 113
diamonds, 34, 46, 114
Dias, Bartolomeu, 23, 28
Dias, Pedro, 62–63; letter from, 63
Dias de Novais, Paulo, 28
Dinamérico, José, 116
diseases, 110, 113, 126; slaves
   decimated by, 33
Dom Affonso I, 25; letter to João II
   urging a stop to slave trading,
   26–27; spreads Christianity, 26
Dom João III, 45
Dom Pedro I, 36, 49
Dornas Filho, João, 66; quoted, 3
duana, 129
duana cafamo, 129
duana imbuno, 129
duana indaro, 129
duana mavero, 129
duana ofú, 130
duana sengo, 130
Duarte (king of Portugal), 21
duque, 130

Eanes, Gil, 21–22
East Indies Company, 33
Efik (language): contributions to
   Spanish American dialect, 85
Egypt, 18
ei, 130
Elia, Sílvio, 74
Elmina, 33, *36*, *39*, 46, 58
Elói, Sebastião, 109, 115
embuá, 130
encomienda, 40
engonhá(r), 130
Equiano, Olaudah, 43
escutante, 130
Estado de Minas, 51, 67
Estudos afro-brasileiros, 71
Ethiopia, 29
ethnicity, 38, 186–87

etymological categories, 140–41
Ewe-Fon (language), 13; contributions
   to Spanish American dialect, 85
exoa, 130

faim, 130
falar africano, 6, 8, 72, 119, 121, 122,
   149–64, 192; defined, 12
favelas, 50
fazendas, 47, 50, 113, *113*, 114, *114*,
   119, 120, 122, 246n4; as center of
   colonial Brazilian life, 120;
   defined, 13
feitorias, 22, 23, 33, *36*, *39*, 45, 46,
   56, 58, 87; defined, 13
Ferreira, Ângela, 108, 166
Ferreira, Marlenísio, 108–9, 166
fimba, 130
fojo, 130
Fontes Pereira, José de, 29
França, Agnaldo, 109
Freire de Andrade, José Antônio, 49
fricatives, 169
frize, 130
fuá, 130
fuzlio, 130

Galera's Bar, 106, *107*
Galicia: as Christian dominion, 16
Gama, Vasco da, 23
gamboa, 130
ganga, 130
ganzipe, 130
gatuvira, 130
gender, 178, 187
Geographia (Ptolemy), 20
Ghana, 22, *36*, *39*, 46, 54, 55, 58, 61;
   as supplier of gold and diamonds,
   17
glides: Bantu, 174
Goiás, 4, 11, 12, 14, 34, 70, 104, 112,
   113, 114, 116, 121
gold, 19, 20, 21, 31, 32, 46, *155*, *157*,
   164; Brazil as leading producer of,
   34; discovery of, 34, 110; effect on

decision to colonize, 111; mining, 46, 114; and minting of coins, 17; scarcity of, 22; slaves exchanged for, 23; as trade item, 39, 45
Gold Coast, 23, 40
Gomes, Fernão, 22
Gonçalves, Antão, 22, 39
Gonçalves Baldaia, Affonso, 22
Gouveia (Jesuit priest): advocate of military conquest, 28
grammatical influences, 197
grimpa, 131
grumetes, 40, 41; defined, 13
guaxaúna, 131
gudunhá(r), 131
Guinea, 22, 45
Guinea-Bissau, 40
gumbo, 131
gunga, 131
guriô, 131

Haitian Revolution of the 1790s, 84
Haitian slave rebellion (1791), 43
Helvécia, 65–66
Henry the Navigator, 21, 22, 55
Hispanic dialects: connection among, 87

Iberian Peninsula, 37, 85; Moor-Christian division of, 16
Ibiapaba mountain range, 30
ibn Battuta, Muhammed, 38
Igbo (language): contributions to Spanish American dialect, 85
imabe, 131
Imbangala, 42
imberela, 131
imberela de omenha, 131
imbuá, 130
imbuá de sengo, 131
imbuete, 131
imbuete de indaro, 131
imbuno, 131
incaca, 131
Inconfidência Mineira, 35

indaro, 131
indaro de cumba, 131
indaro de cumba imbuno, 131
indarumim, 131
ingazeiro, 131
inglaterra, 132
ingombe, 132
ingomo, 132
ingrimo, 132
ingugiá(r), 132
inharra, 132
inhoto, 132
injequê, 132
injó, 132
injó de banzo, 132
injó de grade, 132
injó de marafo, 132
injó de zipaque, 132
injoquê, 132
intertwined language, 80–83
ivory, 19, 22, 26, 45

Jagas, 27
Jamaica, 94
jamba, 132
janga, 132
jangorô, 132
jargons, 85
Jefferson, Thomas, 43
Jequitinhonha River, 30
jerico, 132
Jesuit priests, 26, 28, 33, 45, 59–63, 242n9, 244n17; expelled from Brazil, 35
jibundo, 132
jifeto, 132
jijumba, 132
jinguba, 132
João VI (king of Portugal), 36
John, Prester, 21
John II (king of Portugal), 25

Kalunga (communities), 121
kalunga: meaning of word, 94

Kayapós, 112; devastated by European diseases and slavery, 113
Khoi people, 25
Kikongo (language), 64, 93, 94, 118, 121, 125–35, 137, 138, 139, 146, 150–58, 160–63, 174, 175; and Africanisms, 140; and Africanisms in Brazilian Portuguese, 165; as Bantu language, 8, 192; contributions to Spanish American dialect, 84; greatest language influence in Brazil, 62; meaning of word, 49; similarities to Spanish and Portuguese, 11, 147–48; slaves as speakers of, 103; and source of Calunga's origin, 6
kimbo, 133
Kimbundu (language), 49, 63, 66, 68, 121, 146, 166, 179; and Africanisms in Brazilian Portuguese, 165; and Bantu languages, 8, 192; coexisted with Portuguese in Afro-Brazilian communities, 64; contributions to Spanish American dialect, 85; conversion through conquest, 28; greatest influence in Brazil, 62; and infinitives, 193–94; lacking in attributes and inflections compared to Portuguese, 197; preverbal inflections, 194; *quilombo* setting fundamental to, 118; similarities to Spanish and Portuguese, 11, 147–48; and source of Calunga's origin, 6
Kormakiti Arabic, 82
Kriyol, 58
kukiá(r), 133

La France Antartique, 32
lançados, 22, 57, 59; defined, 13; as middlemen, 56
La Pèlerine, 32
Latin American Spanish: possible African influence on linguistic characteristics, 87

Laytano, Dante de, 71
Lengua, 90
León: as Christian dominion, 16
lexical Africanization, 142
lexical items, compared, *149–64*
Liberia, 22, 43, 54
Língua do Negro da Costa, 64, 68–69, 120, 141, *149–64*; similar in grammar to Calunga, 196; verbal paradigms of, *196*
lingua francas, 65
Língua Geral, 30, 59–61, 118, 119, 139, 141, 242n9; defined, 13
linguistics, 6, 8, 9, 10, 11, 12, 30, 40, 52–100; and linguistic fossils, 165; and linguistic syncretism, 117
liquids, 170
Lisbon, 18, 20, 23, 25, 27, 29, 36, 40, 45, 62
liturgical languages, 4, 62, 64, 65, 66, 72, 85, 141
Lobo Antunes, António, 241n2
lorri, 133
Lower Guinea, 45
Luanda, 25, 28, 33, 41, 45, 46; Musseque neighborhoods, 77. *See also* Angola
lubra, 133
Luís, Joaquim, 104; dialogue with Daniela Bassani Moraes, 6–8
lumbalú (funeral ritual), 93; defined, 13
Luso-African population, 22
Lusophone, 53, 78; and Lusophone countries, *16*

Ma'a, 82
Macedo Soares, A. J. de, 69, 73; quoted, 52
Machado Filho, Aires de Mata, 67, 147
macura, 133
Madeira Islands, 22
madubim, 133
mafuim, 133
maiaca, 133

INDEX 273

maiembe, 133
maioral, 133
Maipures, 31
malamba, 133
malambre, 133
malara, 133
Mali kingdom, 17
Malocello, Lanzarote, 20
malombo, 133
malombo de sanjo, 133
malumbí, 133
malumbim, 133
malungo, 134
mambi, 134
Mammeluks, 18
mangoheiro, 134
Manin, Tunka (king of Ghana): al-Bakri's description of, 17
manjira, 134
mapium, 133
marafa, 134
marafa de uíque, 134
marafa de vinhango, 134
marafo, 134
marangola, 134
Maranhão, 31, 32, 45
maroon slave communities, 241n7
massa de camboque, 134
massango, 134
massongo, 134
massuango, 134
mataco, 134
Mato Grosso do Sul, 14, 34
matumba, 134
matura, 134
Mauritania, 22; *feitoria* established at, 39
mavero, 134
Mbanza, 25
Mbundu, 40
mestiços, 35
micota, 134
milongo, 134
Mina, 46
Mina-Jeje (language): defined, 13

Minas (slave group), 112
Minas Gerais, 12, 67, 119, 121, 122, *149–64*; African-born or mulatto population, 47; Afro-Brazilian speech communities, 148; and *bandeirantes*, 110; and clandestinely held slaves, 50; evolution of Calunga in, 109–10; freed slaves of African origin, 246n2; gender imbalance in, 112; importation of slaves, 46, 111–12, 146; labor needs of, 35; makeup of *quilombos* within, 118; mines of, 34; proportion of blacks to whites in colonial period, 120; studies of Afro-Brazilian language in, 66; and teaching of African and Afro-Brazilian history, 51; westernmost region of, 14
mirante, 134
missosso, 134
mixed language, 80, 82, 191; and cryptolect, 83; defined, 13; "fast," 83; lessons to be learned from, 83; as rare and exotic, 81
mocambos, 49
mocó, 134
mocó de espirro, 134
mocota, 134
mongo, 135
monzape, 135
Moors, 19, 37, 52–53; conquest of Iberian peninsula, 16
morphosyntax, 4, 6, 65, 69, 74, 77, 80, 82, 85, 103–4, 176–98; and Africanisms, 147; Africanized lexicon maintained, 79; changes brought about due to being uprooted and transplanted, 140; composed of rural Portuguese grammar, 121; deviations, 72; reduced structures, 68
Mozambique, 45, 46, 62; final region of slave trafficking, 45; as source of Brazilian slaves, 61–62

274 INDEX

mucafa, 135
mucafo, 135
muchinga, 135
mucota, 134
mufete, 135
mumbacho, 135
mumonha, 135
mungo, 135
mungue, 135
munzá, 135
muquifo, 135
murrudo, 135
muxima, 135
muxito, 135

Nagô, 46; defined, 13
nagoma, 135
nanga, 135
nanga cafamo, 135
nanga imbuno, 135
nango mavero, 135
nani, 135
nasal consonants, 170
nasal vowels: as allophonic, 172
Navarro: as Christian dominion, 16
Ndongo Kingdom, 28, 62
negation, 183–84
Negros Congos of Panama, 85, 89–90, 93, 95–100; as cryptolect, 99; defined, 13; exaggerated grammatical characteristics of, 96; single locus of origin of, 100; speech compared to Palenquero, 95
New York Herald Tribune, 37
nhoto, 135
Niger-Congo languages, *54–55*
Niger Delta, 23
Nigeria, 13, 43, 54–55, 56, 61, 65; formerly Kingdom of Benin, 58; as source of Brazilian slaves, 61
niguciê, 135
niguciê de sengo, 135
Nina Rodrigues, Raimundo, 64–65
Nkuwu, Nzinga, 25

Nzinga, Mbemba, 25

ôa, 136
Obra nova de Lingoa g.al de mina (Peixoto), 63
ocai, 136
ocaia, 136
ocai de banzo, 136
ocaio, 136
ocai ofú, 136
ocai santo, 136
ocaizim, 136
odara, 136
ofú, 136
O Futuro d'Angola, 29
O injó da calunga (Ferreira), 109
omeia, 136
omenha, 136
omenha de mavero, 136
omenha de urungo, 136
omenha de vinhango, 136
opira, 136
opô, 136
orirá(r), 136
orofim, 136
orogongi, 136
orongoia, 136
oropemba, 136
Ortega y Gasset, José, 246n1
Os africanismos no dialeto gaúcho (de Laytano), 71
ossumba, 136
otaca, 136
otata, 136
Ouro Preto, 63, 67, 110, 112, 113, 146; *falares africanos* in, 121; as major city in Minas Gerais, 34
Ovimbundu, 40

padrão (stone cross), 25, 30
paim, 136
Palenquero, 87, 88, 90–94, 96, 99, 189, 244n17; defined, 13; grammatical characteristics of,

INDEX 275

91–93; speech compared to Negros Congos, 95
Palmares quilombo, 63, 64, 116, 117, 119
Panama: and slaves from Congo/Angola region, 95
pandú, 137
papa rato, 137
Papiamento, 87, 88, 99
Papiamentu, 99
Pará, 31, 45
Paracatu, 113
Paraguay River, 31
Paranaíba River, 112, 114
Paranapanema, 30
Paraná River, 31
Patrocínio, José do, 50
Patrocínio, Minas Gerais, 5, 104, 108, 109, 112–14, 115, 124; and informants, 9; origin of name, 246n5; size of, 4
pegante, 136
People's History of the United States, A (Zinn), 48
periá, 136
Pernambuco, 32, 33, 34
Petter, Margarida Maria Taddoni: quoted, 123
Philipp, Karl Friedrich, 29
phonotactics, 171–72, 173
pidgins, 85, 120; defined, 13; and pidginization, 81
pixiê, 136
plantation model, 21
Pombal, Marquês de, 35
ponto de conena, 137
ponto de mirante, 137
ponto de poente, 137
ponto pisante, 137
Portugal, 16, 17, 19, 39; and agricultural independence, 20; as Christian dominion, 16; civil war in Angola, 29; "classroom Portuguese," 78; colonial policy in Angola, 28; colonization of Cape Verde Islands, 57; colonization of four islands, 23; explorations, 15, 18, 20; improvements in maritime technology, 21; and *padrão* with etching, 25; and presence outside Europe, 20; relations with Congo, 26, 27; and slave trade, 22, 28, 33; war with Ndongo Kingdom, 28
Portuguese language, 88; foreign talk variety of, 56; pidgins and creoles, 8, 55–61
"Portuguesement": and rural dialect, 191
Portuguese syllabification: and Bantu-derived words, 173
Príncipe, 22, 26, 45, 58, 60, 87; and Cape Verde Creole, 59; as stopover for ships, 58
puco, 137

Queen Maria I (Portuguese ruler), 36
quicumbi, 137
quijongo, 137
quilombola: defined, 13
quilombos, 8, 49, 113, 116, 119, 120; defined, 13–14; and necessity of common language, 117–18; unknown social organization of, 119; as symbol of resistance and refuge from slavery, 49
quimba, 137
quimbim, 137
quimbimba, 137
quimbimbá(r), 137
quimbota, 137
quimbundos, 48
quimimbá(r), 137
quinda, 137
quindú, 137
quinhama, 137
quinhamá(r), 137
quinhamba, 137
quiombô, 137
quissanda, 137
quitata, 137

quiunda, 137
quizumba, 137

Raimundo, Jacques, 70–71
Recife, 45, 71
reisados, 68; defined, 14
Relación (Cabeza de Vaca), 84
relexification, 81, 83
retroflex, 171
Ribeiro, João, 70
Rio de Janeiro, 30, 45, 46, 146; and clandestinely held slaves, 50; as Portuguese colonial capital, 34; as principal entrance port to Minas Gerais, 112; and Queen Maria I, 36
Rio Grande do Norte, 31
Rio Tejo, *23*
Rodrigues Arzão, Antônio, 110

Sagres navigation school, 21
Salvador, 13, 25, 33, 45, 46, 64; as first Portuguese colonial capital, 34; and slave shipments, 112
Sandoval, Alonso de, 88
sanja, 137
sanjo, 137
sanjô, 137
Sant'anna, Affonso Romano de, 51
santo, 132, 138
São Francisco River, 31
São Paulo (state), 12, 14, 50, 121, 146, 148, 149–64
São Salvador, 25
São Tomé, 22, 26, 45, 60, 87; fertile soil for growing sugarcane, 58; as stopover for ships, 58
Sãotomense, 60–61
São Vicente: first declared Brazilian city, 32
sarava, 138
saravá(r), 138
secret language, 67–68, 81, 104, 106, 108
semá, 128, 138
semá cor de indaro, 138

semá de mucota, 138
semantic categories, 142
semá ofú, 138
semi-creole: defined, 14
semi-creole hypothesis: opponents of, 73–79
sená, 138
Senegambia, 40
sengo, 138
sengue, 138
senguê, 138
Senna, Nelson de, 71
Serra da Canastra, 4
sertão: defined, 14
Sertão Mineiro, 14
shackles, handcuffs, and branding iron, *39*
Sierra Leone, 22, 40, 43, 54
Silva Neto, Serafim da: quoted, 71–72
Silveira, Fernam de, 55
silver mines, 28
Sintra, Pedro da, 22
slaves and slavery, 21, 22, 23, 32, 33, 58, 111, 114; abolition in 1888, 64; from Angola for Portuguese colonies, 28; Bantu-speaking, 8; and Brazil, 44; desperate measures undertaken by, 48; escaped, 49; first written reports of Portuguese spoken by, 69; influence on Brazilian culture, 4; likely multilingual, 60; as majority of Brazilian population, 8; male versus female slaves, 42; management of, 40; numbers of, taken to Brazil, 3–4; role in building Americas, 43; slave coast, 23; slave dungeon, *36*; transport to Brazil, 3; in urban concentrations of South America, 84. *See also* slave trade
slave trade, 8, 15, 35, 37–51; abolition of, 43; and consent of Africans, 39; history of, 37; infrastructure of, 41; and Jesuit priests, 26; and public

opinion, 42, 50; and skills, 46. *See also* slaves and slavery
Smith, Adam, 18, 24, 31
Sousa, Martim Affonso de, 32, 33
Souza, Gabriel Soares de, 110
Souza, Glauce de, 108
Souza, Inácio de, 105–6
specialty vocabulary, 141
Speech of the Negros Congos of Panama, The (Lipski), 95
spices, 17
Standard Brazilian Portuguese (SBP), 166
Stanley, Henry Morton, 27
Steele, A. T., 37
stone depiction of Portuguese caravel, *18*
stone wall, *113*
sucaná(r), 138
sucano, 138
sugar and sugarcane, 22, 32, 34, 37, 84; Brazilian cultivation of, 45; and demand for labor, 26; and African slaves, 35, 40, 50; and Madeira Islands, 21; new boom, 84; as principal strength and substance of wealth, 33; and São Tomé and Príncipe, 76
sumate, 138
Summary of the Antiquities and Wonders of the World (Pliny), 20
Surinam, 88
suruba, 138
Swahili, 81, 147, 246n1
syncretic language, 80

Tabatinga, 67
tamangô, 138
tatá, 138
terreiros, 48
Tietê River, 30
tipoquê, 128, 138
tipune, 138
tipungo, 138
tipungue, 138

Tiradentes, 35
Tordesillas (1494), Treaty of, 29, 30; violation of, 34
Torre de Belém, *23*
Tremembés, 112
Triângulo Mineiro, 4, 104, 112, 114, 116, 118, 119; and Brazil's former slave population, 8; defined, 14; Portuguese settlements in, 113
Tristão, Nuno, 22, 39
tropeiro, 143; defined, 14
tunda, 138
Tupi (language), 13, 139
Tupi-Guaranis, 30, 59
Tupinambás, 30
Tupiniquins, 30
Tupis, 31
Turks, 18
tutus, 48

uanjá(r), 138
uí, 138
uíque, 138
umbundu, 138
Umbundu (language), 103, 118, 124–36, 138–40, 146, 147, 148, 149–65, 173, 174, 175, 176, 177, 179, *179*, 186, 187; and Africanisms in Brazilian Portuguese, 165; and Angola, 242n8; and Bantu languages, 8, 192; contributions to Spanish American dialect, 85; greatest influence in Brazil, 62; and source of Calunga's origin, 6; and strong convergences with Kikongo and Kimbundu, 11, 148, 166
United States, 43, 48, 94; abolition of slavery, 50; and percent of population of African origin, in 1790 census, 241n5
Upper Guinea, 22, 40, 45, 57
urano, 139
urungo, 139
urungo de omenha, 139

vapora, 139
Vasconcellos, Diogo de, 49
Venetians, 18–19
Venezuela, 84, 94
vernaculars, partially restructured, 243n12
Vespucci, Amérigo, 31
viango, 139
Vicente, Gil, 55, 57
vinhango, 139
vissungos, 67; defined, 14
von Spix, Johann Baptist, 29

Wadan: and gold trading, 22
Wealth of Nations, The (Smith), 18, 31
West Central Africa, 40, 42
West Indies Company, 33
wheat, 20, 21, 37, 47
women: difficulty in interviewing, 9–10
word-final rhotics, 170
words: altered from source language, 148; changes in, 140; festivals and social life, 145; flora and fauna, 143–44; food and drink, 143; human body and clothing, 144–45; people and relationships, 144; reinterpretation of, 147; reinterpreted as single lexical units, 147; several pronunciations of, 147; *tropeiro*, 143; verbs, 142, *180*, *194*; work and money, 145

xaxatá(r), 139
ximbado, 139

Yáñez Pinzón, Vicente, 29
Yoruba (language), 13, 46, 48, *55*, 62, 63, 64, 67, 71, 132, 136, 139; contributions to Spanish American dialect, 85; and formation of Afro-Brazilian, 65

Zaire River, 23, 24
zingrim, 139
zipaque, 139
zoeira, 139
"Zong affair," 43
zueira, 139

www.ingramcontent.com/pod-product-compliance
Lightning Source LLC
Chambersburg PA
CBHW021340230426
43666CB00006B/356